ALSO BY STEVEN LEVY

Crypto: How the Code Rebels Beat the Government—
Saving Privacy in the Digital Age

Insanely Great: The Life and Times of Macintosh,
the Computer That Changed Everything

Artificial Life: The Quest for a New Creation

The Unicorn's Secret: Murder in the Age of Aquarius

Hackers: Heroes of the Computer Revolution

The Perfect Thing

How the iPod Shuffles Commerce, Culture, and Coolness

Steven Levy

Simon & Schuster Paperbacks
New York   London   Toronto   Sydney

To Andrew and Allie

SIMON & SCHUSTER PAPERBACKS
1230 Avenue of the Americas
New York, NY 10020

Copyright © 2006 by Steven Levy
Afterword copyright © 2007 by Steven Levy

First Simon & Schuster trade paperback edition September 2007

SIMON & SCHUSTER PAPERBACKS and colophon are registered trademarks
of Simon & Schuster, Inc.

For information about special discounts for bulk purchases,
please contact Simon & Schuster Special Sales at
1-800-456-6798 or business@simonandschuster.com

Designed by Elliott Beard

Manufactured in the United States of America

10 9 8 7 6 5 4 3 2 1

The Library of Congress catalogued the hardcover edition as follows:

Levy, Steven.
    The perfect thing: how the iPod shuffles commerce, culture,
and coolness / Steven Levy
        p. cm.
    Includes bibliographical references and index.
    1. iPod (Digital music player) 2. Apple Computer, Inc. I. Title

ML74.4.I48L48 2006
006.5—dc22   2006050270

ISBN-13: 978-0-7432-8522-3
ISBN-10:   0-7432-8522-0
ISBN-13: 978-0-7432-8523-0 (pbk)
ISBN-10:   0-7432-8523-9 (pbk)

Contents

Contents

iPod Timeline

October 2001	Original iPod
July 2002	Second-generation iPod (touch-sensitive scroll wheel)
	PC-based iPods
April 2003	Third-generation iPod, with four buttons above the wheel
	iTunes Music Store opens for Mac users, with 99-cent downloads
October 2003	iTunes and iTunes Music Store for Windows
January 2004	iPod mini, 35 percent smaller, in five colors
July 2004	Fourth-generation iPod, with click wheel
October 2004	iPod photo with color screen
	Black and red U2 iPod Special Edition
January 2005	iPod shuffle: no screen or wheel
September 2005	iPod nano replaces mini
October 2005	Fifth-generation "video" iPod
	iTunes store sells music videos and TV shows

September 2006	Second-generation iPod nano: smaller, color aluminum skin
	iTunes store sells movies
October 2006	Second-generation shuffle: postage-stamp-size
March 2007	Apple TV: connects iTunes and Internet to television
June 2007	iPhone: touch-screen iPod, Internet navigator and . . . phone

iPod Timeline

Perfect

❯Just what is it about the iPod?

It weighs 6.4 ounces and consists of a few layers of circuit boards and electronic components, covered by a skin of white polycarbonate and stainless steel. It's slightly smaller than a deck of cards. On the front is a screen smaller than a Post-it note, perched over a flattened wheel. It doesn't have an on–off switch. If you didn't know what it was, you might guess that it was a sleek, high-priced thermostat, meant to control temperature in a high-priced condominium. A very sexy detached thermostat that feels very good when you palm it. But you almost certainly *do* know what it is—a portable digital music player that holds an entire library of tunes—because it is the most familiar, and certainly the most desirable, new object of the twenty-first century.

You could even make the case that it *is* the twenty-first century.

It arrived in October 2001, bringing the promise of pleasure to a world in transformation from its comforting analog roots to a disruptive digital future. The world did not fete it with parades. In October 2001, the world had its own problems. The newcomer was welcomed by fans of Apple Computer, the company that makes the iPod, and there was a generalized feeling that a new twist in gadgetry had arrived. There were some glowing reviews in newspapers and magazines. But . . . *this?* No one expected *this.*

Here's what *this* is. The triumph of the iPod is such that the word "success" falls far short of describing it. Its massive sales don't begin to tell the story. When Apple began work on the crash project that would become the iPod, its leaders saw the device as an enhancement of the Macintosh computer—which despite a recent rejuvenation had not gained more than a 4 percent share of the PC market. To that end, the iPod was seen as somewhat of a breakthrough, a significant one with the potential to nudge the company in a new direction. But none of the wizards at Apple headquarters in Cupertino, California, could know that the iPod would become the most important product in Apple's history since 1984's trailblazing Mac computer (if not more important). No one thought that within four years it would change Apple from a computer company to a consumer electronics giant deriving almost 60 percent of its income from music-related business. No one thought the iPod would change the music business, not only the means of distribution but even the strategies people would use to buy songs. No one envisioned subway cars and airplane cabins and street corners and school lounges and fitness centers where vast swathes of humanity would separate themselves from the bonds of reality via the White Earbud Express. No one expected that there would be magazine covers and front-page newspaper stories proclaiming this an "iPod Nation." No one predicted that listening to the iPod would dethrone quaffing beer as the most popular activity for undergraduate college students. And certainly no one thought that the name of this tiny computer *cum* music player would become an appellation to describe an entire generation or a metaphor evoking any number of meanings: the future, great design, short attention span, or just plain coolness.

But that's what happened.

Type "iPod" into the Google search engine, and you will get more than half a billion hits. If you focus your search to see what ordinary people are saying about it, type the word "iPod" into a blog search engine like Technorati or the search field in craigslist, you will be injected into a vast collective cerebrum of 'pod gazing, as people natter endlessly about how they love their iPods, what they play on their iPods, and how the world would end if they lost their iPods. (Some people actually use the iPod platform as a means of conveying their passion—recording their thoughts on "podcasts" to be downloaded and played . . . on iPods!) Nearly everyone who owns one becomes obsessed with it. How gorgeous it is. How you get your songs into it. What it's like to shuffle them. How long before the batteries run down. How it changes the way you listen to music. How it gets you thinking about what greatness is in a product. Or in life.

But you do not have to own an iPod, or even see one, to fall within its spell. The iPod is a pebble with tsunami-sized cultural ripples.

It changed the high-tech industry, particularly Apple. By the end of 2005, Apple Computer had sold more than 42 million iPods, at prices ranging from $99 to $599 (most sold in the middle range). What's more, at that time the iPod had about 75 percent market share of the entire category of digital music players. Its online digital music emporium, the iTunes Music Store, has sold more than a billion songs at 99 cents each, representing about 85 percent of all legal paid downloads, a market that barely existed before Steve Jobs herded the nasty cats running record labels and got them to agree to his way of selling music. The success of the iPod also created a "halo effect" that boosted the sales of Macintosh computers. Since the age of iPod began, Apple's stock price has increased more than 700 percent.

There is a fascinating story behind the development of the iPod, an apotheosis of the method by which one of the world's most innovative companies, with clear eyes and unbounded ego, surveys the competition in a rising new product category, decides it can create something a quantum leap better, and, in barely the time it takes to hear the songs on an iPod hard drive, designs and manufactures something that exceeds even the company's own stratospheric standards.

It's the symbol of media's future, where the gates of access are thrown open, the reach of artists goes deeper, and consumers don't just consume—they choose songs, videos, and even news their way. Digital technology gathers, shreds, and empowers, all at once. Mix, mash, rip, burn, plunder, and discover: these are the things that the digital world can do much more easily than before—or for the first time. The iPod, and the download dollar-store that accompanies it, makes sense of those things without making our brains hurt.

It's a six-ounce entanglement of cultural signifiers, evoking many things to many people. Headline writers and cultural critics talk of an "iPod Generation." This can mean a number of things—sometimes it's just a shorthand way of saying "young people"—but generally it's used to depict a mind-set that demands choice and the means to scroll through ideas and ideologies as easily as a finger circles the wheel on the iconic front panel of an iPod. "It seems to me that a lot of younger listeners think the way the iPod thinks," wrote Alex Ross in *The New Yorker*. "They are no longer so invested in a single way of seeing the world." Sometimes the object's name is used simply as a synonym for anything that plays music; when Dartmouth neuroscientists isolated a cranial source of music memories that fills in the gaps when you're listening to familiar music and the song temporarily cuts out, headline writers knew just what to call that function of the auditory cortex: the "iPod of the brain."

It's a journalistic obsession. Sometimes the iPod gets media coverage not because there's any particular news but just because it's, well, there, and it reeks trendiness, and media types feel good when they write about it. "Nothing fits better in the 'timely features' slot than a headline that includes the word 'iPod,'" wrote William Powers in *The National Journal*. Powers later elaborated in an e-mail: "Journalists tend to be liberal-arts types, fairly techno-illiterate. When we encounter a machine that is easy to operate, we like it. When we encounter one that is easy and *fun* to operate, we are besotted. We 'get' the iPod, and getting it makes us feel tech-ish."

It's also a near-universal object of desire. Some people complained about the cost of the iPod, which was originally $399. (The price tag eventually came down to about half of that for a model—the nano—with equal storage, a color screen, and a slim profile one-third the size of the classic iPod.) But the allure of the iPod is such that even a princely sum is considered a bargain compared to its value. Take the dilemma of the burgeoning dot-com called Judy's Book, whose goal was collecting local knowledge on neighborhood businesses. How could they get a lot of reviewers, really cheap? By offering an iPod to anyone submitting fifty reviews. Figuring the $249 cost of an iPod mini, that's five bucks a review—and, if a sweatshop critic drops out before reaching fifty, Judy's Book pays nada! Laid out in cash terms, it's a lousy deal. But it's not cash—it's an iPod!

No wonder iPods have replaced toasters as bank premiums for

Perfect

opening new accounts. Every time I go to my Chase Bank ATM for a cash infusion, the screen greets me with images of a nano and a shuffle—the enticements for opening a new account to pay my bills online. That's tempting. But would I actually choose *a place to live* in order to snare a free iPod? That's the premise behind the ad I saw for the Stuyvesant Town apartment complex in Manhattan one day, headlined "Download Your Music . . . Upgrade Your Apartment." A similar promotion at Century Towers, a Chicago high-rise, helped fill eighty empty units. "One of the first things they'd say to me after signing the lease was, 'Do I get the iPod now?' " Sharon Campbell, the building's leasing director, told *The New York Times*. Campbell also said that dangling the $249 iPod mini before renters was a better attention getter than the previous enticement of two months' rent, worth between $1,500 and $6,000. So coveted is Apple's little device that the word itself can be shorthand for "adored possession," in a not necessarily benign materialistic sense—as when *The Wall Street Journal*'s movie critic talks of a character's inability to see his baby as "anything more than a commodity—a little iPod in swaddling clothes."

And of course, if someone gives you an iPod, it's glorious. Even if you already have one. Even if you have six. Just owning another of those polished digital gems jacks up the endorphin level. Think of the playlists you'll load!

Some even see God in the iPod. Sal Sberna, the forty-seven-year-old pastor of the Metropolitan Baptist Church in Houston, has constructed an elaborate Gospel of the Gizmo in a series of sermons devoted to "iPod Theology." He seizes on the design of the iPod to dramatize one's faith. "The reason the outside of the iPod is so simple to use and so beautiful to look at is because of the way they designed the inside," he told his congregation. "And so when Jesus talks to us about simplification, it must start on the inside."

And, oh yes, it's a great way to listen to music.

The title of this book, you may have noticed, is *The Perfect Thing*. The iPod is not perfect, of course. There's no power switch, the batteries can fade like a winter sunset, and the songs you buy from the iTunes store are layered with an occasionally annoying set of software rules called "digital rights management." It picks up scratches perhaps too easily. But I use the word "perfect" for two reasons. The first is that the iPod's astounding success has come from a seemingly uncanny alignment of technology, design, culture, and media that has thrust it into the center of just about every controversy in the digital age. In each area, the iPod has made a difference. So don't think "perfect" as in flawless—more in the spirit of a perfect storm (in a good way, of course).

The second reason is that just about anyone who owns an iPod will at one point—usually when a favorite tune appears spontaneously and the music throbs through the earbuds, making a dull day suddenly come alive—say or think the following: "Perfect."

How did all this happen?

I had gotten the Apple letter the week before, an invitation to another one of Steve Jobs's carefully choreographed, exquisitely casual shows. It was to be held at Apple's headquarters in Cupertino on October 23, 2001. The most interesting thing about the invitation was the teasing addendum: "Hint: It's not a Mac." Usually, I would have hopped on the plane to see the latest wrinkle in the consistently fascinating saga of Jobs. His return to Apple was a great business story in itself, but what was novel about his whole career was its unapologetic and unprecedented grafting of 1960s values—everything from rock and roll to cracker-barrel Buddhism—into the corporate world. Jobs was one of the world's greatest salesmen, a guy who outsuited the suits when it came to mastering the pulleys and levers of global high-tech product development and man-ufacturing, a chief executive officer of two companies traded on the NASDAQ (Apple and Pixar Entertainment). But I'd also seen him stroll into his boardroom on a weekday with scissor-cut shorts almost up to his balls and a pair of flip-flops. All of this—the aus-tere authority of the Zen poet, the playfulness of Mick Jagger, and the showmanship of David Copperfield—would be on display at this event. And if recent history were any guide, the product would be worth writing about.

But I didn't go. I attended the launch much later, via the anti-quated medium of a videocassette tape that had captured the event. The location of the actual event was a small auditorium called Town Hall, which is actually inside one of the white Apple build-ings off I-280 that were added to the campus in the early 1990s. As usual for those events, Apple's chairman and chief executive officer, Steven Paul Jobs, dressed in the jeans and long-sleeved black mock turtleneck that he always dons for these soliloquies, strolled onto the stage, without introduction. "We have something really excit-ing for you today," he said. "We lured you here today with the promise of a great digital device that's not a Mac, and that's what we intend to do."

The event proceeded like a striptease. Layers of information were peeled back, the anticipation increasing as the nitty-gritty moment approached and the mystery was dissolved. Jobs began with the equivalent of shedding his gloves: he demonstrated a few of Apple's latest "Digital Hub" products, Macintosh applications that let users master the mechanics of moviemaking and burn their own DVD disks. Then, turning to the great surprise he had prom-ised, he discussed the reasons behind it. (Off came the shoes.) Then he described its attributes and charms. By the time he got to the iPod itself, he had discussed its market placement, its technical components, its interface, and its clever scroll wheel, which allows you to trace your finger along a circular track surrounding the "select" button and quickly zip through a list of the artists, albums, or songs on your iPod. (Outer garments removed.) His descriptions were punctuated with spontaneous expressions of awe at the product. *Isn't that fantastic?*

Finally he said, "Let me show you."

The screen behind him displayed the first image of the iPod—from the side. It was a slim, shiny line, like a cigarette case someone in a noir film would pull out in a nightclub. (*Bam*-budda-boom.) Then, "Let me show you the back, because I'm in love with it." (A shiny steel rectangle; imagine a silver soap dish. *Chick*-chicka-boom.) Then a three-quarter view of the back and the side. "It's really, really durable. It's beautiful." (Waaaah-waaaah-chicka-*boom*.)

Finally, he said, "This is what the front looks like."

Full frontal! You could see the austere white obelisk with its display screen barely bigger than the face of a wristwatch; below the screen was a white-on-white bull's-eye. The object looked clean and alluring but—since it seemed to have no precedent—somehow mysterious. The crowd had barely had a chance to absorb what was on the screen when, suddenly, Jobs produced the actual item in all its nakedness, palming the gadget out of his jeans and holding it up like a pearl fished from the ocean. "This amazing little device holds a thousand songs—*and fits in my pocket,*" he announced, as if *he* almost couldn't believe it.

He put it back into his jeans.

"So . . . iPod," he concluded. "A thousand songs in your pocket." He paused, in case anyone hadn't grasped that point and needed repetition to let it sink in, then added, "This is a major, major breakthrough."

It wasn't until the end of his spiel that Jobs revealed the price: $399. This did not get any applause. In fact, you could almost sense a wave of skeptical calculation moving through the room. Four hundred bucks seemed a lot of money for a little doodad like that.

With benefit of hindsight, the launch was remarkable both for what Jobs emphasized and for what he did not. He was directly on the mark with its core concept. "The coolest thing about it," he said, "is that a whole music library fits right in your pocket." But the implications of what that meant were barely hinted at. The idea that it could let you shuffle your whole music collection was mentioned once, but casually, in the context of a laundry-list recitation of features. Jobs also hit the mark with how easy it was to synchronize the iPod with songs on your computer and how quickly these songs could move from the computer to the device—in mere seconds, because of the high-speed FireWire cable. But he also devoted an awful lot of energy to extolling the relatively minor virtue of using the iPod as a spare hard drive. It was almost as if playing music weren't quite enough and he needed a deal sweetener.

As is common in Steve's launches, the event ended with a video created for the event, a minidocumentary with commentary from talking heads inside and outside the company, as well as loving cinematography of the electronic guest of honor. The most memorable remarks came from musicians. First up was the techno-deejay and sonic experimenter Moby, who at that moment was enjoying a brief period at the top of the music industry heap with an album that not only sold millions but provided a sound track for movies and commercials. The bald, bespectacled mix-master looked like the computer-support nerd your phone company sends to hook up your DSL line, but that was part of his post–rock star appeal. (He had no idea, of course, that within a couple years the iPod would be many times more popular than he.) "I'm having a hard time getting my head around the fact that you can transfer an album onto this in ten seconds," he marveled. "If I was sixteen years old, I think I would be able to deal with that a lot better." He continued to gush. "The design is really cool. I don't know who your product designers are, but, boy, you're not paying them enough. . . . I might have to steal your prototype."

The Smash Mouth singer Steve Harwell zeroed in on the ease-of-use theme. "It doesn't take a rocket scientist to figure this out. And I ain't no rocket scientist, let me tell you. Super simple—five buttons and a scroll pad. You've got a whole record store in this damn thing. This kicks every other product's ass!"

The final musician who seemed to be channeling a script directly from Steve Jobs's PR machine was the smooth soul singer Seal. Like the others, he was fondling the iPod as if it were a pet mouse he adored. "Do you remember what it was like to get your first Walkman? Do you know that feeling?" he said. "I haven't picked up any MP3 player [yet] that has made me go, 'Wow, okay, I want to carry this everywhere I go. OK.' *Everyone's* going to want to have one of these."

All in all, quite a show. Though, as I mentioned, I didn't make it in person. Those days I wasn't traveling. It was, after all, little more than a month after 9/11, and I, like just about everyone else in New York City, was depressed. My eleven-year-old son had seen the collapse of the Trade Center towers from the roof of his school before my wife rushed to pick him up. And now the gap where the towers had stood loomed larger than the towers ever had.

I'd come to work at *Newsweek* early on that blindingly clear day, having arranged some meetings. The first was with a design guru at Compaq. "Hey," he told me, "a small plane just hit the World Trade Center." Then we had a meeting in a small conference area on the seventeenth floor of our building near Columbus Circle, the "back-of-the-book" floor. The conversation was interrupted as people passing by us mentioned bigger planes, another collision, other planes missing. We cut the conversation short. Just then, arriving early, was my next appointment: Apple Executive VP Phil Schiller, who'd come to show me the new Power Mac desktop computer. He had a technician with him to handle the three boxes of equipment he had brought and to set up the unit. It was almost ten A.M. "I'm sorry, Phil," I said. "But I have to go downstairs to a meeting. You can use the phone here if you like."

Schiller stared at me dully. Like everyone else, he was having difficulty processing the events unfolding a few miles downtown, and in Washington, and on another plane as yet unaccounted for. "We're not going to have any meetings anywhere today, are we?" he asked. I regarded this as a rhetorical question.

It would take Phil Schiller five days to get back to California. Other people at Apple were stuck in Europe. But with the exception of some managers checking out suppliers in Asia, almost all the people working on the iPod were at home in the Bay Area. At Apple's headquarters in Cupertino, Steve Jobs was sending an e-mail to Apple employees:

> *I'm sure you've heard about today's extraordinary and tragic events. If you want to stay home with your families today, please do so. For those of you who want to come to work, we will be open.*
> *Steve*

By the time of Apple's iPod press conference in October, the plane crashes had been followed by a wave of anthrax attacks. We even had a scare at *Newsweek;* someone came down with flu symptoms and recalled having opened a strange letter the week before.

On October 22, the day before Apple's announcement, an e-mail informed us of the new procedure for receiving mail. Clean rooms and latex gloves were involved. We had fallen into a Stephen King flick.

Although I did not fly across the country for the Apple announcement, I did follow the news carefully. Steve Jobs is maniacal in attempting to maintain total stealth in his operation, but a cat of this magnitude could not be fully bagged, and news was leaking that the "not a Mac" was some kind of digital music player. The prospect did not exactly thrill people. Digital music players—also known as MP3 players, in reference to the encoding algorithm that compresses music into files—had been around a few years already, but novelty was their main, if not their only, virtue. They generally held too little music, had impenetrable interfaces, and looked like the cheap plastic toys given to losers at carnival games. It seemed a stretch to assume that Apple, a company whose previous forays into pure consumer electronics had been undistinguished, would dramatically change this landscape. In an article published on CNET before the October 23 launch, a couple of financial analysts expressed disappointment that Apple would take its eye off the ball and waste resources on what was probably a fool's errand. An analyst at Technology Business Research named Tim Deal wondered, "What kind of money is to be made in these products? Intellectually, it makes sense to create a new device to fit into their digital device strategy, but right now it's a tricky time to be introducing new hardware."

I don't recall being so negative myself: I made plans to write about this new toy, discussing with Apple when we might be able to photograph it. In no case, my PR contact said, would Apple send us one to arrive until after the Tuesday launch. They weren't even about to put one into a Federal Express box on Monday, afraid that someone might rip open the box and discover Steve Jobs's big secret. In-stead, Apple would dispatch a pair of couriers from Cupertino to hand-deliver the new product to a few select tech writers. Apple's spokesperson made it clear that they would deliver to no designee, only me. Maybe, I thought, I *should* have flown out to see this.

It was sometime in the afternoon of that launch day that the Apple couriers reached *Newsweek*. They had been racing up and down the Atlantic seaboard spreading iPods to tech writers; their previous stop had been *New York Times* reviewer David Pogue's house in Connecticut. So they didn't have time to do much of anything but leave the box. The packaging was a distinctive cube, with a picture of Jimi Hendrix that evoked the excitement of his volcanic performance in *Monterey Pop*. It opened up as if one of Tiffany's finest gems were inside. There was the iPod. It was beautiful.

There was also a stack of fresh CDs in case I didn't have my own collection to feed into iTunes and then load into the iPod. The discs were a nice touch. The musical selection was crisp and connoisseur-friendly, managing to include music of undeniable popularity without discarding the prerogatives of snobbism. It seemed to be a Steve Jobs musical version of Woody Allen's list in *Manhattan,* of things that made life worth living. Jobs's list included his idol Bob Dylan, of course—the very best Dylan, the legendary 1966 concert from the Royal Albert Hall. Sarah McLachlan, Moby, Nirvana, Ella Fitzgerald, *Jagged Little Pill,* Glenn Gould's *Goldberg Variations.* Miles Davis (*Kind of Blue,* natch). Yo-Yo Ma. *A Hard Day's Night.* (I think choosing this CD over the predictable *Sgt. Pepper's Lonely Hearts Club Band* was particularly clever, a nod toward the freshness that really sticks with us from the Beatlemania days.) Dave Brubeck's *Take Five.* Nothing even remotely embarrassing. Of course I planned to plunder my own CD collection once I got home and load my own music into the iPod.

But before I left the office to play with my new toy, I took my prearranged call from Jobs. He sounded out of breath. It was a quarter after one Cupertino time, and he had been chatting up his new product almost from the moment he had left the stage. As interviewers go, Jobs is a classic self-starter. He always has a message to deliver, and he does so with unstinting enthusiasm.

I asked him how many iPods he thought Apple would sell. "There are seven and a half million Mac users with FireWire," he said. "I'll be glad to tell you how many they sell, but I don't do predictions." But he did do proclamations. "iPod," he said, "will be a landmark product."

I wondered what his personal experiences with the iPod were.

"I haven't been able to use it in public," he said. "But I find myself turning on music. Last night my wife was going to sleep and I put on my headphones."

What were you listening to?

"Moby."

The subject turned to September 11. A lot of conversations back then did that. Jobs said that after the attack, Apple had given the introduction a lot of thought, fearing that the wrong note might offend. "I think that we're feeling good about coming out with this at a difficult time," he said. "Hopefully it will bring a little joy to people." Such questions led to a discussion of Apple's relatively low-key iPod launch event, which in other circumstances might have been held in a big city—if not San Francisco, maybe even New York. "It's a tough time," Jobs finally said. "But life goes on. It must go on."

It turned out that the next day was the eve of another major computer industry launch: Microsoft's Windows XP. In contrast to the Apple event, this was a long-awaited rollout. Unlike an Apple event, the presentation itself would be suspense-free: the new operating system had been under examination for literally years, and hundreds of thousands of people had already installed it in beta test format. Everything that could possibly be known about it (except the extent of its security vulnerabilities, which exceeded every assumption, including Microsoft's) had been covered in the press. Nonetheless it was an improvement over previous versions of Windows, an official Big Deal that would be worth billions of dollars of profit to Microsoft. After some hand-wringing about whether it would be appropriate to stage the event in New York City so soon after the tragedy—and after a meeting with Mayor Rudy Giuliani to confirm that Gotham was ready for it—the festivities were on.

The evening before the launch, Microsoft hosted a small dinner for a group of journalists. I have lots of experience talking to Bill Gates and do not break into tears (as some journalists have done) when he yells, "That's the stupidest thing I ever heard!" so the Microsoft PR team seated me next to the chairman. It was always interesting to talk to Bill Gates and Steve Jobs within a day or two of each other. Gates, as Apple competitor and Apple developer, has a long and complicated relationship with his fellow personal computer pioneer Jobs. They have a sort of mutual envy society: Jobs lusts for Gates's market share, and Gates wishes he had Jobs's charisma and his adoring press clips. Jobs knows how to reach the heart, but Gates rules in matters of the head—and the bottom line.

I brought along my new iPod.

The evening wasn't much different from similar Bill gang-bangs (*he* banging *us!*) with lots of questions for the Microsoft founder, who sometimes dazzled us with his panoramic take on the marketplace and other times admonished us about our total stupidity on this or that issue or ignorance of some footnote in the history of PC software. At the end of the meal, just as the other guests at the table were pushing away their chairs, I pulled out the iPod and put it in front of Gates.

"Have you seen this yet?" I asked.

At that point Gates went into a zone that recalls those science fiction films where a space alien, confronted with a novel object, creates some sort of force tunnel between him and the object, allowing him to suck directly into his brain all possible information about it. Gates's fingers, racing at NASCAR speed, played over the scroll wheel and pushed every button combination, while his eyes stared fixedly at the screen. I could almost hear the giant sucking sound. Finally, after he had absorbed every nuance of the device, he handed it back to me.

"It looks like a great product," he said.

Then he paused a second. Something didn't compute.

"It's only for Macintosh?" he asked.

Yes, it was. (Then.)

Over the next few days, I began to play with the iPod Apple had sent me. I loaded a lot of my music into my black PowerBook G3. It took about five or six minutes to rip a CD into iTunes but, once that was done, only a few seconds to load an album's worth of songs into the iPod itself. I was impressed by how quickly that happened and how easy it was. (Don't tell anyone, but I also loaded a bunch of songs I had downloaded during the days when Napster offered the world's music for free.) The sound was excellent, though the white earbuds didn't fit me too well. (I later replaced them with pricier Shure buds.) I must have spent the better part of a night pulling CDs from my shelves and loading songs. I walked everywhere with my iPod—the subway, the streets, down the halls of *Newsweek* to get my mail.

Then I discovered shuffle.

There were lots of different ways to sequence music on the iPod.

One was to painstakingly choose song by song, obviously a work-intensive method that wouldn't allow for any flow. Another was to simply pick an album and let it play. A more ambitious approach was to use the iTunes software on the computer and organize sets of songs in playlists. But the best way, I discovered, was to find the setting that said "shuffle," click through the menus till you got to a list of all your songs, pick a starting place, and go. From that point, your whole collection would resequence itself in glorious chaos. It was like my own private radio station that played only songs that I liked—after all, I had put them there.

I also began to cultivate a nice relationship with the actual device. It felt very good to hold. Spinning my thumb on the scroll wheel was satisfying. The smooth silvery back felt so sensual that it was almost a crime against nature. And it didn't hurt that at least until November, when stores began selling the iPod, I possessed a valuable, hard-to-get little wonder.

One day sitting in the subway, I plugged in the iPod and the world filled up with the Byrds singing "My Back Pages." The faces around me suddenly became characters in a movie centered around my own memories and emotions. A black-and-white moment of existence had sprung into Technicolor. I held my iPod a bit tighter.

Something odd began to happen. As the days passed and I bonded with my iPod, my spirits lifted somewhat. Maybe it was just a recovery process that would have happened anyway, but it seemed hastened by the daily delights of the music that appeared on my iPod. President George W. Bush, whom I disagree with on almost everything, would say something very similar almost five years later: "I'm a bike guy," he remarked, "and I like to plug in music on my iPod to hopefully help me forget how old I am." I wasn't exactly *forgetting* about 9/11, but I was getting excited—once more—about technology and its power to transform our world.

This meant a lot. I am a technology writer. What had compelled me in the first place to devote my career to chronicling the digital revolution was my belief that this was the biggest story of our time. I have often expressed the thought, to the point of boredom to those close to me, that hundreds of years from now, if humanity survives its penchant for self-destruction, people will look back at these decades and wonder what it was like at the time everything changed. Now, living in a city where an awful smell still wafted uptown into my apartment window from the World Trade Center site, that condition about survival was suddenly looming larger. Could it be that the biggest story of our time was *not* how digital technology was taking humanity to another level but how the age-old dark impulses of war and violence were driving humanity to a base level? Part of what I loved about the tech beat was the wild optimism of the people I wrote about, the hackers who think you can tweak the innards of anything to make things work right, the messianic visionaries who believe that binary bits are the essence of existence itself. The computer era was barely a half-century old, the Internet boom wasn't even a *decade* old, and already these developments had made the life my son leads drastically different from my own teenage existence. And it was only beginning. I was proud to think that it might be possible that some of my own writings might preserve the stories of this time and give the people of the future— unimaginable bionic descendants of us analog-bound humans— an idea of what the people who had made it happen were like.

But now I wondered. How could you devote your energies to documenting the Internet, cool gadgets, and the future of music when all this darkness was afoot? Interrupting those bleak questions came iPod, and in those days and the years since its introduction— despite not much good happening in the global arena—I regained my confidence that technology is still the hallmark of our era.

Perfect

It wasn't until I began researching this book that I learned what had happened in Cupertino on September 11 after Jobs sent his e-mail to Apple employees. Though they were welcome to remain at home that tragic day, the people working on the iPod team were faced with a dilemma. They were building an important product with the end in sight, but now their very concept of what was important had suddenly shifted. They wondered, considering what had happened on the other side of the country, whether coming in to work was appropriate or not. But they felt uncomfortable at the prospect of doing nothing, and they couldn't think of what would be more appropriate than finishing their jobs. One by one they fired up their sports cars and drove to Infinite Loop, the address of the gleaming white buildings on Apple's campus, to help get the iPod out the door. It would, as Steve Jobs hoped, "bring a little joy to people." And much much more.

Following are some reflections on a perfect thing.

Identity

❯Those not familiar with the psychodemographics of the Big Apple's underground transit network should know that the L train takes an unusual path. Unlike the major underground lines that snake from Brooklyn to Manhattan and from there head to Queens or the Bronx, the L train begins in so-called pioneer neighborhoods of Brooklyn, home to artists, intellectuals, and young folks on starter salaries priced out of the former Bohemian outposts of SoHo, Greenwich Village, or even the more recently gentrified areas of middle-class Brooklyn. Its path through Manhattan is a crosstown victory lap on edgy Fourteenth Street, the fault line between hip and hopeless in New York City. Thus it has gained a sort of cachet as the subway line for the city's cultural vanguard— those who define cool rather than seek it.

So it was perhaps inevitable that the L line would be the scene of the so-called iPod Wars, described in April 2005 by Trace Crutchfield, writing for a local magazine, *The Brooklyn Rail*. According to his account, while waiting for the L in the Metropolitan Avenue station beneath Brooklyn, he was the victim of a taste attack. The perpetrator was a young woman garbed in seventies punk style—"just about the spitting image," he wrote, "of the singer

Poly Styrene of X-Ray Spex." The one variation from period costume: white earbuds. She pulled out her iPod and thrust the screen to within a few inches of his face. He was thus forced to deal with the identity of her "currently playing" tune. It was by a long-forgotten power punk seventies band called the Rezillos. Hip. Very hip. *Post*-hip. Then she pointed to Crutchfield's jacket pocket, the location to which his own spiraling white earphone cord led, indicating that he should show her what was on *his* 'pod. He reluctantly pulled it out, fearing that it would display a choice that was mortifyingly more prosaic than hers. It was, in fact, a pathetic Pet Shop Boys tune, the sort of thing that Nick Hornby would listen to on a bad day. He was not just defeated. He was humiliated.

This was but the first of many such iPod Wars Crutchfield says he experienced or witnessed, not only on the L train but elsewhere in the city. The winner of these musical sumo matches is the one who, by some sort of silent mutual consent (both people are, of course, wearing headphones), has cued a song that would win the approval of even the most pedantic *Village Voice* rock critic but be totally unknown to all but a microscopic fraction of the listening public. You are guaranteed to lose if you have something that was discovered recently but already popular enough to garner record reviews in the likes of *Rolling Stone* and *USA Today*. So when Crutchfield is caught with the Shins—who are edgy only to someone who hangs in baby-boomer circles, the sort of people striving to score primo tickets to Paul McCartney concerts—he knows he's blown away when a guy with a mustache counters with a song from a band called Turbonegro.

Have you ever heard, or heard of, Turbonegro? I haven't. Which is exactly the point of these wars. A powerful advantage accrues to those who not only know of but *know*—and deeply appreciate—a band off the radar of anyone whose name is inked on a mortgage.

You are wired. You have Edge Cred. Crutchfield's account may have the whiff of the apocryphal—I ride the subway all the time, and though white earbuds are as common as tabloid newspapers, I have yet to be confronted by a blue-haired punkette trumping my Steve Earle with a track from Deerhoof. But "that is the way it really went down," he confirmed to me via e-mail, and I can believe it. Such incidents strike at something deep in Planet iPod. Furthermore, Crutchfield's account confirms more closely documented observations of how music on one's iPod affects status.

Playlist is character.

Musical one-upmanship is nothing new. But the portability of the iPod and the transparency that comes from exposing an iPod screen to an observer make the otherwise private device a potential broadcaster of one's taste. In part because of those factors and in part because the ubiquity of the iPod amplifies such concerns in the media and in Web sites like MySpace.com (where musical choice is as much a badge of identity as is gender or geography), we seem to be immersed in an age of musical voyeurism. Not to mention musical exhibitionism. As a result, we're learning a lot about what songs people like to listen to—and a lot about the people who listen.

Obviously, exalted status comes from cool music libraries. Such libraries distinguish one as a thinking person, a discerning individualist, a lover of fun, a blender of high and low culture, and a bird dog in unearthing undiscovered gems. So valuable is a great collection that some people fret whether the iPod's ease of use, combined with the Internet (on which all fruits hang lower), allows one to concoct a plagiarized personality from an undeservedly spicy playlist. Michael Crowley, writing in *The New Republic*, had his tongue only partly in cheek when he charged that rock snobbery, a practice to which he admits, has become an endangered species—because the "dark side to the iPod era" is that it is too easy to access the cool stuff. "Thanks to the iPod, and digital music generally, anyone can milk various friends, acquaintances, and the Internet to quickly build a glorious 10,000-song collection," he writes. "We are suddenly plagued by musical parasites." He expressed his complicated emotions when his friends plundered his record collection (with his permission, but not the Recording Industry Association of America's). He was instantly shot through with regret: these dilettantes weren't worthy of owning his hard-won rarities. Crowley morosely contemplates a grim future where one no longer attains alpha-hood by possessing a copy of Bob Mould's cover version of the Gram Parsons classic "Hickory Wind." "When everything's instantly available online," he moans, "the thrill is gone."

This sort of gripe is actually a familiar elitist refrain in the digital age, when one can routinely access information in seconds that once required a week of library excavation to retrieve. Stripped to the bone, it's a complaint about the playing field being leveled. Or, as *The New York Times*' music critic Kelefa Sanneh put it, "Obscure ain't what it used to be . . . it's getting harder to find any music at all that's hard to find."

Well, so what? Could it be that there are better ways of valuing music than by the difficulty it takes to acquire it? One of the nicer things about the iPod era is its tendency to stretch a meat-and-potatoes music fan's collection to include exotic tastes once reserved for the Dr. Demento crowd. But only the true gourmands of audio will be able to winnow down their playlists to pick out the choicest cuts to beard the pretender on the L train. Meanwhile, really weird sounds created by fans who build on the work of the artist have become possible for the first time—mixes and mashups and celestial cross-fades. For discerning denizens of the emerging all-digital world, the real thrills are just beginning.

In any case, the iPod era doesn't mark the end of snobbism but a scary acceleration of it. The ability to easily compile one's favorite songs in one place may make it easier to accumulate a collection of dazzling obscurities but also increases the culpability of those whose libraries are less than stellar. When anyone can get hold of previously unattainable B sides of 1950s singles, live cuts from long-out-of-print concert compilations, and whispered-about but seldom-heard gems from top artists moonlighting under pseudonyms, it's an Everest-level challenge to construct a collection that blows someone's mind. (One for-instance: just recently a well-known blog revealed the existence of a quick-and-dirty 1966 recording session intended to cash in on the popularity of the *Batman* TV show—the album, released by a toy company, was an amazing jam session with members of the legendary Blues Project and the cosmic jazz giant Sun Ra. Some weird Web site let you download it free. Having *that* in your library would make you an L train god—before the word spread and everyone else got wind of it, too.)

The idea of defining oneself by what you listen to isn't exactly a new concept. People have always judged and been judged by what they listen to. When I was in high school in the 1960s, you were labeled by whether you listened to Motown or the irreverent noises of Dylan, Hendrix, and the Lovin' Spoonful. (Since we didn't have iPods, we tipped our tastes by clothing: the Motown crowd wore highboy collars and the folk-rock "dirties" wore T-shirts and jeans.) The annotated personal playlist is a tradition that goes back to the early pages of *Downbeat* magazine, and it's been more than a decade since an innovative chain of record stores called Hear Music began to recruit artists to select a set of tunes that deeply influenced them. The purpose is as much biography as buying tips. (Hear Music was subsequently purchased by Starbucks, which seems to use the CDs it sells as an expression of what the company represents, a musical version of a mission statement.) But in the iTunes store and elsewhere on the Internet, this practice has been amplified to breakout status. On Apple's iPod downloading head-quarters, you can find more than a hundred celebrity playlists, not just those of musicians—Avril Lavigne digs Lesley Gore; Barry Manilow confesses that "Tom Waits is my favorite male singer"—but movie stars and athletes such as Sharon Stone ("Just Like a Woman") and Dale Earnhardt Jr. ("A Horse with No Name"). Else-where on the Net, it's common for bloggers to list favorite tunes, and on social Web sites like MySpace.com, your song preferences are the link that potentially binds you to new friends.

On iPods themselves, this practice has been ground down to the nub. Simply handing over your iPod to a friend, your blind date, or the total stranger sitting next to you on the plane opens you up like a book. All someone needs to do is scroll through your library on that click wheel, and, musically speaking, you're naked. It's not just what you like—it's *who you are.*

Not just celebrity mags but the entire mainstream media have caught up to this. A common feature is "What's on your iPod?" The CNN anchorman Aaron Brown confided to *Golf Connoisseur* that his library encompasses "everything that Paul Simon has ever done; everything from early Dylan and Norah Jones to a John Denver song that I hope no one asks me about." The singer-songwriter Ben Lee provides *Wired* with a list ranging from Creedence Clearwater Revival to Conway Twitty and Loretta Lynn's "You're the Reason Our Kids Are Ugly." An arts reporter for *The Birmingham News* is startled to hear that the conductor of the Alabama Symphony Orchestra has loaded his silver mini not with classical music but with Broadway show tunes and that song by Harry Nilsson about the lime in the coconut. Talk show hosts also pop the question, sometimes to people you wouldn't expect, as when David Cameron, the leader of the British Conservative Party, was ambushed with the query on BBC Radio One. The question is not reserved for rock stars and politicians—countless newspapers, magazines, and blogs use "What's on your iPod?" as a cheap man-in-the-street space filler.

Sometimes a celebrity does not bother to wait until someone asks. *Newsweek*'s Devin Gordon was having a routine interview with the actor David Thewlis about his role in a new Harry Potter movie when the thespian suddenly erupted into an ode to 'pod. "I'm as passionate now about music as I was when I was 16!" he said. "I spent the entire afternoon the other day on this roof in Morocco just listening to all my songs in alphabetical order so I'd have no idea what was coming next and it was amazing. It's the greatest invention of the 21st century!"

Bruce Willis decided to clue the world in to his iPod fetish by publishing the news on his Web site. "Being that I am a musician, a lot of people have asked me about my take on the whole Internet downloading, Internet swapping, music piracy issue," he wrote. "So here it is in a nutshell: The Internet has turned me on to amazing music that I might otherwise have never heard of. As a Mac enthusiast I have taken the iTunes playlist concept to a new level." (He goes on, but I won't.)

"iPods seem to have a special place in celebrities' hearts," says Karen Wood, the president of Backstage Creations, which stuffs the fabled "goodie bags" presented to anything-but-needy movie stars and rockers as sugar coating for the chore of attending awards shows and red-carpet benefits. The glitterati began asking for iPods in 2002, and since then, no swag bag has been complete without a mini or, more recently, a nano, though musicians appreciate the multigigabyte capacity of the full-size units.

In part because it's hard to imagine even almost-famous personages going through life without someone laying a free iPod on them, the question of *whether* a celebrity has an iPod rarely arises. (During one of Jobs's famous keynote presentations, the Apple CEO for some reason asked Madonna, her live image from London beamed on a giant screen behind him, if she had an iPod. The Material Girl looked stunned for a minute before replying, *"Duu-uuuh!"*) If one does ask, it is usually in the context of a dipstick plunged into an oil pan of apparent cluelessness, in the hope that the supposedly out-of-it subject will surprise and delight everyone by saying, "You bet I have one of those babies!" If the answer is negative, the whole incident is kind of embarrassing, as it was during a New York City mayoral debate held in October 2005 at the Apollo Theatre in Harlem between the Democratic candidate, Fernando Ferrer, and the Conservative, Tom Ognibene (a blank podium was reserved for the incumbent, Michael Bloomberg, who declined to participate). Among a series of lightning-round yes-or-no questions posed by a cable TV reporter ("Should police officers be required to live in the city?" "Do you oppose the use of eminent domain in Atlantic Yards?") came the wild card: "Do you own an iPod?"

Neither did. Which was surprising, because by then, politicians seemed almost as likely as graphic artists and college students to have them. (Had Mayor Bloomberg been at the debate, he would have answered in the affirmative. He uses his iPod to listen to Spanish lessons.) It really wasn't much of a shock when Elisabeth Bumiller of *The New York Times* broke the news that President George W. Bush had joined the Order of White Earbuds. In July 2004, Bush's twin daughters presented him with a forty-gig iPod, whose storage space he had barely dented the following spring, when Bumiller's article appeared. At that point the president had not yet dared to navigate iTunes; his personal assistant, Blake Gottesman, took on the mantle of First Downloader, patronizing Apple's online store to provide the content for the presidential 'pod. Some tunes were also downloaded by Bush media guru Mark McKinnon, leading fair-use copyright activists to speculate about White House infringement.

What's on George Bush's iPod? Bumiller, unhesitatingly embracing the "Playlist Is Character" ethic, got the list and promptly recruited a rock critic from *Rolling Stone* to expound on the significance of the sonic selections that accompany the president on his frequent midday mountain-bike rides. Typical boomer stuff, sniffed the Stoner, with the exception of some vintage George Jones, which won grudging approval. The nadir seemed to be "My Sharona," a musical preference successfully suppressed until after the chief executive was safely reelected. Bumiller's sources duly acknowledged that many of the artists on Bush's iPod disliked the president but also noted that any list of modern musicians that stipulated support of the Bush administration would be severely impoverished. Ultimately, McKinnon—who himself once wrote songs for Kris Kristofferson's publishing company—cautioned Bumiller not to read too much into the list. "No one should psychoanalyze the song selection," he said. "It's just music to get over the next hill."

Bumiller's article caused a minor sensation. Undoubtedly, the impulse that led the White House to go public with the news of the presidential 'pod was cultural spin doctoring, an attempt to connect with the millions of young people who doted on their own iPods. The impulse of Bush's critics, however, was to mockingly assemble proposed playlists for the POTUS Pod, an exercise conducted far and wide among denizens of the blogosphere. The president might well be wary of the set that Katrina vanden Heuvel, the editor of *The Nation*, prepared for him; it included Kid Rock's

"Pimp of the Nation," and R.E.M.'s "The End of the World as We Know It." Responding to her choices, more than three hundred readers of that left-leaning opinion journal piled on with their own suggestions for sound tracks to best augment a Camp David mountain-bike workout. The Bush-haters' hit parade included "American Idiot," "War (What Is It Good For)?," and Frank Zappa's "The Torture Never Stops."

Eight months later, in a December 2005 Fox News interview, the playlister-in-chief spoke directly about his iPod. It was clear that he'd become pretty familiar with the artists on his iPod. He'd added Alison Krauss (good), Aretha Franklin (better) . . . and the Archies (oh, well). Though well known for his penchant for order in his daily schedule and his overall loathing of the unexpected, the president surprisingly gave his official endorsement for shuffling, though it wasn't quite clear if he understood that this was the name of a smaller iPod as well as a feature. "I put it on shuffle," he bragged. "Lightweight, crank it on, and you shuffle the shuffle . . . put it in my pocket, got the ear-things on . . . and if you don't like it, you got your little advance button. It's pretty high-tech stuff." All in all, President Bush was much more impressive with his iPod use than his counterpart in England, Tony Blair, who admitted to television interviewer Michael Parkinson that while he had an iPod, "I'm not very good with any aspect of it." Blair left it to his daughter Kathryn to load his iPod with tunes, specifically those of Christina Aguilera. (Ouch.) By April 2006, Bush was sufficiently obsessed with the iPod that he made a pretty good joke about it in a speech about competitiveness at Tuskegee University:

Here's another interesting example of where basic research can help change quality of life or provide practical applications for people. The government funded research in microdrive storage, electrochemistry and signal compression. They did so for one reason: It turned out that those were the key ingredients for the development of the iPod.

I tune into the iPod occasionally, you know?

Was Vice President Dick Cheney left out in the iPod cold? No, he was not. His daughters, Liz and Mary, bought him an iPod for his birthday in 2004, and told *USA Today* that the Vice President used it to listen to . . . the Carpenters. Very typical, it seems, of the songs that populate Playlists for Undisclosed Locations. Even Liz Cheney was moved to make an endearingly dead-on editorial comment on Dad's iTunes library: "Ugh." Nonetheless, Cheney's iPod would become very important to him, as illustrated by an incident on Air Force Two during a late-2005 flight back from a quickie visit to Iraq. A glitch in the plane's electrical system shorted out most of the power outlets. One was working in the back of the cabin, and reporters were taking turns using it to power their computers. Then they were abruptly disconnected—on the orders of the vice president. "When Cheney said his iPod needed to be recharged," the Associated Press reported, "it took precedent above all else and dominated one precious outlet for several hours. The vice president's press staff intervened so a reporter could use the outlet for 15 minutes to charge a dead laptop, but then the digital music device was plugged back in." According to the AP account, keeping the VeepPod charged "is a priority for his staff."

Could there possibly be an iPod owner uncooler than the vice president? Yes, there could. In the summer of 2005, word came that Queen Elizabeth had a silver iPod mini. No word of its contents, but much mordant speculation. It seems reasonable to assume, though, that if she had downloaded "God Save the Queen," it was not the Sex Pistols' version.

The next beat in this drumroll is obvious: the pope. Yes, in March 2006, an employee of Vatican Radio gave the visiting pontiff an iPod, engraved on the rear with the legend, in Italian, "To His Holiness, Benedict XVI." Besides radio broadcasts, the iPod contained classical music by Beethoven, Chopin, Mozart, and Stravinsky. According to the Catholic News Service, "Hundreds of radio journalists, sound engineers and support staff lined the radio's hallways to greet the pope, and present him with gifts, mostly special in-house productions such as CDs and books on church, religion, and the pope." But it was the two-gigabyte white nano presented by the station's tech support guy that most impressed His Holiness. "Computer technology is the future," he said.

In a way there's something comforting about these reports of iPod adoption by people who seem incongruous in the digital world. It paints a telling picture of how even the most cautious humans have been adjusting to the furious pace of the modern world. Ever since, say, electricity, society has had to endure a steady succession of disruptions in the name of progress. Forward-thinking folks have always embraced novelty and been quick to identify the virtues of an unexpected new technology. (Think of Edith Wharton, who by 1902 had equipped her Berkshire estate with electricity, telephones, and a hydraulic elevator, and who bought a motorcar two years later.) Some have always held back for a spell, either not seeing the necessity for something like a moving picture box in their home or feeling intimidated by the demands that this development might make on them. Eventually they come to see the value of the invention, and there is a moment in time— when the newfangled object has shifted to a mass phenomenon but is not yet so common that using it draws no comment whatsoever—that unlikely people hop on the bandwagon, albeit with a bit of vertigo.

Of course, some people take a *long* time to get up to speed. Penn State icon Joe Paterno, who began coaching the football team when 45-rpm records were the rage, was once asked about one of his players' having been caught using an illegal file-sharing Internet program. "What the hell is download music?" he wanted to know.

He need only have asked his athletes, because even among sports figures the iPod has become a form of expression, and to inquiring sportswriters a subject's playlist can be as revealing as a diary. "If you want to plug into Laveranues Coles' inner life," begins a *New York Times* story about a wide receiver for the NFL Jets, "borrow his iPod." It turns out that although Coles is a taciturn type, his playlist is the eloquent evidence of a secret he had previously kept from even his closest friends—that for three years, beginning when he was ten years old, he had been abused by his mother's boyfriend. The 343 songs on the iPod are, claims reporter Karen Crouse, "emotional fingerprints" that provide a window to Coles's pain as well as the therapy he uses to heal himself. A rap called "Motivation," whose lyrics in part go "Anything that don't kill me make me better," is Coles's favorite. "Basically it's about people bringing you down," the twenty-seven-year-old told the *Times*.

Fortunately, Coles plays football and is not subject to the rules that govern his basketball colleagues. In November 2004, Toronto Raptors star guard Vince Carter was stunned by an NBA edict that terminated his practice of conducting pregame warmups while plugged into his iPod. A glum Carter told the Toronto *Globe and Mail* that the ban might well harm his game. "I focus in when I have music on," he said. A sentiment that resonated in the 2006 Winter Olympics, when America's half-pipe snowboarders would actually *compete* while blaring Death Cab for Cutie and AC/DC into earbuds or speakers set into the hood of their custom-made Burton snowjackets. When Hannah Teeter gold-medaled to the tune of "Communicate," she brought fame to previously unknown Strive Roots—not incidentally, her boyfriend's band.

But the most powerful means of examining someone's playlists don't require the assistance of reporters or even the aggressive tactics of L train duelists. iTunes itself has several means of enabling voyeuristic explorations of someone's musical tastes. Though the clothing designer David Li's prototype shoulder strap with an electronic readout that reveals what song is currently playing on your iPod has yet to hit the market (the product, Li writes, "is intended to encourage social connectedness by making this hidden information visible"), there is an electronic equivalent built into Apple's instant messaging program, iChat: an electronic status line that informs everyone on your buddy list what tune you're listening to—a chance to impress friends by your early adoption of Sufjan Stevens or embarrass yourself by a weakness for the *Best of Bread*.

Another iTunes feature works on a network of connected computers by allowing you to expose your entire music library to anyone on your local network, or "subnet." (It's up to the user to determine whether he or she will block this feature, but lots of people don't realize that sharing is the default option.) Using a special, Apple-designed wireless protocol called Rendezvous (the name was later changed to Bonjour), you can scan the libraries of total strangers who just happen to be within a few hundred feet of you. By clicking on a song from the list, it's also possible for a free rider to stream that song from someone else's computer to his own. And *they can't see you looking*. It's like rifling through someone's music collection while they've stepped out to buy milk for the coffee. For the past few years, whenever I'm at a tech conference, I flick on iTunes to scour my immediate wireless neighborhood, trolling for interesting tunes. In my experience the wireless connection is usually insufficiently robust to stream songs without hiccups or dead stops, but I'm fascinated to see what other people have loaded into their libraries.

Naturally, when you look at someone's music, you make judgments. An eclectic and knowing collection raises your opinion of the collector. By some accounts, a really good playlist can even generate an aphrodisiac effect. In a blog posting, the tech writer Mitch Ratcliffe reported on a lunch with Apple's Tony Fadell, who told Ratcliffe about grateful e-mails he'd received from collegians on campus networks. Apparently these male students were beneficiaries of midnight visits from female students who'd scanned the guys' playlists on the campus networks and were so impressed that they craved an instant hookup.

A great story, albeit with the dubious ring of a letter to *Penthouse*. But social scientists are hard at work actually *documenting* this stuff. Amy Voida, a graduate student at the Georgia Institute of Technology, began a formal study of the behavior of people who have access to one another's iTunes playlists. She began her project while spending a summer internship at Xerox's Palo Alto Research Center (the same place where, in 1979, Steve Jobs and a team of Apple engineers made a visit to view the original graphical user interface, a trip that became part of history when the ideas reemerged in the original Macintosh in 1984). Though Voida was not a Macintosh user and didn't even have an iPod then, many of her colleagues at PARC's Ubiquitous Computer Group were hard-core iTunes lovers, and they agreed to work on the project with her. Voida's test bed for study was a Silicon Valley tech company with about 175 employees (she promised to keep its identity confidential) that allowed her access to its computer network so she could track the playlists available and who looked at them. Then she interviewed the heavy users among the twenty or so workers who participated in this benign musical surveillance.

The conclusion? "iTunes' interface plays a critical role in terms of allowing an audience to examine and judge a collection, thereby creating an impression of a co-worker," wrote Voida and her four coauthors.

One participant in the study was humiliated by the realization that his list was not solely a reflection of his own respectable tastes but also included some lame-o songs that he had downloaded for his less discriminating wife. "To get a little insight into what I'm about, it'd kind of be inaccurate, 'cuz there's, you know, here's Justin Timberlake and there's another couple of artists on here that . . . Michael McDonald, you know," he told the researchers, apparently so upset that he was unable to speak in coherent sentences. "Some of this stuff I would not, you know, want to be kind of associated with it."

Knowing that people could see your lists and judge you by it changed not only the social dynamic but the playlists as well: people stocked their collections not solely with what they liked but what they thought would raise their status among coworkers. The academics writing the paper instantly recognized this as an example of what the renowned sociologist Erving Goffman long ago termed "impression management."

Voida and her coauthors also documented how viewing the playlists of others could widen someone's tastes. "There were people that definitely found things that were similar to artists that they already liked that were new artists that they hadn't listened to before, and people just kind of ate that up," she says. But it could be dangerous to depend on someone else's playlist. "There was one gentleman who was in the middle of listening to a brand-new artist he had found on somebody else's music library and the person whose music he was listening to left the company," Voida says. "This guy was really upset that he was in the process of discovering this new music and it disappeared underneath him."

When Voida presented the paper, entitled "Listening In: Practices Surrounding iTunes Music Sharing," to the American Computing Machinery Conference of Human Factors in Computing Systems, she prefaced the talk with a whimsical introduction that included PowerPoint slides of the playlists of the various authors of the paper. "One of the guys," she says, "apparently has music taste that's so hip that he was contacted by the Stanford University radio station, and he was asked to come guest-DJ for them."

Now, *that's* impression management.

What if you don't want others to see? Fortunately for introverts and Kenny G. fans, iTunes lets you shield your playlists from others on the network. And the people who challenge you on the L train can't *make* you show your screen to them. As Dr. Jennifer Hartstein, a child and adolescent psychologist in New York City, explained to a reporter for *The Atlanta Journal-Constitution*, revealing playlists to someone else can be an emotionally risky act. "It might let you learn more about me than I want you to," she warns.

On the other hand, *intentionally* opening the iTunes kimono can be an adventure in itself, strangely intimate and ultimately fulfilling. In the pursuit of all things iPod, I set out to make a musical bond with another open soul. I figured my friend Stacy, who is rarely spotted on the streets of Greenwich Village without earbuds fixed to her first-generation iPod, would be a perfect candidate. She had alerted me to the abundance of choral music on her iTunes, but I was ready for anything. All we awaited was an opportune moment when I had my own iPod ready to plug into her computer, whereupon I would give the fateful answer "yes" to the dialog box that asked me if I were sure I wanted to replace all the songs in my iPod with those in her iTunes library.

(This sort of opportunity was not envisioned by the iPod's software designers but is a consequence of the subtle interaction between iTunes and iPod. Though many owners of the device assume that the iPod is the storage container of their songs, the songs really live on the computer. An iPod is essentially a satellite of the iTunes software application; when you dock the device to the computer, the iPod checks the changes made to iTunes since the last time you docked and updates the iPod to mirror the current collection on your computer.)

I was not alone in wanting to try this form of exploration. John Schwartz, a reporter for *The New York Times,* had written about his experience after buying a fully loaded iPod from his friend Ken; before wiping the disk clean and replacing it with his own music collection, Schwartz thought he'd spend some time in "Kenworld," his buddy's musical territory. He not only discovered some cool new tunes but accumulated insights about his pal. "Outside his iPod, Ken is pleasant but reserved," he wrote. "But his selections show an unbridled feeling I had never glimpsed; he treasures the passionate Tori Amos and has a goofy soft spot for Air Supply. I know him better, and I like what I know."

But what if Schwartz *hadn't* liked what he discovered? Would the musical geography of Kenworld have made Ken radioactive in real life? I wondered whether spending time with Stacy's iTunes would affect our friendship. It wasn't so much the choral music that worried me but the danger that she might harbor a fondness for hokey pop songs. I wondered if I should try someone else instead.

In the summer of 2005, I did enter into someone else's iTunes zone. It was the result of an impulsive exchange with a woman I hardly knew, a former dot-com executive whom I ran into at an informal tech conference in Sebastopol, California. We'd fallen into discussion about—what else?—iPods. She was describing her tastes, which sounded quirky but were apparently imbued with a definite aesthetic. On a whim, I asked her if she would fill up my shuffle with a representative sampling of songs from her collection. She gamely agreed, and I pulled the 240-song device out of my bag and passed it to her. A few hours later, she pressed the newly loaded white bar into my hand.

It was a few days before I dared plug my Shure earbuds into the newly loaded shuffle. I guess I should mention at this point that my new 'pod-mate was an athletic blonde in her thirties. (She later wrote me that she had ruined two shuffles "due to sweat getting into the internal electronics from the back plate during my long runs.") So I would be remiss if I did not admit that the exchange of songs had something of an erotic charge to it. This was enhanced by the utter weirdness of her selections. I felt as though I had stumbled into someone else's brain, and in this unfamiliar territory, there was little to hang on to. Some pieces sounded like trancelike sound tracks to low-budget horror films. Then there was atonal music that sounded like electrified Stockhausen. There was free-form jazz with saxophones on the brink of panic. There were vocal selections ranging from menacing tunes from a shredder to ballads sung by hiccupy women. This was music chosen by someone who is unperturbed by the screeching of fingernails on a blackboard. On live records of the Grateful Dead, I usually skip past the spacey, unstructured drum solos; I suspect those are the only parts this woman listens to. The only major overlap between her library and mine seemed to be the totally mellifluous but lyrically cranky Aimee Mann; these songs seemed like islands of stability in a churning sea of cacophony, attitude, and menace. In short, it was

Identity

her soundscape, and I was just a tourist. There was plenty of fodder to imagine what personality had put together this collection—clearly someone with daring, whimsy, a craving for some hard edges, and a perfectly reasonable fondness for Ms. Mann. (Unless, of course, there was considerable impression management involved.)

Though a two-way exchange wasn't part of my original scheme, I returned the favor, filling up the shuffle with a selection of songs from my own library and sending it across the country to my new-found friend. Dr. Jennifer Hartstein, the psychologist who warned about exposing one's playlist, would not be surprised at the deflation of my ego that followed. A few days after receiving the shuffle, the recipient gently informed me that what I had thought was a respectably edgy set of tastes was really the musical equivalent of a stuffed, comfortable couch. "Your song selections are very consistent," she wrote, as if bending over backwards to be polite. "So far, the songs have covered rock/alt/country and blues. All clearly sung interesting lyrics, and even the instrumentals would easily support lyrics. It seems that half of the music is from 2000 on, but there are selections from other recent decades. While I couldn't write/read/paint to this music (because the clear lyrics would keep grabbing my attention) it is very much good traveling music. Is that how you use your shuffle?"

That hurt. I had secretly prided myself on what I considered to be a wide-open, if not daring, contemporary musical taste. But when passed through the unbiased ear canal of a neutral observer, this painstakingly acquired collection was exposed as baby-boomer comfort food. Despite the fact that lots of the songs were recently recorded, by musicians young enough to be grandchildren of the Beatles, I now realized that these newer tunes, albeit performed by sneering guitar bangers or alternative folkies of near-Mennonite austerity, were almost without exception all too clearly descended from the folk-rock, blues, and R&B I was hooked on in the sixties. Much of my music expressed the same woe-is-me lyrics that moved me back then. "A few other things I noticed about your musical selections," wrote my partner in this experiment. "You listen to the words. You also don't seem to like singing that involves more of a yelling kind of style. You like smooth, or rough voices, but not screechy. You like acoustic instruments."

In other words . . . wimp!

Viewed competitively, I could be called the loser in a transcontinental version of the L train wars. But the exercise taught me (once I got over the shock) that comparing playlists should be viewed not in terms of a smackdown but rather a learning experience. iTunes surfing is not merely a revelation of character but a means to a rich personal narrative, navigated by click wheel. At one point the universal goal of the literate was to write the Great American Novel. Then it moved to the Great American Screenplay. And now, the Great American iTunes Library.

Origin

❯A thousand songs—an entire record collection—in your pocket? It sounded like a dream. But a small team working for a big company in Silicon Valley understood that digital technology had put that far-fetched scenario within reach. They set out to create a supercool device that you could take on the road, then happily scan through oodles of songs transferred from your CD until you found the one you wanted. Or, if you preferred, you could shuffle through your whole library. After months of hard work, they accomplished their task.

Apple's dynamic effort to create the iPod? Nope. The team described above did not work for Apple. They were computer scientists at Digital Equipment Corporation's Palo Alto research division, and they did their work in 1998 and 1999—more than two years before Apple developed and released its music player.

Before the iPod, there was the Personal Jukebox.

In 1998, the first digital music players were just beginning to appear—but they used memory chips that held barely one CD's worth of music. Andrew Birrell, a British-born, Cambridge-educated computer scientist, first came up with the idea to create a music player that used the tiniest hard disk drive possible, then a

2.5-inch drive that went into notebook computers. It would store a *hundred* CDs' worth of music. He began the project with his colleague Ted Wobber in May 1998. It was something to occupy the researchers as their once-mighty company, DEC, was being acquired by the Houston-based PC maker Compaq. (Within a few years, Compaq itself would be bought out by Hewlett-Packard.) "We saw it as a really cool thing that we'd like to actually own, and I guess we reasonably thought that other people would like to own it, too," says Wobber.

Over the next year they managed to solve problems of energy management, sound processing, navigation, and integration with personal computers until they finally had something you could hold in your hand—something that held a hundred of your CDs. It could fit in a pocket, sort of. Not a pants pocket, certainly not a shirt pocket, but a big pocket in your jacket or parka. Using its menus, its seven-line screen, and six buttons to navigate, you could find the song you wanted to play—eventually. But it worked.

It would have made quite a splash if Compaq had begun the rigorous process of getting the price down, perfecting the interface, and smoothly synchronizing the PC software. But as Dave Redell, who was in the DEC research development group (which tries to get researchers' creations into the product pipeline), explains, the project was a victim of a sad corporate soap opera. "When Compaq bought Digital, they basically got the whole research thing completely by accident. Once they found out it was there, a number of the VPs started putting plans in place to kill it. We tried pretty hard to interest product groups, but they didn't have the vision that this thing could have a very wide audience. Maybe it was because they couldn't see form factors which would be smaller and priced less, or maybe it was because they looked at us and said, 'Well, who are you?' "

The Personal Jukebox team tried a last-ditch scheme to convince Compaq to market the device. They would give units to Compaq's top executives for Christmas 1998. They worked like mad to produce enough prototypes to give to forty key people who would presumably be blown away and immediately start production. What happened? "The executives' kids got hold of them," sighs Redell.

Meanwhile, the researchers realized that even in the months since they'd begun the project, the technology to make a digital music player had taken a big step. It was possible to build something smaller, for less cost, than the first-take device they'd completed. "We said, 'It's not too late, let's do this.' And they wouldn't pay any attention to us," says Wobber. Meanwhile, Redell was determined to get the Personal Jukebox on the market, even if it had to be licensed to another company. Every one of the big consumer electronics companies he approached turned him down. Finally he found an obscure Korean company called HanGo. "They were the only guys who had the guts to do it," says Redell.

Introduced at the Comdex show in November 1999, the PJB 100 was a strange product—an awkwardly sized box that was oriented horizontally, like a movie screen, rather than vertically, like the iPod. ("We all knew that the thing was too big and heavy," says Redell. "But we had a little belt clip thing for it so you didn't actually have to have it under your shirt, making you look sort of Quasimodo-like.") Its plastic case was colored an icy blue, somewhat evocative of the recently released iMac. But a few tech writers who reviewed it were sufficiently excited to report that some sort of revolution had begun. "The MP3 that changes everything," proclaimed *Popular Mechanics*.

In any case, the PJB had a number of shortcomings: a barely adequate interface, mundane jukebox software, and dead-slow uploading. The screen had no backlighting, and the memory buffer was skimpy, so the music skipped when you bumped it. HanGo's marketing was minimal. The cost—$799—was beastly. And the name, PJB, sounded like a dyslexic ordering a peanut butter and jelly sandwich. It never won a following. Like the wizards of Xerox PARC, another Palo Alto research division of a great company whose head was located eastward, the DEC scientists will dwell forever in a destination that they never booked—the limbo populated by creators doomed to see their great ideas realized, and hugely improved upon, by companies with more visionary bosses.

But in early 2000, when the PJB was shown at the Consumer Electronics Show, Apple Computer was late for its date with destiny. And who knows how or when Steve Jobs would have made his move were it not for a fateful, and painful, encounter with a long-time software partner of Apple's, a company called Adobe.

Jobs once walked me back along the chain of events that had led to iPod. Square one, he told me, was FireWire, the name of a means of quickly moving masses of digital information from one gadget to another. (The technology is also known as iLink.) Apple had invented it in the early nineties, but the first to exploit it were Japanese electronics companies, which put it into their camcorders. "But nobody, including Apple, put it on a computer," says Jobs. That changed in 1999, when Apple came up with the iMac DV, an upgrade to the new iMac the company had introduced earlier. "We put a FireWire port on it," says Jobs. "This was a big deal back then—we could get digital video into the computer without any adapters. That was huge."

At that point, Jobs approached the software developer Adobe, which had a Windows program that was the leading tool for consumers editing digital scenes captured by camcorders into their own home movies. Apple had enjoyed a long and fruitful relationship with Adobe; Jobs had given the company its first big break in 1985, when he picked it to provide the fonts and output system for Apple's groundbreaking laser printer. But by 1998, Adobe clearly felt that supporting Apple's platform was a lousy use of its resources, arguments to the contrary from Steve Jobs notwithstanding. Jobs's summary is terse: "We asked them to port it to Mac, and they refused."

The rejection was a rude wake-up call for Jobs, a reminder that no matter how nifty his computers were, many of the best software developers began and ended their consideration with the Macintosh's minuscule market share. If Macintosh were to have applications that would distinguish it as *the* machine for creating personal media, Apple would have to write them itself. It was a necessity that was bound to mother some smokin' inventions, because (in Jobs's thinking, at least) who could possibly come up with more spectacular applications than Apple? So Apple embarked on what it came to refer to as the Digital Hub strategy. The idea was to produce the world's greatest portfolio of consumer software, available only to those smart enough, cool enough, and thinking-different enough to buy an Apple computer. The first one would be iMovie, a spectacularly easy-to-use tool to transform camcorder clips into home movies—a far better application for beginners than Adobe's was. iMovie, with its brushed steel look and intuitive controls, was certainly a spiffier movie-editing tool than anyone had ever seen. "That evolved into the group that did iTunes, and iTunes was what led us to do iPod," says Jobs.

In retrospect, it seems odd that the idea for some sort of iMusic program hadn't come first. Apple employees were passionate music lovers. "It's in our blood, and we love it," says Jobs. But as the new millennium was dawning, Apple was ignoring music, even if music *was* in its blood. Tens of millions of people were downloading songs on Napster. People with Windows computers were burning CDs. And Apple was nowhere. The only software it supplied for music was a little application that let you stream the songs from a CD through the tiny Macintosh speakers. The idea of playing music that was stored on the computer itself, as a digital file, hadn't occurred to the wizards of Cupertino. Apple's iMac and even its machine for professional media producers, the Power Mac, offered no way to "burn" music onto a disk. As late as early 1999, there was only one third-party application that let Macintosh users play MP3s, and it wasn't Apple's—it was a quick-and-dirty port of one of the first digital jukebox applications, WinAmp. The Mac version was called, in case you missed the connection, MacAmp.

If Apple didn't see the opportunity, some of its most passionate developers certainly did. In 1999, Cabel Sasser and Steven Frank, based in a Portland, Oregon, apartment, were writing a software utility pack that would provide a grab bag of goodies for Mac users. When working on an audio player, Sasser and Frank realized that what the Mac really needed was a cool MP3 app, so they shifted their energies to creating what they would call Audion, a robust digital music playing program that fit the character of the Mac. Unfortunately for them, a rival group had the same idea.

This was SoundJam, created by a team of top Cupertino refugees. In the early 1990s, Bill Kincaid had worked on the Copland project, slated to be the next big operating system on the Mac. He left in March 1997, and was working for a start-up, spending what spare time he had between his job and his family on his road-racing hobby. One day, while driving to a track where he'd take his Formula Ford for a spin, he heard an NPR report about the Diamond Rio, a little gadget that could play an hour or so of digital music encoded in something called MP3. It was the first time Kincaid had heard of MP3. But what really got his attention was the reporter's comment that the players didn't sync with the Macintosh. Suddenly, Kincaid had a new task added to the top of his stack: fixing that problem.

It was not surprising that Kincaid hadn't heard much about MP3 players; the Diamond Rio was pretty much the first one anyone had heard of, and it was still largely underground. Rio's "PMP300," released in September 1998, was only the second attempt at storming the U.S. marketplace. (The first was a flash-in-the-pan spring 1998 effort called the MP3Man from an obscure Korean company, Saehan.) It was a stumpy little box that held only twenty-four songs but a pioneer nonetheless.

Kincaid quickly got in touch with the Diamond Rio people and even talked to some of their engineers in Taiwan. "I realized pretty quickly that I could design the interface hardware and the driver support [the physical connector and the software translator that would let a Rio talk to a Macintosh] but I was not the right guy to write a 'Rio Manager' app," wrote Kincaid in an online account of his quest. "I've never been a UI programmer, but I knew a really good one—Jeff!"

He was referring to Jeff Robbin, whose Apple roots went back to 1992, when he worked there as an intern while pursuing an MBA. A Chicago native, he'd taken computer science as an undergrad and was broadening his view of the business world when he landed his dream internship in Apple's operating system group. "I loved it so much that I couldn't think of anything else and came back full-time as soon as I graduated in 1993," he says. He also worked on Copland, but the troubled Apple of the mid-nineties was a mess. In early 1997, Robbin left the company, but not the platform. He became one of the best authors of utility programs for the Mac, including Conflict Catcher, a valuable little application that identified which programs would simply not get along with each other. For this alone, many Mac owners owed Jeff Robbin a big debt, even though they had no idea who he was.

So Bill Kincaid called Robbin. "There's this Rio MP3 player that's pretty cool," Kincaid said. "We should make it work with a Mac." Robbin had never worked on music projects before but agreed that it sounded like a good idea. They began a small company called SoundStep but kept working from their respective homes. Robbin arranged for the publisher of Conflict Catcher, a small firm called Casady & Greene, to distribute the product. During the following months, the pair learned all they could about MP3, digital signal processing, and other music-related geekery. Their plans for SoundJam became more ambitious, and by the time they were readying it for release, the program was much, much more than an interface for the Rio—it was a full-featured digital jukebox that even had hippy-dippy light shows that filled the screen while you played your songs.

In the summer of 1999, SoundJam beat Audion to market by a few weeks. For the next few months, the two teams would enjoy a heated competition. Though each group would have liked to envision the other roasting in some special hell, the rancor was tempered by the fact that each team respected the other's technical prowess, and when Sasser would run into Robbin at a Macworld Conference, the chatter was collegial.

And why not? In a sense the fate of both would be determined not by which company made the cooler "skins" for its interface but by what would happen when Apple got into the game. If the mothership in Cupertino decided to make its own music player, it would immediately decimate the potential marketplace for Audion and SoundJam. On the other hand, there was always the likelihood that Apple might not want to start from scratch—which meant that the possibility existed for a big buyout, and maybe a job at Apple.

Apple indeed was interested. By then it was beginning to dawn on Jobs and others that the company was blowing a chance to become a big player in what should have been a great stage for Apple. "I felt like a dope," Jobs later told *Fortune* magazine. "I thought we had missed it. We had to work hard to catch up."

Buying a company that had already taken a stab at Mac-based music software would make up some time for Apple. Audion was already in talks with AOL, so when Apple asked for a meeting "about the future direction of Audion" in June 2000, CEO Cabel Sasser had to demur. But SoundStep was not so encumbered. In any case, the guys who'd written SoundJam had another advantage over the Audion guys: they were Apple corporate veterans. Robbin in particular was still regarded highly in the company for his work there. A deal was cut to buy SoundStep and hire Robbin, Kincaid, and a third Apple veteran, Dave Heller, from the team. Then the real work began: transforming a somewhat quirky third-party program into an official Apple program. In the spirit of iMovie, Sound-Jam would be totally remade into iTunes.

"When Apple decides to take something on, you know, we really take it on full throttle," says Robbin. "SoundJam was sort of a Swiss Army knife of features—it had everything but the kitchen sink in it, and yet it was missing some of the core fundamentals that made iTunes . . . iTunes." The most fundamental element of all, of course, was the trademark conviviality that characterizes just about everything that Apple does. Steve Jobs would not tolerate a program that was ugly or acted ugly. "Apple takes complicated concepts and makes it just incredibly simple and easy to use," says Robbin. "Even in this very first version of iTunes, it was about bringing digital audio to the masses. It was about tying in with the iMac, and CDs, and CD burning, and it was just about digital audio as being a focus for the company."

In only four months, the team produced the first version of iTunes. With its brushed-silver look borrowed from iMovie, it was not just a huge step up from SoundJam but a leap beyond the juke-boxes available on Windows machines. Jobs proudly made it a centerpiece of his keynote speech in the January 2001 Macworld Conference & Expo.

Among those in the audience were the designers of Audion. The competition between Audion and SoundJam had been an all-out feature war with all sorts of bells and whistles. But under the iron fist of Apple's simplicity cops, the new iTunes was stripped down, cleaner, and many times friendlier than anything that had come before. It gave people the ability to search for their songs at lightning speed, a task performed without forcing you to go into some clumsy mode of specifying whether you were looking for the title, the artist, or the album. "iTunes was of course brilliant," concluded a stunned and disheartened Sasser of Audion. "It was a way to take a complicated digital music collection and make it easy. Sure, it was limited, but man, it was easy." It was also the end of Audion. Eventually, after trying to compete for a while, Sasser and his colleagues pulled the plug mainly because, as Sasser wrote in his farewell, "iTunes is, you know, actually pretty awesome."

But an awesome digital jukebox could be only so useful. What good was it, really, if the means of actually *hearing* digital music was crummy? You could archive and organize tunes to your heart's content, but the whole exercise fell down when you simply wanted to play back the music and dance and all you had was the crappy speakers in your computer. iMovie worked with great camcorders. (iPhoto, the application created as the photography spoke in the Digital Hub, would take advantage of amazing digital cameras.) The iTunes team had made sure it was possible to hook up a Macintosh to the portable MP3 players then available. But the Apple brass had come to a conclusion about those devices.

Every single one of them sucked.

"Everybody had the same story," says Greg Joswiak, who was then a Macintosh marketing manager. " 'I got it, it was cute, and now it's in the drawer.' And that means no second-time purchase. That means no telling your friends how cool it is. Because it isn't cool."

It fell to Apple's senior vice president of hardware, Jon Rubinstein, to do something about that. Known as Ruby to Apple insiders, he had been with the company since February 1997, predating Steve Jobs's second coming by about six months. This marked a reunion between the two, as Rubinstein had been Jobs's key hardware lieutenant at NeXT (the company Jobs founded when he was booted out of Apple in 1985). Rubinstein, who grew up in New York City's lower West Side (near Hell's Kitchen) and studied electrical engineering at Cornell, considered himself temperamentally suited to work with the sometimes tempestuous Jobs. "We complement each other," he says. "With Steve pushing me, I achieve things that I wouldn't be able to do on my own. I think I bring a balance and a deep understanding of technology, and I'm pretty good at building teams and getting products out the door."

The question was whether it was possible for Apple itself to build something that could redefine the whole field of digital music—to bring the functionality and breadth of iTunes into a device that you could put in your pocket. This seemed like a foray that was out of character for the company known for Macintoshes and little else. Rubinstein, however, notes that Apple's Wi-Fi transmitter, the AirPort, was an example of the company going beyond computers into the device world. So when Rubinstein promised

Jobs that he could make something about the size of a pack of cards that would play a library's worth of music, it wasn't such a wacky suggestion.

Would Jobs fund that project?

It was certainly worth looking into. Rubinstein decided to bring in someone to initiate the process. "I needed someone just to explore, to validate that what we were thinking made sense," he says. Going outside the company to fill that role was no big deal. "It wasn't particularly unique," says Rubinstein. "One of the things I tried to do when we restructured the hardware division many years ago was get a really good mix of Apple people and people from the outside. I bring in tons of interns every summer to keep a steady stream of college hires going, and we also bring in senior people so that they have varied experiences." Anyway, he adds, just about all the top guys at Apple were already really busy with Macintosh projects.

After quietly asking around his contacts in the Valley, Rubinstein heard from a trusted friend that there was one guy, currently unattached to any of Apple's competitors, who had what sounded like the ideal background and experience. Ruby tracked down the prospect and gave him a call on January 23, 2001.

Anthony Michael Fadell was on a ski slope in Vail, Colorado, when his cell phone rang. The 32-year-old engineer was taking a rare few days off. He had recently started a small company and was more than happy to continue with it. He liked the control of heading his own firm; too many times while working for someone else, the fiercely independent Detroit native wound up feeling cheated.

This call was from *Apple*. All his life, Tony Fadell had idolized that company. When he was twelve, he'd combined a summer's money he'd made caddying with a contribution from his grandfather to buy an Apple IIe personal computer. He became an ace programmer and started three companies before he graduated from the University of Michigan. His first job out of college, in 1992, was at a start-up called General Magic, working beside two of the stars of the legendary team that had created the Macintosh, Andy Hertzfeld and Bill Atkinson. It was like joining a basketball team and finding yourself teammates with Larry Bird and Dr. J.

Unfortunately, the General Magic handheld communicator was a flop. From there, Fadell had a weird few years at the Philips corporation. Concerned about its overly staid reputation, the Dutch conglomerate had offered Fadell, still in his twenties, the chance to head its new mobile computing group. He was by far the youngest manager at that level in the entire titanic company. Even if Fadell had had a steady temperament and been mature beyond his years, this would have been controversial. But he embraced the role of execupunk and became a walking culture clash. He'd sometimes show up at work with bleached hair, and at meetings he would blast anyone within earshot. When a *Fast Company* reporter asked him where he'd be if he'd grown up before computers were invented, he responded, "in jail." Nonetheless, Fadell headed the development of handheld, Windows-based PDAs (the Velo and the Nino) that sold a half million units. Working on these, he was one of the first to understand the importance of digital audio and MP3—and how one might implement the technology in small devices. He was eventually promoted to vice president for business development, responsible for the company's Internet and digital audio strategy. He got the idea of creating a home digital entertainment unit with a hard drive–based jukebox to store thousands of songs and talked to RealNetworks to develop some of the software. Then he accepted a job at Real, figuring that he'd have a better chance to ship a challenging product with a company still in touch with its start-up mentality. But in part because of a disagreement over whether he'd move to Seattle, he quit after only six weeks.

Now Fadell was developing the idea with his own company. He'd hired twelve people already and was working out a partnership with Samsung. But here was Jon Rubinstein, telling him to come in and talk about a project. At Apple! So Fadell took the meeting. Of course, Ruby couldn't tell him anything *about* the project, because of Apple's near paranoia about keeping secrets. All Fadell knew was that Apple was offering him an eight-week contract to do *something* that it thought he was qualified to do. What could he say but yes?

Only after agreeing did he learn that his job was to put together an MP3 music player that would work with iTunes and would not suck. Essentially he'd have to build a small computer—because, once you get down to it, that's what an MP3 player is, something with a nice visual interface that runs the database program that stores the digital song files, then performs the high-speed mathematical processes that make those files into the same Jimi Hendrix and Yo-Yo Ma tunes that you'd hear on a CD player. No one mentioned that this product might transform all of Apple and set the technology world, the business world, and especially the music industry on its head. Because no one suspected it would.

Fadell set about researching the world of MP3 players. (One product that fell beneath his radar was the PJB 100, which by 2001 had sunk from obscurity to obsolescence.) His experience with handheld devices helped him in the next part of his quest, to become very familiar with the components that might be used to build a better one, Apple style. Ruby had already been looking at some of these pieces, particularly the brand-new 1.8-inch hard drive made by Toshiba. Despite its diminutive specs, it held five gigabytes of data—enough for 1,000 songs.

To those who had followed technology for a while, the cost and capability of such a component were sort of a crazy joke, one of a series of absurdities unleashed by Moore's Law. As a yardstick of how ridiculously compact and capacious this hard drive was, consider the situation when Apple unveiled the original Macintosh in 1984. The computer badly needed a hard drive, but they were so expensive that including it in the package would have almost doubled the $2,500 price. When one finally appeared as a third-party peripheral almost a year later, it was half the size of a shoebox and cost around $2,000. It held ten megabytes (a megabyte is one thousandth the size of our now-familiar gigabyte), which seemed like an enormous amount of storage at the time. Ha! *The entire capacity* of that 1985 disk drive is insufficient to store the single MP3 file of Neil Young's "Down by the River."

Now Toshiba had a five-gig disk drive so small you could swallow it, with enough capacity to pack in three days' worth of music—a thousand songs—and its cost was measured in tens of dollars, not thousands. Mind-boggling, to be sure. But that rate of advancement is an everyday fact of life to people who work in technology. Apple's methodology was based on securing the very latest implementations of these astounding advances—and driving the price down to levels that would have its suppliers pulling their hair out. Apple could get those suppliers to bend to its demands mainly because it was Apple. A big deal with Apple meant that your factory would be very busy; just as important, having Apple as your customer provided credibility for a new technological advance, at least among those in the know. (It was forbidden, however, to openly enlighten others about this; Jobs's wrath was fearsome when suppliers boasted about their role in providing parts for the company's jewels.)

Another factor that Rubinstein had determined early on was

that the new device would use the FireWire technology to load songs. "Before that, everyone was using [the much slower data transfer standard] USB 1," says Rubinstein. "You can't move music over USB 1. It just doesn't make it a usable product if it takes four hours to download your songs."

Fadell was assigned a partner in his efforts, a sort of consigliere who would provide him an interface to the sometimes confusing Cupertino culture. Chosen for the task was Stan Ng, a hardware marketing manager who had been with Apple for six years. Ng and Fadell quickly got to the nub of what was required. " 'In your pocket' became the mantra for the product, because that was definitely the size and form factor that hit the sweet spot," Ng says. "There were products out there that were small but that held maybe twenty or thirty songs and didn't have great battery life, and other products had a hard drive but they weighed over a pound and didn't fit in your pocket. We wanted to create something that merged the best of both worlds."

Apple demanded total stealth, so on their quest Fadell and Ng would talk to people but not really tell them what they were working on. Not even people inside the company. Eventually Fadell came to identify the key components, gauge the possible dimensions, and blue-sky an interface. He began to make models of what an Apple MP3 player might look like, cutting pieces out of foam core boards and gluing them together. He finally came up with one that he felt was ideal: a box slightly bigger than a cigarette case with a sharp screen toward the top end and navigational buttons below. But when he held his model it felt too light. He went to his garage and recovered the old tackle box he'd used many years ago when he'd gone fishing with his grandfather. Still inside were old fishing weights. After pounding them down with a sledgehammer, he stuck them into the model to provide a heft that approximated what the final device might feel like. He showed it to Rubinstein, who was delighted.

Fadell's contract ended in early April, and a meeting was scheduled for him to bring his conclusions to the Apple executive team. He had more than done his homework, not just on the project but on the politics of presenting it to Steve Jobs. He came to the meeting with not one but three different versions. Two of them were sacrificial lambs that he felt would rightfully be rejected, setting the stage for the third one, which he was sure was the perfect solution to Apple's problem. The hard-drive model would be expensive— Fadell priced it out at around $400—but such a leap forward that people would want it. Before the meeting, Fadell and Rubinstein hid the model of this favorite under the large wooden bowl that Jobs kept in the center of the long table in the fourth-floor conference room.

The key people were all at the meeting: Rubinstein; Jeff Robbin; Apple's worldwide marketing vice president, Phil Schiller; and of course Jobs, who had been in contact with Ruby on the project but had yet to meet Fadell. The session started out with Ng showing the usual sort of marketing slides—stuff about the market potential, the competition, how horrible the current choices were, and the question of whether Apple could innovate. Jobs, as always, kept things moving with his interruptions. Then Fadell took over. He laid out potential parts on the table—a 1.8-inch hard drive, a small piece of glass for the screen, various battery alternatives, a sample motherboard—and began instructing the group on the fine points of handheld economics, the current pricing curves of memory and hard-drive storage, what the latest battery technology was, and the kinds of displays one could use.

Executing the Goldilocks gambit, Fadell showed his first model; it had a big slot that could accept either a hard drive or a flash memory card to hold music. This was a clumsy solution and not well received. *Too complicated,* Jobs sniffed. Then came the second proposal, a device that would store tunes with dynamic RAM memory; it would be cheap and hold a bunch of songs, but if the battery died, the songs would vanish and you'd have to reload. *That will never sell,* grumbled Jobs. Finally, Fadell went back to the table and began grabbing the pieces he'd used to demonstrate what parts were available. As if constructing a Lego device, he snapped them together, creating something that might now be considered iPod-esque, and handed it to Jobs. The silence said, *This is more like it.* Then it was time to show Jobs the more polished model under the bowl, with the angling weights and mockups of buttons on the front to control the software. This time Jobs's pleasure was obvious.

Just right.

There was another surprise to come. At that point Phil Schiller asked, "Can I bring out my thing now?" He went out of the room and came back with a number of different-sized models of a play-back device—big ones, tiny ones, in all sorts of shapes. They all had one thing in common: a wheel-shaped contraption on the front. The idea, Schiller explained, was that by using a single finger, tracing the circular pathway on the wheel, you could easily scroll through lists—of songs, of artists, of albums. To select something, you'd press the bull's-eye in the center of the wheel. What's more, as your finger moved around, the pace of scrolling actually accelerated, so you could go through long lists at a fairly brisk pace.

(Schiller later explained to me that the idea had crystallized at an earlier meeting with Jobs and Rubinstein. "All the other MP3 players had these little plus and minus buttons to go down a menu one song at a time. We were going to hold a *thousand* songs on this thing—you can't hit the plus button a thousand times! So I figured, it you can't go up, why not go around?" His only fear was that by putting a circle in the middle of the device, people might think there was a speaker installed and would find it frustrating when no sound came out.)

Jobs asked Fadell if he could build something like that, and Fadell said he could.

The project was a go.

It's worth pausing here to note a couple of things about the device Apple wanted to make, and why the elements of success were in place at that very moment. With the tiny hard drive and Fadell's compact form factor, the iPod would be small—easily acing the "in your pocket" standard. With the high-speed FireWire technology, the device would be fast; it would load songs at lightning speed, eliminating one big complaint about previous players. With the scroll wheel—and the inevitable clever software touches that Apple would add—it would be easy to use. With the iTunes software from the Macintosh built in—and with the iPod seen as a satellite of that software, instead of a foreign device that required complicated high-tech handshaking—it would sync effortlessly with a music library. And if Apple's industrial design team performed its usual witchcraft, it would be utterly beautiful. It was a recipe for something, well, perfect.

Now there was the question of a deadline. It was logical to expect a task like that to take at least a year. By their working very hard, it could be done sometime in 2002. But that ignored a more important deadline. This was a classic consumer product, nailed down to unyielding seasonal economics. And the lion's share of sales would come during one season. The Apple people made this crystal clear to Tony Fadell. "I'll never forget the conversation," says Greg Joswiak. " 'Tony, we've studied the math here and we're brain surgeons, and we think Christmas is gonna be big.' " Nonetheless, it was far from certain that producing a breakthrough device—and one that was a considerable departure from Apple's usual products—could be completed in not much more than six months.

The formal code name was P-68. Dull, to be sure, and devoid of significance, but years earlier a clever code name had gotten Apple into trouble. One of its original PowerPC computers had been casually dubbed "Sagan" (because its chip could perform "billions and billions" of calculations). When its namesake, the astrophysicist Carl Sagan, heard of this, he was outraged, considering it to be an unauthorized commercialization of his name. He threatened to sue, and Apple changed the code name to the seemingly unobjectionable BHA. (Somehow it leaked out that the acronym stood for Butt Head Astronomer.) Since then, code names at Apple were oblique by fiat. Nonetheless, informally, people in the P-68 project also used a more evocative term for the project: Dulcimer.

Even at this stage, Fadell was not sure he wanted to commit to Apple full-time. He was still the head of a twelve-person company and was wary of working for others. He had been on too many projects that had wound up in the dustbin of high tech and was wildly vacillating on whether he should accept the offer. The issue came to a head on the day Fadell and Ng were scheduled to present the project to all of Apple's key development people for the first time. Before the meeting, Fadell had scheduled sessions with a few top executives, desperately seeking assurance that he was doing the right thing. The final session was with Jobs, who called not long before the four P.M. meeting. The conversation dragged on, and by the time Fadell made it to Rubinstein's conference room, he was a half hour late. Everyone was grumbling about the wait. Then Rubinstein told everyone that the meeting might have to be canceled—either Fadell was going to agree to work at Apple, or everything was off. Fadell couldn't believe it. "Is this the way everyone gets hired at Apple?" he asked. Finally, he agreed.

"I twisted his arm pretty hard," admits Rubinstein, but if the project were to continue, Fadell, who had impressed him during the contract period, would have to be on board. "I said, 'I'm doing this for your own good.' He didn't quite see it that way at the time. I think now he understands."

Fadell was in for the ride of his life, a process that would in some ways compare to the development of the Macintosh, whose origin tale had attained mythic status in geek circles. But he still resented what he considered a demeaning ambush. He would even quit the job twice in the next few months. (Eventually Fadell became Rubinstein's successor when his boss retired in March 2006.) But Fadell had little time to stew over Ruby's pressure play, as he, Ng, and another Apple executive had to leave almost immediately for Asia to nail down suppliers and manufacturers; otherwise it would be impossible even to consider making the insanely optimistic holiday deadline. They went to Hong Kong, Korea, Shanghai, and Taiwan, never revealing exactly what Apple wanted to build but presenting the specs for the particular work they wanted. The final meeting was in Taiwan, with a company called Inventec. Inventec had worked on the Apple's ill-fated but adventuresome handheld Newton organizer. The group toured the demo room and the factory, and felt that they had finally found a match.

Fadell's hardware team represented just one of several work flows on the project. The creation of the entire iPod system would rely on many people in various divisions at Apple, as well as outside contractors. Jeff Robbin, who had become the head of Apple's iTunes division, was in charge of the team that would develop music playing software inside the iPod as well as a new version of iTunes that would work hand in hand with the new device. "From the beginning it involved working on the user interface, working on just the design of how it operated," says Robbin. "We had to figure out how iTunes was going to sync the content onto the 'pod, how the 'pod was going to access that information, how we could do a database on the device that was just incredibly simple to use. And then there were even little details that were an interesting challenge around simple things, like being able to unplug the device without having to unmount it. Making it into a product that my Mom could handle, that was the goal."

In addition, Apple's ID wizard Jonathan Ive and his team would work on the industrial design that would make the iPod so cool. This involved not only sketching but checking out the latest in polycarbons and tooling.

Other tasks would require outside support. Just because Apple was inventing the scroll wheel did not mean that it had to reinvent the wheel in every particular. For some key aspects of the player—from the chip set to the audio electronics—Apple wondered whether some other company might be doing work that would form a basis for the hardware structure of its own player. As it turned out, a company called PortalPlayer was. Founded only in 1999, the company, based in San Jose, just down the road from Cupertino, had been working on designs for MP3 players for a number of other companies. Recently, its executives had realized what the people at Apple (and DEC) had—that tiny disk drives could revolutionize music players.

"The people making those disks didn't care about the music business, they cared about computer notebooks," says Richard San-quini, an engineer who began consulting for PortalPlayer around then and later became its chairman. "We said, 'Hey, this will go into notebooks, but this will make a real big difference in music players.'

At that time we had no customers; we said, 'We think that it's going in that direction, and we've got to do a better job.' "

Considering this, it wasn't surprising that Apple would hook up with PortalPlayer. "Everyone in the Valley kind of knows each other and what you're doing," says Sanquini. "How many MP3 companies can you have? They saw a couple things in our company that differentiated us. One, we really, really understood the total solution technically, and we provided the silicon and a very primitive kind of operating system. They would be able to take our platform and spend their time on the application software." In addition, PortalPlayer had been working hard at one of the trickiest tasks that Apple had to accomplish: power management when it came to starting and stopping the hard drive, an energy-draining process that would have to be handled so that the batteries didn't wheeze to a halt halfway through a long Grateful Dead jam.

The PortalPlayer people were thrilled when they heard Apple's plan. The Asian companies they had been working with to develop MP3 players were eager to make products. But Apple had a *vision*. Jobs's wizards had thought out every aspect—not just storage but the way the music would have to be uploaded at high speed, the flexibility of the interface, the rechargeable batteries, the feel of the product in your hand. It made sense for PortalPlayer to throw all its cards in with Apple. The would-be subcontractor didn't even blanch when it heard Apple's goal of having the iPod out by Christmas.

PortalPlayer also had relationships with other subcontractors that could supply the best specialized components. This helped further extend the geographic roots of the iPod, which already included the hard drive from Japan, the manufacturer in Taiwan, Korean memory chip, and a Texas Instruments connector for the

FireWire transport. For instance, PortalPlayer brought in a high-quality audio-processing chip from Wolfson Microelectronics in Edinburgh, Scotland.

There was another major part of the project that also required some outside help: the layer of software that would mediate between PortalPlayer's hardware platform and the top-level Apple software that presented options to the user and integrated itself with iTunes. Though Apple's software skills were unparalleled, the time crunch made it nearly impossible to produce a debugged system that would work with the unique chip set of the new device. The solution came fortuitously one day when Jeff Robbin was interviewing a former colleague for a job on the Dulcimer software team. Mike Neil, then working for a small firm called Pixo, wasn't told what sort of project he was being interviewed for, but once he learned who was involved (Fadell is a gadget guy . . . Robbin is an MP3 guy . . .) he had a pretty good idea what it was. "I'm not interested in the position," he said. "But at Pixo we might have some technology that could help you out."

Pixo had been founded in 1994 by yet another Apple refugee, Paul Mercer. Mercer, who worked at Apple in the 1980s and early 1990s, was known as "the gadget guy." He worked on the handheld Newton device, but his pet project was actually a tiny pen-based gizmo code-named Swatch that could actually run the Macintosh operating system. (Apple never produced it.) In 1994 he left Apple and founded a company devoted to bringing Mac-style technology to handheld devices like PDAs and phones. He called it Pixo "because we're pixel-pushers." The company, consisting mostly of former Apple-oids, got several rounds of funding and worked for various consumer electronics clients. By 2001, Mercer had left the firm (he was still consulting) and had turned over the technology responsibility to Neil and an engineer named Jeff Miller.

Apple suggested that Mike Neil come up with a proposal on what Pixo could do for Apple. He did even better. "We built a little prototype. In a couple of days we whipped out a little example of a simple MP3 player, using the concepts from iTunes, so it had playlists and all that kind of stuff." He brought it in to show to Ruby, Fadell, and Robbin, and played a tune for them. "I think it was Eric Clapton, from the *Unplugged* album," he says.

Ultimately, Pixo was hired to write the software that would work on top of the PortalPlayer chips. The Apple interface experts would modify what the Pixo people did. The terms of the license were never made public, but Mercer ruefully claims, "Let's just say that Apple got the deal of the century." Pixo was a logical fit because the company had a portable computer code that could easily be adapted to the custom chips—and since they had been Apple-schooled, Pixo's system got along famously with the Macintosh. (In 2003, the company went out of business and Apple was able to buy Pixo's iPod-related intellectual property for itself. The rest of Pixo's assets went to Sun Microsystems.)

Just because Pixo was providing software didn't mean that its employees were entitled to know all the details about the iPod. The prototypes, which were never to leave the Apple campus, were phonied up to hide the true nature of the design. The Plexiglas-based models were about a foot wide, controlled by huge buttons. "Basically they were trying to disguise the fact that it was this little cigarette case–sized thing," says Mike Neil. "Of course, if you flipped it around and you looked in the back, there was a motherboard that was the size of a quarter in there. So it was pretty obvious that it was going to be a small device."

The Pixo people didn't have direct contact with Jobs but could guess when he'd been involved. "Usually when you work on a software product, you try to schedule a build in the middle of the week, so the testers can test it. But Apple always wanted things on Friday. I think what was happening was, they were giving the build to Steve, who would take it home for the weekend and play with it. Then on Monday we'd invariably get a whole bunch of requests to change this, tweak that, do all that kind of stuff."

The PortalPlayer team was getting similar feedback from the CEO. "They'd have meetings, and Steve would be horribly offended he couldn't get to the song he wanted in less than three pushes of a button," a PortalPlayer engineer, Ben Knauss, later told *Wired News*. "We'd get orders: 'Steve doesn't think it's loud enough, the sharps aren't sharp enough, or the menu's not coming up fast enough.' Every day there were comments from Steve saying where it needed to be."

One particular area where the Pixo people sensed Jobs's finicky standards was the character font used for the menus on the screen; a lot of alternatives were tried out before the final selection of the one called Chicago, a style that had actually been created for the menus in the original Macintosh.

The Apple people, of course, had full-contact sessions with Jobs. He would pick up the device and say what he liked and what he didn't like, and he would fire questions at everyone, pushing hard—*What are you going to do about it?* It was Jobs who told everyone what the device would be called. "He just came in and went, 'iPod,' " says one team member. "We all looked around the room, and that was it. iPod. And we're like, 'Where did that come from?' " (Excellent question, and one that proved increasingly elusive the more I pressed people at Apple about it. Finally, I was able to corner Jobs on it and he said that to the best of his knowledge the name sort of *emerged,* not exactly in a form of immaculate conception but in a lengthy back and forth among him, his marketing people, and Chiat\Day. "The ad agency loved it," he told me. But I get the distinct impression that the iPod moniker won out not because of its brilliance but because Jobs had had enough of the naming process and the hour was getting late.)

Sometimes his pronouncements would astound his employees. When one of the designers said that obviously the device should have a power button to turn the unit on and off, he simply said No. And that was it. It was a harsh aesthetic edict on a parallel with his famous refusal to include cursor keys in the original Macintosh. In Jobs's point of view, all that was needed was forward, back, and pause buttons, arranged around the circumference of the wheel. (After much effort, his team eventually convinced him of the necessity of a fourth button, called "Menu," that would move you through the various lists of available options.)

On one hand, the lack of an "On" button really isn't a big deal, since once you touch any other button on a dormant iPod, the device comes to life. And Jon Rubinstein contends that the lack of a power switch is not a Steve Jobs quirk but actually a companywide policy that reflects a reality of the digital age. "There's this mythology that it's really good for your system to turn it on and off all the time," he says. "It's not. It's much better for the machine to just sit there in that mode than it is to turn it on and off constantly. We design the systems to go into very-low-power sleep states, and we have various levels that take different amounts of time to come out of, and so depending on how long you've left it idle, it'll keep going into lower and lower power states. And eventually it'll turn off."

That's a fascinating concept—that as you leave your iPod alone, it goes from a light snooze to a high-REM deep sleep. But in practice, this isn't always ideal. When new iPod owners try to turn off the device, they often wind up wildly pushing buttons before finally discovering that the solution is to hold down the "Play" button on the wheel for three seconds or so. (Huh?) Eventually

Apple took to shipping iPods with a plastic film over the controls, an overlay that clearly delineated which button one should press to turn the damn thing off.

Nonetheless, Jobs's maniacal attention to detail and harsh way of communicating proved incredibly effective in producing products that were many cuts above the clunky efforts of his competition. Other companies were happy simply to do a good job; Jobs's efforts wound up in museums. If sometimes his autocratic stance resulted in something quirky—like omitting a power switch—such anomalies were more than compensated for by the suave elegance and downright desirability of what he drove his minions to create. Jobs's ideal customer was someone who was just as discerning as he was. He wanted a product that people would lust for, and he would tolerate no warts that might spoil the experience. And in the case of the iPod, there was no problem communicating the need for excellence to those working on the project, because this was a product they all desperately wanted for themselves. The long hours brought the team together; sometime during that summer Fadell even took a group skydiving.

Everybody at Apple seemed to love music passionately, and the more they worked on the iPod the more they realized that they had a chance to make a product they would kill to have in their own pockets. "All of us working on it were so excited to be working on it, it was kind of a dream project," says Jeff Robbin. "Certainly we were working long hours, we were all working together late at night, and it was highly energized. But it was just an incredible team project. There were no boundaries. The software guys, the hardware guys, the firmware guys, everybody worked together. It was a pretty amazing experience."

It got even more amazing as the ambitious goal of making a holiday deadline actually looked feasible. One of the first signs came in August, when a song was played on one of the physical prototypes. The prototype was actually a circuit board containing the hardware chips and hard drive. A group of people working late at night realized that they were close to that milestone and worked harder until the unit played music. They took turns listening on a set of headphones that had originally come from someone's old Sony Walkman. The first song, by the way, was "Groovejet (If This Ain't Love)" by Spiller, a house music dance tune with vocals by the British diva Sophie Ellis-Bextor. If you think that's weird, consider that the second song was "Theme from the Big Country," from the sound track of the 1958 William Wyler movie starring Gregory Peck, Jean Simmons, and Burl Ives (who won an Oscar for his role). If you download the piece, you can imagine the thrill of the iPod team, passing the headset around to pipe in this sprawling Copland-esque orchestral piece—on their little squirt of a music player!

Copy protection of songs wasn't part of iTunes or iPod, which happily accepted songs in the free-flowing MP3 codec. But Steve Jobs was concerned about piracy, so he did take modest steps against it. Until very late in the process, the iPod's designers intended not only to let people load songs from their Macintoshes onto the devices but to enable a reverse process: the ability to add songs to a computer *from* an iPod. But Jobs, obviously convinced that this two-way sync would make it too tempting for people to plug their iPods into a friend's computer to download entire collections of songs, mandated that the sync would work only one way. Likewise, one day Jobs announced that iPods would come packaged in an outer wrapping that said, "Don't steal music." What about other languages? he was asked. "Put multiple languages on it," he said.

Everyone seemed to have a moment of enlightenment when the clouds parted and it was clear that something amazing was emerging. For Jobs, "It all clicked for me when we designed the user interface. We had the wheel, and we started to lay out the menus and argue about this and that, and it took us about a week where we had most of it done, and once you saw the user interface and how easy it was going to be to get around and how well the wheel worked and how well the concepts of the user interface worked, then it was really clear that you'd be able to [navigate through] a thousand songs. Having a thousand songs in your pocket wouldn't be that exciting if you couldn't navigate and access them easily. Once that user interface clicked, it was like, 'Oh, my God, this is gonna be so cool.' "

Significantly, that interface made the experience special even for those who had been intimately involved in designing it. For Stan Ng, the head-slapping moment came when he took his own prototype home for the first time. "I probably had eighty or ninety CDs' worth of music on my Macintosh, and transferring down superfast over FireWire and then being able to pick any music, any album, whenever I wanted to was a feeling of freedom, of empowerment. It was just magic. I don't know how else to put it."

While such informal experimentation was the closest thing to market research Apple performed, there were all sorts of tests to make sure that everything worked, especially when the device came into contact with the physical insults it would face from users in the real world. The most fragile piece was the hard drive. "No one had really ever put such a tiny hard drive in a device that was really pocketable," explains one engineer. "So we were doing things like dropping hundreds of disk drives in these models to figure out if they were going be robust or not." The testers set up robotic arms that methodically dropped the drives—some on their own, some in cases—from different heights to see how high they could fall and survive. The hard drives were like digital crash test dummies. Apple figured that an iPod should be able to withstand a thirty-inch tumble, and the dummy disks passed the test.

Meanwhile, in Taiwan, another problem emerged only days before the launch: Apple's engineers found a glitch in one of the circuit boards that would be sandwiched into the compact layered innards of the device. One of the "traces" (the microscopic wire connections) was missing, a flaw that would crash the unit in certain conditions. This was apparently something that the factory itself was not equipped to fix in the forty-eight hours or so that was required to meet the schedules. So the Apple people were grilling taxi drivers in Taiwan to find back-alley-garage production shops that might be able to take in thousands of boards and quickly make the fix so that the modified boards could be delivered to the factory to immediately be assembled into the first run of iPods.

"It was a very scary time," says Rubinstein. "But we had to stay focused on the product. And we had a product launch scheduled, and so we just kind of kept nose down and kept cranking." Rubinstein was under additional pressure, because on October 13, he was scheduled to be married. In fact, the launch was postponed a week past its original date, to October 23, so he could return from his honeymoon.

Soon before the launch, the first production iPods arrived, ready for the lucky first wave (like me) who would receive them in advance of the thousands that would be snapped up instantly when Apple began selling them to the public in November.

Looking back on the process, Jobs waxes philosophical. "If there was ever a product that catalyzed what's Apple's reason for being, it's this," he says. "Because it combines Apple's incredible technology base with Apple's legendary ease of use with Apple's awesome design. Those three things come together in this, and it's like, *that's what we do.* So if anybody was ever wondering why is Apple on the earth, I would hold up this as a good example."

A few days after the launch, Jobs threw a celebratory lunch for forty or so of the core people who had worked on the product. He thanked the team not only for making a great product but for taking all of Apple in a new, limitless direction. For the meal, he sat down at a table with a few unfamiliar faces and asked those he didn't recognize who they were and what they did. One of the youngest engineers, hired only a couple of weeks earlier and clearly not briefed on Apple personnel, answered Jobs's questions and then had one of his own. "What do *you* do here?" he asked the guy he clearly hadn't recognized as his CEO.

That got a good laugh in Cupertino. But as the iPods rolled off the assembly line, the fun was just beginning.

And what about the DEC computer scientists who worked on the Personal Jukebox? "In the back of our minds, it was 'Gee, this could've been Compaq,'" says Ted Wobber, who with Andrew Birrell now works at Microsoft's research facility in Silicon Valley. "But practically speaking, I'm happy for Apple and happy that such products are available on the market. They're very useful. And, you know, I enjoy owning one."

Cool

❯Dr. Carl Rohde is a cultural anthropologist at the University of Utrecht in the Netherlands. He studies coolness. He lectures, writes scholarly articles and books with titles like *Symbol Soup: The MTV Generation and its Symbols,* and consults on coolness for dozens of companies, including Adidas, Coca-Cola, Wrangler, and General Motors. Twice a year he heads the European Cool Hunt, which is, according to his curriculum vitae, "120 cool hunters all over Europe continuously searching for cool people, cool places, cool mentalities, cool trends. And for the reasons why it is cool."

"Cool" is a term that seems as strongly linked to the iPod as white earbuds, the Apple logo, and gripes about battery life. So certainly the Professor of Cool would be missing a major trick if he did not identify the 'pod as a central player in global coolness in the twenty-first century. And Dr. Carl Rohde does not disappoint. "It's a totally cool product," he says. "We have documented this, beginning at the time when iPod started its march to the number one position, which it actually has now."

So it's official: the iPod is the coolest thing in the world, a fact that in itself isn't so illuminating. (Just look at that little puppy—what's the first word out of your mouth?) The bigger question is how much the iPod's coolness is responsible for its commercial success, as well as its place in the culture and in our fluttering hearts. What's more, since the iPod's status is now so beyond dispute, by understanding *why,* we can learn not only about the iPod but about coolness itself, and what it says about ourselves.

The task is trickier than it sounds, in part because of the broadness and ubiquity of the C-word. It's flung about so often that one may be excused for dismissing the whole exercise as hopeless, on the grounds that "cool" is an all-purpose descriptor for anything that tips the scale on the positive side. On the other hand, as Dr. Rohde's consulting contracts indicate, the quality is something that commerce must pursue. Coolness is not merely an attribute of a commodity; it *is* a commodity. Yet part of its essence is that it's inherently elusive. Maybe it's possible to buy coolness, but if it *looks* as if you've bought it, it isn't cool. Coolness is also a constantly moving target. Sometimes an object, trend, or pop song begins life in the zone of total uncoolness, but with the passage of time a subtle redefining of aesthetics or desirable behavior occurs and it winds up (at least for a time) in the zone of total coolness. To people grounded in rationality—like the propeller-heads who live and breathe technology—the whole subject can be incredibly frustrating.

I once found myself in a heated discussion with Bill Gates about the nature of cool. I had said something pretty obvious from my point of view: that the Tablet PC, Microsoft's pen-based laptop, despite being the beneficiary of the hard thinking and technological virtuosity of many brilliant people, was simply not cool. And the iPod was. This observation incensed Gates. By that measure, he claimed, cool can be defined simply by reporting the marketplace's reaction to a product. "It sounds to me like you're saying volume equals cool," he charged. That's not it at all, I replied; coolness is not necessarily tied to profits. He challenged me to come up with an example of something cool that didn't sell well. Okay, I said, what about rock bands universally revered by trend makers (like the Velvet Underground in their heyday) but with sales that didn't track to their heady reputation? He didn't buy it. "Only cool to a small amount of people," he sniffed. "In a sense, to be cool, you've got to have high market share. High market share is something that comes after hard work and making the hard decisions. [When it first came out], Microsoft Word was as uncool as it could possibly be. I mean, *Microsoft Word?* Not cool! But then, it [eventually] redefined the word processing category."

But, Bill, I said, remembering the time I showed him his first iPod, didn't you think the iPod was cool even before it became a commercial success? "It's an irrelevant question," he sniffed. "I knew that music player devices would sell well. And I knew as soon as they got this high [sales] volume, *you* would declare it cool. As night follows day."

Our disagreement isn't surprising considering how easy it is to declare something cool and how hard it is to produce something cool. Not to mention how hard it is to *be* cool. There's an element of magic involved that drives pragmatists like Bill Gates nuts. Nonetheless, shareholders often demand that companies deliver that magic on command.

Can cool be reliably produced?

Few have sought the secret as determinedly as the longtime entrepreneur and technologist Yossi Vardi, the godfather of the Israeli dot-com movement. Vardi's greatest success came when he provided the funding and guidance for ICQ, the first instant messaging program. When he first became involved, ICQ was just a program created by some very smart kids. But when ICQ was released on the Internet, with no marketing, it became a viral phenomenon, a part of life for tens of millions of people. Eventually Vardi sold the company to AOL for $400 million. But the amazing way it took off on its own, becoming the passion of millions of people, stuck with Vardi. He became obsessed with the question *What made it cool?* "Every day, for weeks, for months, eighty thousand more people would download this software," he told me one day as we breakfasted at a tech conference. "We began to get love letters, hundreds of love letters. 'ICQ, I love you!' I came to the realization that there must be some genetic code in this thing, something embedded there which created this strong resonance in the heart of the users. I said to myself, 'Okay, now the thing I have to do is very simple. I have to decipher the code. If I know the code, I can replicate it, and if I can replicate it, I can create a production belt.' "

A production belt?

"How do you call that thing that Ford did?"

"Yossi," I said, "that's an assembly line."

"Yes! An assembly line to crank out cool."

For the next three years, Vardi dove deep into the calculus of cool. "I bought maybe two hundred, three hundred books," he says. "I have a whole library on experiences in theater, in storytelling, in software, in architecture, in retailing, in shopping, in traveling. I talked to architects, talked to artists, talked to software makers, talked to people who created wonderful things."

But all that knowledge brought him no closer to the secret he sought. There were many, many lessons to be learned from the astonishing things people have created and the fascinating responses from people who considered those things cool. Nonetheless, Vardi never came close to cracking the code because the more he learned, the more he understood that there was no code to crack. He found himself identifying with the Japanese engineers in a story he heard.

"I don't know if it's true or not," he says, "but I heard that when the Japanese wanted to create the Lexus, they took three hundred engineers and they told them, 'Go and see why the Mercedes is cool.' And they defined all these very implicit, tacit things in the Mercedes, like, for instance, the click of the door. You know, when you close the door of the Mercedes, you have a very distinct noise. And they found that in order to achieve this noise, the entire rim of the door has to touch the chassis of the car at once, along the whole rim. If you have the formation of the door at one point touch before the rest of the rim, you don't have this click."

In other words, you couldn't re-create that Mercedes feeling by isolating the noise and then jimmying up a door to replicate that noise. What was cool about the sound was the way it revealed how the click had gotten there to begin with. "The click came as a consequence of the way the door was, the care they took to make that," says Vardi, "and that was a consequence that stood for the perfection of the door."

Vardi ultimately concluded that you cannot produce coolness on demand. The only thing a company can do is strive for perfection and hope that the gods smile on it.

And yet . . . there is Apple Computer. The C-word has been consistently linked to Apple's products. Most emphatically, the iPod has taken on that adjective almost as a birthright. What is the link between coolness and iPods? Is trendiness a significant component of the iPod's success? Why has the world of fashion embraced the iPod? Why won't your kids accept a generic substitute, which plays the same damn songs an iPod does?

Apple itself does not generally cite coolness as a reason to purchase its products. Once I directly asked Jobs whether he had tried to make the iPod cool. "No," he said, "we try to make it great. *We try to make it great.*" At a 2004 press conference, someone asked him what would happen if iPods were no longer considered trendy. He looked at the questioner as if she'd tried to feed him a cockroach. "I don't think we're seeing something trendy," he said. "It's a product that's truly revolutionizing the way people listen to music. You don't spend $250 or $300 for something because you want to be trendy."

Oh, really? It certainly is no secret that people often spend *thousands* of dollars because they want to be trendy (though they will rarely explain their purchase in just those words). There is an entire economy devoted to the pursuit of trendiness. Jobs is certainly not unaware of this, and though he professes to disdain such cultural climbers, he is surely aware that Apple is a beneficiary of such trends. On the other hand, he seems to imply that his company deserves its exalted cultural status, while its competitors do not. In a November 2003 article in *The New York Times Magazine*, he dismissed companies that tried to pursue innovation for its own sake—as opposed to Apple's approach of hitting the target by making great products—as "somebody who's not cool trying to be cool."

Coolness *does* matter to Apple. A case can be made that Steve Jobs has devoted as much energy to Apple's image as he has to its computers. He introduces television ads at his launch events as if they were new products themselves, instead of Madison Avenue concoctions produced to sell objects. When a new ad campaign breaks between launches, he instructs his minions to generate coverage of it in major publications. It's not uncommon for me to get a call from an Apple PR person asking if I would be willing to view a commercial under a nondisclosure agreement and then get an exclusive Steve Jobs interview about it, timing *Newsweek*'s coverage so that we hit the streets just as the ads hit the air.

Jobs builds his brand the way Michelangelo painted chapels. One of the first things he did when he returned to the company in 1997 was to develop an advertising campaign to rebrand Apple in people's minds as a company apart from its competitors. His vision for Apple since the day he cofounded it was that it would be regarded not as a faceless corporation but rather as a company that *meant* something. "My goal," he told me in 1983, "is to become a ten-billion-dollar company with soul." In 1997, the way to tell people that the soul was back, he concluded, was to link Apple with cultural icons who exemplified the characteristics that he wanted people to think of when they thought of Apple. People who thought differently.

Jobs worked on the campaign with Lee Clow, the creative director of TBWA\Chiat\Day. This was a homecoming, as Clow had worked with Jobs and Apple on its famous "1984" advertisement that kicked off the Macintosh in that year. (The commercial, in case you missed the most celebrated 60 seconds in advertising history, depicted an entire dystopian state laid to waste when a young blond woman courageously tossed a sledgehammer into a screen where an Orwellian dictator was blathering instructions. It never showed the product or even mentioned what sort of thing the product was, and it was nationally aired only once, during the 1984 Super Bowl. But people are still talking about it.) Clow and Jobs shared a vision of what Apple had once represented and a desire to regain that idealistic aura. "They asked us to come in and talk about what Apple needed to do to get its focus back," Clow told *The New York Times* in 1998. "It really wasn't hard; it was just to go back to Apple's roots." Originally, Chiat\Day's idea was to show different-thinking people who actually use Apple computers, but when the ad people tested the slogan along with images of true giants whose hands had never touched a mouse—Einstein, Gandhi, and Martin Luther King—they realized that they could make a statement with a much bigger impact.

"The whole purpose of the 'Think Different' campaign," Jobs once told me, "was that people had forgotten about what Apple stood for, including the employees. We thought long and hard about how you tell somebody what you stand for, what your values are, and it occurred to us that if you don't know somebody very well, you can ask them, 'Who are your heroes?' You can learn a lot about people by hearing who their heroes are. So we said, 'Okay, we'll tell them who *our* heroes are.' "

Of course, what we got was a sense of who Steve Jobs's heroes were. He assumed that by associating his company with the people *he* admired, he'd lead consumers not only to think more highly of Apple but be inspired by what Apple stood for! Helping pick out which of these heroes would be the subject of advertisements was, he says, "one of the best parts of my job."

Adding to the mystique of the Think Different initiative was the fact that the ads never identified the heroes by name. Though some visages had Rushmore-esque status—Picasso, Alfred Hitchcock, Muhammad Ali—others, like Maria Callas and Frank Lloyd Wright, were not exactly household faces. "Young people like it because they feel they're not being talked down to," said Clow. "And the knowledgeable people feel it's cool to be among the cognoscenti."

Jobs devoted himself to the ad campaign with his typical fanatical attention to detail. Of course, his idol Bob Dylan had to be among the Think Different crowd. And since "one of my greatest heroes is Gandhi," he says, he worked overtime to secure the rights to the photo he considered the perfect image. "You have to get two sets of permissions, one from the estate and one from the person owning the picture," he explains. "We got permission from Gandhi's grandson, but Time-Life, who owned the picture, said, 'No way.' I had to call [Norman] Pearlstine [at the time, the head of Time Warner's editorial division], and he said okay."

Another Jobs touchstone, John Lennon, was easier. "Yoko said okay for a picture of her and John. I was actually here in California, and I saw her in a restaurant. She came over and said, 'I knew I was going to see you sometime soon, so I've been carrying this picture for a week.'"

By the time the iPod appeared in 2001, Apple had recaptured its mojo, and its simple fruit logo had regained status as a cool indicator in itself. To introduce the iPod—at the time an unfamiliar device that needed some explanation—Jobs felt a fairly traditional campaign was called for. Apple's commercials showed a guy undocking the device and dancing, thus illustrating the iPod's portability and ability to suck songs off your computer.

It wasn't until 2003 that Apple unveiled a much cooler campaign that would be forever identified with the iPod: "Silhouettes." Also created by TBWA\Chiat\Day, these ads exploded in your eye with blinding neon backgrounds. Though the human being was rendered as a moving black silhouette, the iPod itself and its white earbuds were a pure white that visually screamed even more loudly than the bright yellow or green or purple background. At first, the silhouettes were static images on magazine pages, billboards, and bus shelters.

Transferring the campaign to video for television commercials was a fairly intricate process, set into motion for a debut in early 2004, to promote the Windows version of iTunes. In each spot a hot young person—his or her face not seen but often featuring a touchstone of hip minority status, like dreadlocks—would be going absolutely bananas to a wild rock or hip-hop song, typically a brand-new tune by a band that your kid has heard of but you haven't. The Chiat\Day people, using a cutting-edge video house called Company 3, made three versions, each one focusing on a different sizzling genre of music: rock, techno, and hip-hop. All featured a tune from a new band in the genre, and the exposure of the rock group Jet and the dance-oriented Black Eyed Peas helped catapult the groups into stardom. The white earphone cords—painstakingly drawn frame by frame by postproduction artists—would shake wildly, a serpentine invitation to the aural bacchanalia provided to those who partook of the iPod drug. It was an out-of-control party in your head, which justified the neoepileptic fits of the anonymous baggy-pants dudes or miniskirted babes. Finally, the dancer would vanish and on the screen, in Apple's familiar bold Garamond font, would appear all the words you needed to know: "iPod, Mac or PC." And then the Apple logo.

"Without saying a word," wrote Randall Stross in *The New York Times*, "the commercials present viewers with a choice: orgiastic boogaloo-ing with the in crowd, or standing forlornly out of the picture."

But though Apple spent an estimated $200 million for promotion during the iPod's first four years—more than twenty times as much as its rivals Sony, iRiver, and Creative combined—the commercials were only one component of the coolness initiative that augmented the product's massively positive word of mouth. Apple has always had an aggressive Hollywood operation designed to sneak Macintosh computers into TV shows and movies (think of Carrie Bradshaw's black G3 laptop, Seinfeld's iMac, and all those Macs tracking down terrorists in *24*). More often than not, the producers don't need convincing—they come to Apple first. The effort to make the iPod a movie star was destined for success whether Apple asked for it or not.

Take Fox Network's most popular Gen Y television show, *The O.C.*, a prime-time soap. It is insanely influential in the music industry; the tunes that play on its sound track are the contemporary equivalent of the old *American Bandstand* for breaking new acts. The creator of the show, Josh Schwartz, is a lunatic Apple fan. He considers the iPod "the greatest invention since the wheel." (Not the scroll wheel—the *wheel.*) On the dark day when a lowlife thief broke into his black 530 BMW and ripped off his forty-gig iPod, "there was a hole in my heart," Schwartz says, and he immediately drove to an Apple store to replace it. Naturally, he had had no reservations about giving the iPod a recurring role in his television show, so much so that at one point the executives at Fox sent him a letter telling him to stop the free publicity to Apple and consider using generic MP3 players instead—a directive he considered clueless. "I want to show the *iPod,*" Schwartz says. "It's what our audience uses and what our characters would use."

The iPod is also a prize possession in such shows as *Scrubs* and *One Tree Hill.* The psychic detective in *Medium* tracked a killer by a bloody iPod. The lifestyle alchemists in *Queer Eye for the Straight Guy* use iPods to enhance the coolness factor of the hopeless dweebs they make over. And the 5G iPod got the American equivalent of a royal imprimatur when it was listed as one of Oprah Winfrey's "Favorite Things of 2005." (The Queen of Daytime had previously named an earlier model one of her favorite Spring Things, and in May 2003, she presented one to each of 350 audience members.)

Getting iPods into hip-hop videos took a little more micromanaging. Executives at Interscope Records called Jobs to suggest that he send off some iPods to load the prop room for 50 Cent's video of his new song, "P.I.M.P." "One of the things we do is deliver a message of cool," Ron Gillyard, Interscope's head of urban music, told my *Newsweek* colleague Jennifer Ordonez. "We said if kids see 50 Cent with an iPod, it will make the iPod cool to them." That's a rather simplistic equation, but in any case the video turned out to be a full-fledged, um, pimping of the iPod to the world of hip-hop and its suburban wannabes. It shows the notorious rapper prepping for an important meeting of "The Council of Pimps" by scrolling through the menus on his iPod, a device that holds his intense attention despite the potential distraction of half-naked "hos" stalking his bedroom like lionesses at the watering hole. Later in the video, 50 Cent addresses the distinguished Council of Pimps, chaired by the wizened rapper Snoop Dogg. He, too, has an iPod! Niiiice.

In the movies the iPod has played more character roles than Steve Buscemi. It has been a prop or plot point in *The Italian Job, Blade: Trinity, Agent Cody Banks, First Daughter, Legally Blonde 2,* and the Spielberg remake of *War of the Worlds.*

But it would be a huge mistake to attribute the basic attraction of the iPod to the ad campaigns and endorsements. The Lesson of Yossi applies here: it wasn't the commercials that made the iPod cool; the iPod *declared itself* cool from the get-go. As a reporter for the BBC, writing about the silhouette ads, put it, "Unlike 99% of campaigns the creatives' job here is simply not to blow the product's cool." The idea was to enhance the basic coolness components that were already there. Simply filling the screen with an iPod might do the trick—at least in the thinking of the ad geniuses at the Ford Motor Company, which made a commercial for its new Fusion model that begins with an extended close-up of Apple's music player. "The iPod is so iconic that people stop to watch the ad," gushed a Ford spokesperson to *Slate*'s Seth Stevenson, who branded the practice "cool by association." But coolness isn't a transferable commodity. As Yossi would tell you, iPod's coolness comes not from clever marketing or tribe mentality but from *what it is.*

Sure, some people are undoubtedly drawn to the iPod by the buzz around it. In August 2005, a marketing firm called the Diffusion Group set out to find out how many people by asking the question "To what extent does the 'cool factor' pull people toward the iPod and away from other devices?" The authors of the study began by stating the obvious: "It took no time for the iPod to become the chosen device of the ultra-cool set—it was a status symbol, a level of techno-chic that very few could aspire to and even fewer could make happen." But was that still valid four years after its launch, they wondered, when iPods were cheaper and more common and even Dick Cheney had one? The firm conducted a survey that drew responses from seven hundred mobile phone users in Internet households.

The study, released in October 2005, unearthed a lot of interesting factoids. For instance, iPod users groove on rock and roll 20 percent more than the average music consumer—and they listen to hip-hop *50* percent more. Owners of non-Apple digital music players are more likely to plug in to jazz, blues, and classical music.

But was their relationship with the iPod a true commitment or a faddish infatuation? The answer is that they truly, madly, deeply loved the iPod. Yes, there was indeed a percentage—12 percent, in fact—who had gravitated to the iPod mainly to jump on the bandwagon, and those, the Diffusion Group found, were the most likely to switch brands in the future. They're sort of the bridge-and-tunnel crowd of consumers, hooked on someone else's idea of cool. The rest of the vast collection of iPod owners, the millions and millions of others, had bonded more firmly. Their very first experience with shuffle mode seemed to have acted like an imprinting experience. They were in for good.

Nonetheless, part of the enjoyment of owning an iPod certainly seems to be the cachet of owning it. It's a modern twist on the old canard that no one is fired for buying shares in IBM—no one is branded uncool for owning an iPod. And in certain circles it is severely uncool to own anything else. Even the children of Microsoft executives have made it clear to their parents that they will accept no substitute, even if it means betraying the company that issues the family paycheck. Owning one makes you part of something bigger than yourself; when people talk about the iPod generation, you're right there. Especially in the early days of the iPod, when white earbuds were not as ubiquitous as ears, there was a feeling that when you spotted someone else with an iPod, silent high fives were exchanged. "It gives you the feeling you belong to a tribe," says Carl Rohde, the Professor of Cool.

That feeling changed as iPods became standard issue, and the tribe was as likely to include your grandmother as it was Kate Moss. At that point in the life cycle of a hip product—whether a playground-idol athletic shoe or a sneery punk band—there arises a coolness crisis. It's one thing to establish coolness among a knowing minority. But the crossover to a larger audience risks everything. As the Professor of Cool puts it, "You have to all the time reassure the most important target of your coolness, the minority, 'Hello, I'm still cool.'"

Apple managed that shift without losing a beat. In Rohde's view, "The iPod has done this. It has jumped from minority coolness to mass coolness."

The transition is further proof that the iPod's essence—not its marketing or its aura—is behind its popularity. While coolness might have been in the back of Apple's head all along, the company's real drive was for greatness. As Virginia Postrel, author of a perceptive book on the role of industrial design, *The Substance of Style*, explained to me, "Things can be cool because they're exclusive and single you out as an early adopter or somebody with money or somebody with unusual fashion-forward taste. But things can also be cool just because they're really beautiful and people like them. And then they can still be cool if they become ubiquitous."

It is no mistake that Postrel cited the iPod's beauty. She argued in her book that such high style is not a frill but something with inherent value. "Aesthetic pleasure itself has quality and substance," she wrote. "The look and feel of things tap deep human instincts. . . . Having spent a century or more focused primarily on other goals—solving manufacturing problems, lowering costs, making goods and services widely available, saving energy—we are increasingly engaged in making our world special. More people in more aspects of life are drawing pleasure and meaning from the way their persons, places, and things look and feel. Whenever we have the chance, we're adding sensory, emotional appeal to ordinary function."

The iPod turns out to be the canonical illustration of this theory. While there are obviously many factors that make the iPod irresistible—not least of which is its association with music, and not just any music but our own favorite songs, which it plays in heavy rotation—one stands out as launching the iPod to the very heights of the statusphere. This is its universally celebrated, endlessly pleasing, devilishly functional, drop-dead gorgeous design. The aforementioned Diffusion Group study concluded that even when the device became so commonplace that it was embraced equally by the trendsetters and the clueless, its design would keep the iPod on top. "Any short-term impact of a diminished 'cool factor' is unlikely to impact Apple in the long run—assuming it continues its design mastery," concluded the authors of the Diffusion Group study. In fact, a full 13 percent of the iPod owners interviewed reported that its aesthetic design was the *primary* reason they had bought it.

The Professor of Cool isn't surprised. "It just looks beautiful," says Rohde.

"There's a tactile quality to it, and yet it's very, very modern and sleek," Postrel told me. "So it kind of has that nice warm-cool, hard-soft, masculine-feminine, modern-comfortable mix."

Michael Bull, a British sociologist who studies personal audio, has noted that in the digital age, the music itself is obtained as an opaque file with no packaging—the traditional aesthetic components like album art and liner notes have disappeared. "The aesthetic has left the object—the record sleeve—and now the aesthetic is in the artifact: the iPod, not the music."

Not only do the iPod's owners admire the look of their iPods, but frequently (this is alarming) they display signs of a deeper, more physical attraction. You can see this in their interaction with the six-ounce hunk, especially in the early days of the affair. Owners love to touch it; during interviews I notice that discussing an iPod will trigger an urge to take it out of purse or pocket and fondle it, as if it were a small pet that needs reassuring. Maybe they're also assuring themselves that it's not lost. In any case, people can't keep their hands off it. Don Norman, the former Apple guru of user-friendliness and author of *Emotional Design,* has noticed this about iPods. "People fondle these new toys," he says. "They hold it in their hand, turning it around, stroking it. Not only does it look good, it feels good." More to the point is the confession twelve-year-old Josie Lonetti blurted out to a reporter for the *St. Paul Pioneer Press:* "On the first day I got my iPod, I kissed it good night, and my little sister called me an insane freak." We can chalk that up to youth, but what was the excuse of the grown woman writing for *Wired News* who exchanged her original iPod—which no longer worked—for a more powerful new one? She cried so hard that she could hardly breathe and spent two days in mourning, during which she could not bring herself to open the box of the replacement for the beloved (but broken) fifteen-gig "Pigwidgeon." Tales like this abound in the blogosphere and in conversations overheard in college cafeterias.

This fierce emotion is shared by Apple's CEO, by the way. Steve Jobs is very sensitive to any slight, even a veiled one, to the iPod's appearance. Once as I began an interview with him, I took out my microphone-equipped iPod to record the conversation. The device was covered by a translucent plastic iSkin cover. He looked at me as if I'd smeared the *Mona Lisa* with cow excrement. I tried to explain that I wanted to prevent the smears and dings that iPods often attract. He wasn't having any. "I think the stainless steel looks beautiful when it wears," he said. "Probably it's like us. I mean, I'm going to be fifty next year, so I'm like a scratched-up iPod myself." (Ironically, this conversation occurred only days before Jobs was diagnosed with pancreatic cancer.)

So it is that the wellspring of the iPod's coolness is its unmistakable look. How did *that* happen? It turns out that the iPod's industrial design has a clear pedigree. While Steve Jobs has consistently presented the development of the iPod as a team effort, he has publicly singled out the company's industrial design ninja as the guy responsible for the look and visual integration of the device. This is Jonathan Ive. Known within the company as Jony, Ive has continually made design history and put enough Apple hardware into the Museum of Modern Art's design collection to make MOMA an informal annex of the Apple Store. The iPod represents the apex of the partnership between Ive and Jobs. In some quarters people believe him to be the father of the iPod. (U2's Bono calling him "Jony iPod" helped that one along.) That's inaccurate, but it is fair to say that his vision fixed its look.

Jony Ive is a burly guy in his late thirties but appears younger. He's hulky under a loose T-shirt, hair shaved a few nanos short of a dome. Once he speaks, it's clear that he is more aesthete than hooligan. His tone is hushed and respectful, particularly when one of his creations—be it iMac, iBook, Power Mac G4 Cube, or iPod—sits in front of him. The accent is middle-class British. Ive was born in Essex in 1967 and has been in the United States for a decade and a half. Ive's work at Apple (along with Jobs's decision to give him credit) made the designer a celebrity in his own right. In June 2003, the Design Museum in London proclaimed him the winner of its first Designer of the Year award; Ive won both a public vote and a juried competition. The BBC called him "the Armani of Apple." In 2004, fashion, film, media, and design experts polled by the BBC named him the most influential cultural figure in all of Britain. (He beat out J. K. Rowling and Elton John.) And the 2006 Queen's New Year's Honours List bestowed on Ive the title of Commander of the British Empire. But the best accolade comes from his boss: "Working with Jony is one of my favorite things here."

As a child, Ive loved objects and especially enjoyed dismantling them. By his early teens, he understood that his future would be designing new things, and though he was never very good at drawing, he concentrated on art and design at school, matriculating at Newcastle Polytechnic. He then cofounded a trendy London design firm called Tangerine, where he drew up plans for hair combs, power tools, and even a toilet.

Though he was anything but a computer expert, late in his college days Ive discovered the Macintosh and was blown away. "I remember being astounded at just how much better it was than anything else I had tried to use," he once told an interviewer for the Design Museum. "I was struck by the care taken with the whole user experience. I had a sense of connection via the object with the designers. I started to learn more about the company, how it had been founded, its values and its structure. The more I learnt about this cheeky almost rebellious company the more it appealed to me, as it unapologetically pointed to an alternative in a complacent and creatively bankrupt industry. Apple stood for something and had a reason for being that wasn't just about making money." So in the early 1990s, when Apple did a search for a hot young designer to energize what had become a dreary operation, the twenty-five-year-old Ive eagerly took the interview, shaking with fear that he would somehow blow his chance. He got the job offer in 1992 and moved to Cupertino. His hopes were high, not only because he was going to work for what he had assumed was a cheeky company willing to break rules, but because for the first time he'd be inside the belly of a corporate beast, able to pull levers that a consultant doesn't ordinarily get his hands on. Those hopes were pretty much bleached out in the California sunshine. "The company was in decline," he said. "It seemed to have lost what had once been a very clear sense of identity and purpose. Apple had started trying to compete to an agenda set by an industry that had never shared its goals."

Almost five years into this unexpectedly dead-end sinecure, Ive got the break of his career: Steve Jobs became his new boss. Jobs, of course, is an autodidact of industrial design, known globally as a trendsetter in the field. When Jobs was still in his twenties, he once explained his vision of design to me, using as a symbol the object whose name he appropriated to name his computer company. "Fruit—an apple," he said. "That simplicity is the ultimate sophistication. What we meant by that was when you start looking at a problem and it seems really simple with all these simple solutions, you don't really understand the complexity of the problem. And your solutions are way too oversimplified, and they don't work. Then you get into the problem, and you see it's really complicated. And you come up with all these convoluted solutions. That's sort of the middle, and that's where most people stop, and the solutions tend to work for a while. But the really great person will keep on going and find, sort of, the key, underlying principle of the problem. And come up with a beautiful elegant solution that works."

This was a remarkable expression for a businessman, reflecting the classic quest for enlightenment, something one would definitely expect to find in the Zen 101 final exam. Satori, then ship. Jobs believed that semispiritual process was the secret of the Macintosh, the project he described at the time as "the greatest I ever worked on." Jobs later achieved a level of success with the NeXT computer workstation, which, despite being a commercial failure, is now regarded as having been a springboard for a number of significant innovations. And he certainly enjoyed triumphant vindication with the Pixar Animation Studios, which he would build into the world leader before selling it to Disney for more than $7 billion in 2006. But in 1997 no one would have dared place a bet on him to come close to replicating the Macintosh's winning mix of technology and design. Nonetheless, when he returned to Apple, it was exactly that pinnacle of high-tech, groundbreaking, design-driven innovation that he hoped to match and even surpass.

Naturally, Jobs was eager to locate a partner to realize his aesthetic vision for the new Apple. Generally, he regarded the company in 1997 as largely gutted of creativity. On the other hand, as he explained to me not long after he took over, one saving grace was the surprising number of "A and A-plus people" among the company's ranks. These were people who had refused opportunities to take their considerable talent elsewhere because they refused to believe that the dream of Apple was dead. Although Jobs had no qualms in flipping pink slips at the lesser lights, he was more than happy to retain one top employee. No one was more of an A-plus-er than Ive, though the Londoner was frustrated and jaded by then. "I don't know if this is true," Jobs says, "but Jonathan told me that the day he met me, he had his resignation in his pocket."

Ive *has* said that on the day that Jobs returned, work was begun on the iMac, the computer that would begin Apple's comeback on the innovation trail. Jobs went to Ive's house and outlined his design goals while walking around a vegetable garden planted by Ive's wife. The two were clearly kindred spirits, sharing an aesthetic that mixed outlandish novelty with an anodyne Zen sensibility. And Ive couldn't believe how much Jobs understood about physical style; he was even knowledgeable about obscure Italian designs. Though Jobs could often be blunt, Ive claimed to appreciate the straightforward nature of the feedback. "He'll give you three sentences, and as you work they will become more clear," he says. And the iMac set the tone for a collaboration so successful that Jobs made Ive the exception among all creative people at Apple, exposing him to the general public.

But even as the iMac was celebrated for its fresh, delightful look, Ive and Jobs insisted that the source of its coolness was not skin deep, but the result of painstaking attention to detail. "The thing that all of our competitors are missing is that they think it's about fashion, they think it's about surface appearance," Jobs complained to me once. "And they couldn't be further from the truth. The iMac isn't about candy-colored computers. The iMac is about making a computer that is really quiet, that doesn't need a fan, that wakes up in fifteen seconds, that has the best sound system in a consumer computer, a superfine display. It's about a complete computer that expresses it on the outside as well. And [competitors] just see the outside. They say, 'We'll slap some color on this piece of junk computer, and we'll have one, too.' And they miss the point." At a later interview, talking about the first iBook, which had a rubbery satchellike clamshell case, he argued that the very inclusion of a built-in handle had been an exercise in style. "Is that design?" he said of the handle. "I think it is. It's not just about looking good, it's about the use of the product. Not having a latch, is that design? Yeah, we think it's design. The rubber on the product, is that design? Yes. It affects how the product looks and how you feel about the product, but it's also incredibly functional if you happen to set it down too hard."

Perhaps the most aesthetically accomplished computer that Ive designed was the G4 Cube, a breathtakingly compact white enclosure floating in a Lucite frame. The Cube was an important product for Apple—not in the business sense but for its psyche. During an extended session with Jobs and Ive several days before its release, I realized that the Cube was the apotheosis of all they wanted an Apple product to say in design. It was about being brutally minimal. "This is the coolest computer ever made," Jobs told me. "It's our vision of what technology should be and how it should work and what it can do for you. We make progress by eliminating things. It's a much more courageous approach, much harder than living with all this [cheaper] stuff that most people live with. Saying *this is not necessary, we can take this out.* And you're left with just the essential thing." Ive, who had been nodding silently while his boss spoke, chimed in, "We're total fanatics about this stuff!" (Unfortunately for Apple, the sales of the premium-priced Cube were more minimal than Jobs had hoped, and the critically acclaimed machine went down as a glorious overreach.)

But Ive's greatest work will always be the iPod. One day Ive discussed how he had shaped its look. The conversation took place in 2004, just before the release of the fourth-generation iPod. (This was the first full-sized iPod with the "click wheel," distinguished by the buttons embedded in the scrolling circle itself.) Spread before us on a conference table was the new model, flanked by all the previous variations and generations, neatly arranged as props for our meeting. Why, I began, do people feel so emotional toward the iPod, and what might its design have to do with it? "I think it's a complicated answer," he said. "There are so many things that have made it successful. When I talk about 'stuff,' I deliberately focus on—obviously—the design, but I very much acknowledge and am very much aware that it's a successful product because of the whole phenomenal system."

That disclaimer out of the way, he gingerly began to explain how he had crafted the iPod's look. The conversation was like being escorted on a secret tour into the caverns of coolness. "We are surrounded by so many electronic and digital devices that are on a similar sort of scale," he said. "Just think of the hundreds and hundreds of thousands of these. And they're not really very good. They're so instantly forgettable. One of the problems with each of these individual projects is that there's a story behind them of a designer wagging his tail in your face. They're just clamoring for attention. Now, you know how obsessed and seriously we take our design here. But to us, the *music* was much more important than the design. Somehow, I think our goal was about getting design almost out of the way. We wanted to create a very, very new object. But think of how many hundreds of thousands of objects of this sort there have been in the last twenty years! This was a fairly ambitious challenge—not to create another trivial digital small object. The goal wasn't to *try* to make it immediately and instantly recognizable at twenty feet. But it *is*. It is, because of the consequence of the more important goal—just to try to design a product that was efficient, elegant, and simple."

Ive looked down at the table at the row of iPods, from the original scroll wheel model to the mini to the yet-unreleased fourth generation. "What it really was about, in some sense," he finally said, "was getting design out of the way."

Ive believes that a key to that Zen-like goal was the color of the original iPod. The subject of the iPod's glossy white polymer finish is something so deep that it reduces the normally articulate Ive to fits and stutters. "If you think about white," he begins, "white is such a . . . a . . ." He grasps for a word that will capture this chimerical concept, while his eyes devour, as if for the first time, the Moby-esque whiteness of the iPod, a palm-sized slice of Antarctica laid before us. "I mean," he finally continues, "on one hand, it's neutral. But it is such a *bold* neutral. If you just think from an Apple point of view, we started out as the color company"—here he is talking about the first iMac, which added color to what had been the drab beige prison of computing—"and then we came out with these sort of *unapologetic, perfect white products.*" First came the shimmering, almost ethereal Cube. Then the company replaced the outside of the laptop iBook—which debuted in lollipop hues of blueberry and tangerine—with a dense white plastic exterior. It was like the Beatles following up the baroque business of their *Sgt. Pepper* album cover with the naked blankness of *The White Album.*

The iPod was the boldest step yet toward whiteness, an effort directed to the heart of visual simplicity and minimalism, with perhaps a yearning toward invisibility. "Right from the very first time, we were thinking about the product, we'd seen this as stainless steel and white," Ive explained. "It is just so . . . so brutally simple. It's not just a color. Supposedly neutral—but just an *unmistakable, shocking neutral.*"

It's almost as if Jony Ive, a London-born industrial artist, were channeling Ishmael, the narrator of Herman Melville's fabled novel. "In many natural objects, whiteness refiningly enhances beauty, as if imparting some special virtue of its own," Melville wrote in *Moby-Dick*. Ishmael is driven to solve "the incantation of this whiteness," a journey that leads him to ask whether white "by its indefinitiveness . . . shadows forth the heartless voids of immensities of the universe, and thus stabs us from behind with the thought of annihilation, when beholding the white depths of the milky way." At least that's what I *think* Ive is getting at. Certainly the passion of Ive's soliloquy seems at odds with the psychological interpretation of iPod white offered by Luke Williams, an expert affiliated with the celebrated Frog Design collaborative. "Consciously or unconsciously," he wrote, "the iPod materials reference a convention of cleanliness that *everybody* interacts with *every day*—a bathroom." In Ive's view, the null hue is much more in line with Melville's blizzard-level turmoil than with an idyll on the potty.

Ive draws a sketch for me to illustrate the Whiteness of the Pod, how they laid the polycarbon plastic on the rear steel cladding to get "quite a strong, almost sort of halo around the product," rendered so that the chromelike steel is visible from some angles but only subliminally perceived in other angles. The surface itself is a "double-shot polycarbonate," a two-layered concoction wherein an injection molding procedure binds a transparent plastic coating over a layer of solid white.

As this conversation continues, Ive grows more intense. Now he turns to the packaging. It would take a complete additional chapter in this book to fully capture his description of how the fold-open box was designed, how each component fits perfectly in its slot, how opening the box is akin to unwrapping the most carefully packed Japanese artifact. For a full two minutes he talks about the number of decisions and breakthroughs required to settle on the just-perfect way the FireWire cable would be wound and bound and situated in the box.

Clearly he is pouring his heart out. He goes on to describe the exacting considerations behind each curve and tolerance on the unit. There are profound implications behind every degree of beveling and every micromeasurement in the seam between the silvery steel and the snow-colored skin. It's hard to imagine holding such a conversation with the designers working for most other companies. We are no longer in a world where a device like a digital music player has a few screws on the back so service people can open it. A recessed screw on this device would stick out like a lug bolt on a Brancusi. Even an "On" button was considered too much of an aesthetic abomination to be included on this exalted artifact.

"*So much* of what we do is worry about the smallest of details," he says. "We think it's the right thing to do, to care that much, but at the back of your mind you wonder, *will anyone ever notice*? And while I don't think all the people using the product notice or care in a conscious way about every little detail, I do think in the aggregate it's really important, and it contributes to why people like the product."

Now that we've absorbed the shock of the new white of the iPod, he's ready to talk about what might be an even greater triumph in design, the iPod mini. This is the tinier iPod introduced at the Macworld Conference & Expo in January 2004, just as the iPod itself was really taking off in the marketplace.

The mini's defining attribute, of course, was its size, 35 percent smaller than its big brother and almost 50 percent smaller than the original iPod. Steve Jobs has always had an insatiable fetish about miniaturization. The *Saturday Night Live* skit where a Jobs imitator (decked out, natch, in black turtleneck and jeans) introduced in rapid succession a fingernail-sized iPod micro, a confetti-sized iPod pequeño, and a final, literally imperceptible iPod invisa (holding *eight million songs and every photo ever taken*) was a joke rooted in truth. So it was no surprise that just as the original iPod was finding its mass audience, Jobs would exploit the advances of smaller hard drives and lower-tolerance scroll wheels (which in 2002 had gone from a mechanical version to a slimmer solid state version) to shrink the iPod. To maximize space—and do away with buttons entirely—Jobs's team came up with a new twist on the mini's scroll wheel, the original version of the click wheel that was now graduating to the original model. You navigated by clicking on the compass points of the wheel: North for "Menu," East for "Forward," South for "Pause," and West for "Back." "The click wheel was designed out of necessity for the mini, because there wasn't enough room for [the buttons on] the full-size iPod," says Jobs, "but the minute that we all experienced it, we just thought, 'Oh, my God! Why didn't we think of this sooner?' "

This new variation would also feature *colors*—gold, silver, pink, green, and blue—in a striking brushed-aluminum case. And held side by side with the original, it made the white model—acclaimed as the sleek sports car of music players—suddenly look like an SUV.

"The mini was designed with exactly the same philosophy [as the original iPod]," says Ive. "We were trying to take advantage of and exploit the fact that it was a smaller drive and really understand the differences. We made one model taking an approach [similar to the original], using that design vocabulary and form factor, and it was just completely wrong. Then we started to explore very different materials and approaches. We realized we could

Cool

make this in aluminum. Unlike with stainless steel, you could blast it and then anodize it—which is a form of dyeing—and then you could do color in an unusual way."

Another factor that Apple was aware of from the beginning, says Ive, is that from the get-go the smaller version of the iPod should be built with some way of physically attaching it to the user, as if it were clothing. "Most things have stuff that clips onto them, and it's a pretty unpleasant process," says Ive. So the mini was built so you could wear it, either on a plastic belt connector, which was included in the package, or on an armband, which Apple sold for $30. ("There is a new form of jewelry in the land," says Don Norman. "In the past only one technology, a wristwatch, was so commonplace that we strapped it to the body and thought of it as jewelry. Now we have the cell phone, the digital camera—which are merged—and Apple's music player.") Apple's designers tried to figure out how people would attach the device to themselves and what the vulnerabilities would be if they dropped it at that point of exposure, and then tried to engineer it so that if you did drop it at that point, the device wouldn't be rendered dysfunctional. "A lot of what we do will be thankless because it's not obvious, because we refuse to rub your face in it," says Ive.

At first glance, a lot of technology writers, myself included, wondered whether the mini would be a hit. The iPod's little sister was more compact and very attractive, to be sure. But it really wasn't much less expensive. It cost $249, while the big brother dropped to $299. Do the math. A standard iPod with twenty gigabytes of memory—5,000 songs' worth—stored its music at six cents per song. The mini held only 1,000 songs—a quarter per song! Why wouldn't you spend a lousy fifty dollars more and get to carry a music library that was five times as big? Jobs sounded a bit defensive when asked this question after introducing the mini. He first emphasized how great the colors were, predicting that gold would be huge—"I think the hip-hop crowd's going with this one"—and confessing his own preference: "I'm a silver kind of person." He insisted that the lower price would make a difference to some people: "It's easy for us to underestimate, but for many people $50 is a lot of money." He suggested that some people who already owned an iPod might want a second one for the gym. "They're going to want both," he said. "They're going to say, 'On a trip, I'll take my whole library with my iPod and when I go to the gym I take my mini.' " Not surprisingly, considering Jobs's well-known fetish for miniaturization, he extolled its compactness and praised the work of his engineers in making it so small.

Aside from Jobs's guess that gold would be the most popular color (it was the least), it turned out that he was right and the geek critiques were all wrong. We made the mistake of crunching the numbers. Those who followed fashion instead of tech specs—like Virginia Postrel, who from the outset predicted success for the mini on her blog—understood that this smaller, more colorful, more affordable, and even cuter iPod would not only do well but extend the audience of the iPod and drive it even more deeply into the cultural gestalt. "What [Apple] realized is that this is a fashion accessory that people enjoy looking at and wearing, and that it's not just about how many songs it holds," says Postrel, who bought herself a blue mini.

The mini, in fact, became the best-selling iPod of all. Especially among women. When the *Today* show hosted a "Gender Wars" debate between two consumer technology touts in April 2004, both the male and female commentators chose iPods—but while the guy wanted the burly forty-meg white model ("You gotta have the big iPod"), the female commentator specified a pink mini ("It's teeny!"). When her male counterpart tweaked her with a patronizing comment that she might have been a sucker for the cool color, she acknowledged that while she liked the look, the key was that "it just works."

But cool hunters have concluded that the look may indeed have been the clincher for millions of iPod mini buyers. "Never underestimate the wow-factor of design," wrote Carl Rohde in his 2003–2004 *Global Cool Hunt Report,* "even when in quantitative research, respondents hardly ever mention the importance of design as part of their buying decision-making process."

What was the most popular iPod color? Silver. But every time I went into the Apple store in SoHo, especially around Christmas, the shortest stacks of iPod minis—meaning the ones most in demand—seemed to be the pink model.

The mini represented a turning point for iPod. Clearly, the reduced storage capability didn't seem to bother people. In fact, in 2005, a Solutions Research Group study showed that the average iPod owner has 504 songs; a different survey found that the average was 900. Apple Executive Vice President Phil Schiller says that Apple has concluded that a limit of 1,000 songs turns out to be the "sweet spot" for most people, the number that sticks in most people's minds as the most they'll need. (A 2004 Jupiter Research study backs him up further: it found that only 23 percent of consumers said that they'd ever need more than 1,000 songs on their player at one time.) There will always be music nerds who gripe that even 10,000 songs is not enough for their copious collections. But for some people, the ability to hold thousands of songs is a liability—the vast empty space is intimidating, a silent rebuke to one's music-gathering ability.

But then there's Karl Lagerfeld, the renowned fashion designer who instantly took to the iPod and, in no time, went over the top. His iPod lust is symbolic of the way the fashion world has embraced the iPod. "I have 60 i-pods [*sic*]," he scrawls longhand on Chanel stationery. "It's the new way to store music. I can travel with all my music." He explains how Louis Vuitton made him "a beautiful traveling case," which houses his iPod collection and a portable loudspeaker system. Lagerfeld has an elaborate system involving laser-etched codes on the back of various iPods that clarify which sorts of songs each unit stores. Prada, Kate Spade, Gucci, and other designers all got into the business of making skins and cases for iPods, but Lagerfeld topped them all with his own carrying case made for Fendi, dubbed the Juke Box. Selling for $1,500, the gaudy multicolored giant purse—a virtual RuPaul of iPod transport—holds up to a dozen devices.

By the time the mini family got an upgrade in early 2005—adding not only longer battery life and more storage but hotter colors—Apple was more fully exploiting its aesthetic appeal. A press release led off with a message that emphasized couture over chips:

> Your music has never looked so good. And neither have you. . . . With a new palette of colors to choose from, iPod mini caters exclusively to your individuality and sense of style. Pick the color that suits you best—silver, pink, blue or green. Each iPod mini is brighter than ever and completely wearable, ensuring that it will spice up any outfit. Just attach it to the included belt clip or to an optional accessory like the lanyard or armband and you're ready to go out in style.

Indeed, the mini was a fashion object to die for.

Apple tried a further experiment in color with its U2 iPod, a special model with the signatures of the Irish rock band engraved on the rear casing. It was the first black iPod—an ebony tinge as dense as the leather jacket worn by Bono, the group's loquacious lead singer, set off by a fire-engine-red click wheel. "The black iPod is something I coveted—this is a beautiful object," said Bono in October 2004 at a press roundtable session after he and guitarist The Edge performed two songs at the launch event in San Jose. "People want to sleep with it," he added. "My three-year-old loves it. It's sexy, and music should be sexy." After the roundtable, Jobs introduced me to the singer, and as soon as the CEO moved out of earshot, Bono serenaded Apple's design prowess some more. "Working with Jobs was as easy as pie," he said. "We'd call, and he'd be obsessing on the Bakelite. Apple has created an art object for hardware and software to live in."

Art? Indeed, some people have gone as far as to say that the industrial design of the iPod and other Apple products is tiptoeing toward that lofty realm. But Jonathan Ive is reluctant to go there. "The goal of art is self-expression, and the goal of this is for people to be able to listen to music on a device that was cared about, where every detail was worked on and refined and refined and refined," he says.

"I don't see it as art," he concludes. "I mean, I see it as a digital music player."

Cool.

Personal

❯In February 2005, the writer Andrew Sullivan visited New York City and became severely discombobulated. The energizing, cacophonous racket he had associated with New York had fallen silent. Even more disconcerting, the city's formerly boisterous population had apparently been mindjacked by some alien force. Staring at the suddenly quiescent street life, he fingered the culprit. It was the Gizmo That Stole Gotham:

> There were little white wires hanging down from their ears, or tucked into pockets, purses or jackets. The eyes were a little vacant. Each was in his or her own musical world, walking to their soundtrack, stars in their own music video, almost oblivious to the world around them. These are the iPod people. Even without the white wires you can tell who they are. They walk down the street in their own MP3 cocoon, bumping into others, deaf to small social cues, shutting out anyone not in their bubble.

Even Sullivan's own status as an iPod owner—"I joined the cult a few years ago; the sect of the little white box worshippers," he confessed—did not mitigate his sorrow at what had been lost. "Walk through any airport in the United States these days and you will see person after person gliding through the social ether as if on autopilot," he wrote. "Get on a subway and you're surrounded by a bunch of Stepford commuters staring into midspace as if anaesthetized by technology. Don't ask, don't tell, don't overhear, don't observe. Just tune in and tune out."

Has the iPod destroyed the social fabric? Has it transmogrified us into a zombie culture? Has love of our own tunes lured us into aural narcissism, locking us in a cycle of self-love, from our hand-picked music library straight to our brains, via earbuds? It's something an unplugged observer might well ask. In certain places—the gym, the subway, the airplane, the schoolyard—it may seem that the immediate environment, and the people in it, gets less attention than the increasingly inevitable iPod.

Outsiders are getting frustrated at the party they haven't been invited to. To those who depend on making cold connections, it's beyond frustration. Pity the poor beggars and street musicians who must now compete with the personal concerts buzzing in the heads of potential donors. For politicians seeking to press voter flesh, it's a nightmare. "This is a whole new hazard in campaigning!" Gifford Miller, striving to be New York City's mayor in 2005, told *New York* magazine. "We have to come up with something to jam the iPods!" (Miller, of course, lost the primary.)

And it's not just mendicants, pols, and social critics who worry about the effect; even some enthusiastic iPod owners are concerned about the impact on the social dynamic. Wayne Coyne, the singer and guitarist for the Flaming Lips, for instance, loves the access to his music that the iPod gives him but admits, "There's an insulation that happens. I can see space is at a premium in a community like Manhattan, but in a way it's saying, 'I'm with you people, but I don't want to deal with you.' I don't really like that sometimes—I like the idea of 'Let's deal with each other, why not?' "

Coyne's lament is typical of this form of social criticism. But it's misguided. Think of your experiences in the subway and gym before the iPod became standard issue and supposedly made everyone into an extra from *The Village of the Damned*. Did people in those pre-'pod environments spontaneously break out into chatter, exchange intimacies, and otherwise "deal with each other"? No. They avoided eye contact and counted the minutes until the torturous boredom of those social hells might end. Now people happily listen to their favorite music, marvel at how their personal soundscapes enliven their surroundings, and appreciate the cozy (albeit virtual) protective covering that their iPods provide them. Amazingly, *that* seems to make observers crazy.

This wailing and moaning about the iPod's effect on human interaction is actually part of an old story. The complaints fit into a long tradition of neo-Luddite discomfort about the way people tweak their environments—and mess with their minds—to alter their mental and emotional state. Two things always seem to evoke an indignant outburst of "It ain't natural!" One is drugs; the other is technology, applied so as to please ourselves. When the latter is used to get effects as mind-blowing as the former, things become really interesting. (One of the most memorable quotes I've ever gathered in my reporting career came in 1982, covering the US Festival, a huge rock concert sponsored by Apple cofounder Steve Wozniak. At a motel nearby, Jerry Garcia, who was prepping to play a "Breakfast with the Grateful Dead" set, proclaimed, "Technology is the new drugs." Okay, not an original concept, but consider the source.)

Without altering one's chemical composition, the iPod does change your head. Plugging directly into your ears, dominating the brain matter in between, and shuffling your music collection to extract constant delight, it generates a portable alternative reality, almost always more pleasant than the real one. To some, that's scary, and the image of millions of people wandering around with this musical prosthesis has kicked up a sandstorm of criticism, often with a panicky edge.

The iPod, of course, is only the most recent, and most compelling, advance in a movement of portable cocooning that's been under way for decades. Even before personal stereos, some critics had observed the lure of isolated musical environments, which were then mostly found in the semiprivate enclosures of automobiles. In his 1974 book *Television: Technology and Cultural Form*, the sociologist Raymond Williams used the term "mobile privatization" to describe the phenomenon of people forming technological bubbles around themselves, isolating themselves from the scrum of human relations. "What is experienced . . . in the conditioned atmosphere and internal music of this windowed shell," he wrote, is "the pursuit of self-determined private choices." Sounds good to me. But Williams was less into celebrating choice than decrying its effect. Technology, he was saying, was making us into islands, particularly in our cars.

Cars, however, are islands no matter how you cut it. Essentially they're rooms that go places, and often they can be pretty social, even when the radio's on. (Think of the "Bohemian Rhapsody" scene in *Wayne's World*. Anything but antisocial.) Also, the demands of stopping for traffic lights and avoiding pedestrians require a relatively high degree of attention directed outside the bubble. In any case, the bubble itself is a natural outgrowth of being in a car, and only a sociologist would bother to gripe about the isolationist angle. The step that would really upset the social order came when it was possible to wire up an individual in a way that allowed him or her to aurally check out of the environment and withdraw into a private universe while technically present in the "real" one.

The first person to explore this phenomenon seems to be an eccentric amateur inventor named Andreas Pavel. Born in Germany, he was six years old when his family emigrated to Brazil, where Pavel became a citizen. But he frequently moved back and forth, studying social science and philosophy in Berlin. He was a huge and omnivorous music fan, and in the late sixties his odd-shaped house in São Paulo was a gathering place for a wide circle of friends. Bunched into a living room with a high, vaulted ceiling, Pavel and his visitors would sprawl on a huge sectional couch pushed to the center of the room, as if sunning on a beach, and would listen to music boomed from big Stanton speakers. The selections would range from Stockhausen to Javanese gamelan music. Pavel cheerfully recalls that they'd often share a joint or three.

Pavel, then in his midtwenties, came to love those sessions so much that he wondered how he would re-create the experience during a planned long stay in Switzerland. His solution was to hack together a portable, high-quality listening device. He began with a shoe-box-sized Sony cassette player and open-air Sennheiser earphones, a relatively new innovation. He figured out that if you disconnected the Sony's speakers and hooked the speaker wires directly to the earphones, you could get decent sound, and when he got to Europe he had a local radio shop jimmy up an adapter that could help power two sets of phones. (By then he had found even lighter open-air headsets made by Pioneer.) He strapped all the electronic components onto a thick belt. By February 1972, it was ready. He hooked the recorder to his belt, and, accompanied by his girlfriend, a dancer who shared his love of music, headed to the snow-covered woods near Saint-Moritz. In the cassette slot was a new album from the jazz flutist Herbie Mann called *Push Push*. The title track was a spirited collaboration with rock guitarist Duane Allman.

"It was snowing a bit," Pavel recalls. "Very romantic, a wonderful landscape. I put one headphone on my head and one on my girlfriend's head. We went to the most beautiful place in the woods, and I just pressed the button."

The woods exploded in sound, as if Pavel and his snow angel were in one of those heady psychedelic movies of the era. "It was, like, 'Wow! I can't believe that!' A really fantastic experience," he recalls, channeling the excitement of that momentous day as if in a rapturous flashback. "It is like an electronic drug, that thing! It's like the whole band is playing in the woods, at full sound. It is like film, a film experience. We couldn't get enough of it. We played and we walked, and played it and played it."

A funny thing happened when Pavel and his girlfriend were walking through the woods. They encountered some other hikers—the first people to stumble on what would one day become a common phenomenon, earphoned dropouts from reality. "They saw these two zombies, me and my girlfriend, walking in the woods and dancing with this music, but they couldn't understand it!" says Pavel. "Because this was 1972, and until the Walkman came out seven years later, the general public was not used to seeing people walking with headphones."

Despite his ambitions to market his "stereobelt," which he eventually patented, Andreas Pavel never succeeded in directly licensing his idea. He was turned down by Philips, Yamaha, Grundig, everyone. It took the Walkman—which Sony introduced in 1979 and which eventually sold 340 million units—to bring musical mobility and personal audio to the masses. (The iPod would take those categories into another dimension.) Pavel would launch a decades-long attempt to collect royalties from Sony and eventually collected a significant but undisclosed sum. But as far as the world was concerned, it was the Walkman, and only the Walkman, that made it possible to "transport [the] inner landscape of sound with one wherever one goes, simultaneously taking the pleasures of private listening into the very heart of the public world and the qualities of public performance into the privacy of the inner ear," according to the authors of *Doing Cultural Studies: The Story of the Sony Walkman.*

It's no coincidence that the iPod is commonly referred to as the "Walkman for the twenty-first century." There are numerous parallels between Sony's achievements and Apple's. Just as with the iPod Apple jetted the company's already considerable mystique into the stratosphere, the Walkman heightened the aura of a company that had already galvanized the world with its skills at stylish miniaturization. The Walkman, like the iPod, was not only a business triumph but a cultural success. And both have fomented a steady backlash from those who believe that such devices rip the social fabric, reward self-involvement, affect one's mental and otolaryngological health and safety, and are just plain too much fun.

Unlike Andreas Pavel's account of his invention, which seems to have been fairly consistent through the years, the origin of the Walkman has a number of variations. One version attributes the idea to Sony's cofounder Akio Morita, who, on a visit to New York City, was repulsed by throbbing boomboxes and concocted a cocoonish alternative. A variation of that tale attributes the offensive rock music to Morita's children, whose thrashing songs, unwelcome to the classical-music-loving executive, dominated his household. A totally different story gives credit to engineers in the company's tape recorder division; working desperately because their unit had been marked for obsolescence, they converted a portable voice recorder into a stereo device. But Sony's official history pegs the idea to Sony's other cofounder, Masaru Ibuka.

In 1978, Sony was making a portable cassette tape recorder called the TC-D5, the size of a shoebox. Ibuka, then semiretired and the company's honorary chairman, began taking it on transpacific flights with a set of headphones. He'd put on a huge set of earphones and listen to the classical music he adored, in clear stereo. But lugging the device around was a pain. Ibuka knew that Sony made a much more portable recorder called the Pressman, designed for reporters and executives to capture interviews and take dictation. So one day he asked his deputy Norio Ohga if the Pressman could be converted to a stereo, play-only device.

Ohga gave the assignment to Kozo Ohsone, the head of Sony's Tape Recorder Business Division, and within weeks—maybe here is where the desperation part kicked in—they had swapped out the recording mechanism with the electronics required for stereo playback through headphones. To keep the unit at the same compact size, they eliminated the speaker, assuring that this product would forever be wed to headphones. Sony's cofounder Ibuka, dropping in on the project one day, came up with the idea of adding lightweight headphones.

It made sense for Sony to think of a portable tape player. For one thing, though tape cassette technology was pioneered by the Philips company (as a means of supplanting bulkier, harder-to-handle reel-to-reel tapes), Sony had been instrumental in promoting the medium. The Japanese firm had successfully convinced Philips to offer the cassette as a royalty-free world standard. After considerable advances in materials and engineering, cassette tapes had approached, if not equaled, the sound quality of vinyl records, and music was routinely offered in that format.

The project was also consistent with the company's heritage.

After all, the company had made its bones with what was arguably the ur-Pod—the first cheap transistor radio. The company, then called Tokyo Telecommunications Engineering, seized an opportunity that came when the big American companies failed to see the allure of liberating radios from the house and car, a feat made possible by the invention of tiny transistors made by Texas Instruments. The first company to license the technology was a tiny firm in Indianapolis that released a five-inch-high and three-inch-wide one-speaker AM radio called the Regency TR-1 in 1954. The radio cost $700 and the sound was lousy, but it developed a cult following—and even an iPoddish bit of glamour. Producer Michael Todd, in a forerunner to today's celebrity goodie bags, gave them to cast members of his movie *Around the World in 80 Days*.

Sony was in position to top the Regency; it acquired its own license for transistors from AT&T and had wireheads in Tokyo design tinier, more powerful components. In August 1955, the TR-55, the firm's first product with the Sony name, was ready, but a year later an even smaller version, the TR-63, barely more than four inches high, invaded the U.S. The ur-Pod had one white earplug, albeit something that looked like a hearing aid. The device's cultural impact was huge. For one thing, for the first time teenagers could abandon the family radio console and mainline the new "Top 40" radio stations in the privacy of their bedrooms, or as they hung out on the street. "The shirt-pocket-portable or, simply, the transistor (as it was called then) became a metaphor for freedom and independence; the right to express, in music and in things, the style and tastes of youth," wrote anthropologist Michael Brian Schiffer. "The tiny transistor radio had become the symbol of a generation."

In 1979, a more sophisticated Sony was creating what it hoped would be the next generational symbol. There would be two big differences between the transistor radio and the Walkman. The first would be the audio quality—instead of the fuzzy sound that bleated from your first transistor radio, the Walkman's high-response headphones would deliver the sort of intense aural surround that you got at home from your own stereo system. The marvel was that these phones, dubbed the H-AIR MDR-3 (catchy, huh?) were lightweight—50 grams, compared to the 300 or 400 grams of others sold at the time—and "open-air," unlike the astronaut-style cups of conventional phones. The second novelty, of course, was that instead of radio content the music you'd play on the Walkman would be *your* music, encased in what was to become the ubiquitous cassette.

This added a potential level of isolationism to the experience. Instead of connecting with an announcer or deejay at the other end of the broadcast signal, Walkman users would be cocooned into a self-directed feedback loop, listening to their own tapes and inviting the rest of the world to go off somewhere and take a bath. You'd be the only ticket holder in your own great-sounding private concert hall. But what about the everyday interruptions—some from those who considered themselves your "loved ones"—that now would be blocked out by the sonic cone sealed by your new foam phones? Wouldn't they resent the fact that you were in the concert hall instead of interacting with them? Or at least being on the same *planet* with them?

This was an issue that Andreas Pavel had often encountered in his lonely peregrinations with the Stereobelt. His solution to those who looked askance at the spectacle of an earphone dropout was to pass over the second pair of earphones to the affronted party. *Take a hit of this, my friend.* "They would look astonished at me and then I would stop in front of them and, without saying anything, would take one of the two headphones and put it on their head," says Pavel of his strategy to deal with baffled or outraged strangers. "They would usually flip out completely. They would behave as if they were at a party."

No one at Sony, however, knew of Pavel's travels back then. The first person in the company to worry about these isolationist issues was none other than cofounder Morita. One night, he brought home a prototype of the Walkman. To his dismay, he later wrote in his autobiography, "I noticed my experiment was annoying my wife, who felt shut out." This led him to the realization that "it would be considered rude for one person to be listening to his music in isolation." He went back to his engineers and suggested a technological fix for this cultural consequence, an idea that Pavel had already implemented on his forerunner: the Walkman should have not one but two headphone jacks, so people could share music. They implemented this idea inside a week, but soon after Morita tried out the revamped prototype, he found that even tandem earphones could lead to antisocial consequences. On a golf outing, Morita had prepared a surprise for his playing partner, novelist Kaoru Shoki. He dramatically handed the prototype to his friend, and both donned earphones to hear the cassette Morita had inserted: a recording of Shoki's wife, a concert pianist, playing the Grieg concerto. "He smiled broadly and wanted to say something," Morita later wrote, "but he couldn't because we were hooked up to headphones. I realized this was a potential problem."

Morita went back to the engineers with another request: to create a way for the listeners to speak to each other. The Sony team thus created an orange "hot line" button. Pressing it activated a built-in microphone that allowed you to speak directly to your plugged-in friend's earphones.

As with the iPod, produced with breakneck speed to launch by the holiday season, the Walkman development process was an intense effort to make sure the product would be delivered in time for Japan's big selling season, the summer vacation. Morita threw down this challenge at a product meeting in February 1979, explaining, "Our target market is students and other people." The Sony-ites in attendance, mostly younger engineers, technical designers, and marketers, responded with panic but executed with fervor, in part because the Walkman was a product they wanted to own themselves. They made the deadline. On June 22, 1979, Sony unveiled its baby with a degree of showmanship and suspense that Steve Jobs—then a twenty-four-year-old mogul-in-training, beginning to contemplate a successor to the Apple II—might have appreciated. Journalists arriving at Sony's headquarters in the Ginza were directed to buses and handed a Walkman. Not until they arrived at Yoyogi Park—Tokyo's version of Central Park, which was filled every Sunday with crazed Elvis impersonators—were they directed to turn the devices on, to hear a sonically thrilling stereo introduction to the capabilities and virtues of the Walkman.

Sony's official history reports that the journalists didn't know what to make of the weird event. It was *really* weird for those who hadn't been given the sample units. They were among the first to experience what would soon be a common experience—being on the outside looking in as people in their midst checked out of the physical world and into the headphone zone *and they couldn't go there*. "The response from the press was cool," says the history.

And for the first couple of weeks the sales reflected that puzzlement. Sony worked hard to get people to give the Walkman a chance. The company ran a series of print ads that not only emphasized the device's mobility but suggested that this hunk of electronics was a sexy means of self-expression. One typical ad featured a long-legged Western woman in a halter top dancing frantically with her lightweight earphones as a Buddhist monk with conventionally bulky earphones looked glumly on. "In every case," wrote John Nathan in his book *Sony: The Private Life,* "the images reinforced the notion that the Walkman and its stylish headphones were a fashion statement." But ads were only one part of generating a Walkman allure. As Apple would do twenty years later, Sony made sure that the first ones off the production line went to key writers and critics—and, as with the iPod, they recruited musicians to give the first hands-on endorsements. (One big difference: Sony gave its freebies to members of the Berlin and New York Philharmonic orchestras; Apple bestowed its gems upon Moby and Modest Mouse.) Sony didn't have the chance to place Walkmans into television shows, but it did heighten the buzz by sending out ringers—typically young couples—into the Ginza on busy weekends, strolling with Walkman headphones on. By the end of August, the stores were out of stock and clamoring for replacements. Within a year, Sony began selling the Walkman worldwide, and it became an instant global hit. The foreign product intros were held in ultrahip venues like Regine's nightclub in London. The English pop star Cliff Richard even recorded a song inspired by the Walkman:

> *Cassette in my pocket and I'm gonna use it*
> *Stereo, out on the street, you know*
> *Oh oh oh woh woh woh*

The bemused journalistic accounts of seeing people with those lightweight circles of foam over their ears was a precursor of the reports of the next century's invasion of white earbuds. A reporter for *Money* magazine marveled at the "glassy-eyed folks walking around with headphones wired to little boxes hanging around their necks. . . . Those little boxes are portable tape cassette players. . . . It seems you don't have to stay home to listen to your stereo these days." Oddly, some Sony executives had been concerned that people would resist going out in public with a Walkman because the headphones might be associated with a hearing disability, something mildly shameful in Japan at that time. Morita's rejoinder to this was that Sony would create "a headphone culture."

That it did. While the very name of the unit emphasized mobility (on the first ads the word "Walkman" was spelled with two outsize capital "A"s, each of them dressed with a pair of shoes on their feet), the key to the unit was its private nature. Morita's insistence on including a second earphone jack and a button for hot-line communication proved misguided—no one used them. "Although I originally thought it would be considered rude for one person to be listening to his music in isolation, buyers began to see their little portable stereo sets as very personal," Morita admitted. "And while I expected people to share their Walkmans, we found that everybody seemed to want his or her own." Sony eventually got rid of the second jack on most models and eliminated the hot-line button. Despite Morita's wishful thinking, and in spite of a raft of television commercials that showed people from disparate walks of life cozily sharing their music with dual earphones, when offered the chance to keep their music to themselves, they grabbed it.

The Walkman was not about sharing, it was about *not* sharing. It was a *me* machine, an object of empowerment and liberation. "I remember my first Walkman," the venture capitalist Joi Ito wrote on his blog in 2005 (the memory was inspired by his iPod use). "It was the Sony TPS-L2. I was in 9th grade. I had just moved to Tokyo. The Walkman was part of the 'coming of age,' becoming independent, asking a girl out for the first time and becoming Japanese part of my life. I remember the feeling of having music thundering in my head as I walked to school. It made me feel all subversive inside."

Sony itself would come to the conclusion that two impulses—both associated, by the way, with the effects of drugs—were behind the lure of personal audio: escape and enhancement. The first one is obvious: putting on the earphones to wrap yourself in the music of your favorite cassette was a means of shutting out the world around you. "The experience of listening to your Walkman is intensely insular," wrote the critic Vincent Jackson in an essay called "Menace II Society." "It signals the desire to cut yourself off from the world at the touch of the button. You close your eyes and you could be anywhere." Jackson's essay also dealt with the bad vibes beamed his way by bystanders indignant that he chose to reject their aural environment for one of his choosing and, worse, that he had fun doing it. His message to them? "Piss off!"

One woman, cooperating in a sociological study, described her Walkman use in the 1980s as "like an escape . . . getting away from it all. Being sort of transported somewhere else for a while. . . . My parents had divorced. My mother was experiencing a pretty traumatic breakdown at the time. So it was nice to be anywhere. If I didn't have the Walkman, I'd feel what was going around me."

But as Andreas Pavel discovered the first time he used the stereobelt—and as millions of Walkman users found for themselves—escape is only part of the lure of personal audio. There was also what Sony considered the enhancement factor. Some described it as a means of empowerment—the newfound ability to reshape your reality enveloped in a matrix of your own making. "If the Walkman so far represents the ultimate form of music on the move, it also represents the ultimate musical means in mediating the media," wrote the sociologist Iain Chambers. "For it admits the possibility, however fragile and however transitory, of imposing your soundscape on the surrounding aural environment and thereby domesticating the external world; for a moment it can all be brought under the stop/start, fast forward, pause and rewind buttons."

Everybody who ever put on those foam Walkman headphones knew the feeling—first came the rush of hearing really good music untethered to the anchors of a full-size stereo system. Then, as you walked around, the music you were listening to transformed itself into a *sound track*, reshaping your perception of the crappy world you were otherwise stuck in. Andreas Pavel, who was there first, called the experience "the secret theater." The cassette you chose determined the movie that you would be thrust into. A stroll to the store could put you into the role of spear carrier at the opera. Walkman'ing it on the subway could make your fellow passengers look like a lineup from a Marcel Ophuls documentary. Wear it on the roller coaster, and you could be on a scary acid trip. The Walkman, claims the science fiction writer William Gibson, "has done more to change human perception than any virtual reality gadget. I can't remember any technological experience that was quite so wonderful as being able to take music and move it through landscape and architecture."

Herbert Marcuse had earlier bemoaned radio as one more example of "technological reality" violating "the private space by which man may become and remain 'himself.'" The Walkman turned this kind of thinking on its head. The sociologist Rey Chow, identifying the Walkman as "a revolution in listening," extolled the abilities of Sony's device as a means of making a sneering, punkish statement; while zoned out on the headphones, he argued, you are consciously rejecting the reality gruel that The Man has dished out. "This is the freedom to be deaf to the loudspeakers of history,"

Chow gushed. "The Walkman allows me . . . to be a missing part of history."

When the British sociologist Michael Bull studied the habits of Walkman users, he found that they not only used their personal soundscapes to make their surroundings into film sets, but that many of them actually became imaginary movie stars in these ear-cinemas. An alarming number of his subjects confessed that they envisioned themselves as characters in brutally violent films like *Reservoir Dogs* or *Goodfellas*. One guy, riding the bus, "mentally picture[d] myself in *Pulp Fiction* except there would be a few more murders and that Ingrid Bergman, Liz Taylor, Deborah Kerr were in it." *(Deborah Kerr?)* Another subject, whose Walkman was loaded with music from spaghetti westerns, reported that listening to it actually transformed his personality into that of a cold "verbal bounty hunter," shooting his workplace colleagues with "short cool blasts of verbal abuse."

While millions of Walkman users embraced this cocooned freedom, plenty of people were repelled by the spectacle. Some of the criticism came from stuffed shirts who could be relied on to attack any novel means of having fun. When the conservative critic Allan Bloom scolded Americans about their philistine ways in a best seller called *The Closing of the American Mind*, it was no surprise that he fingered the Walkman as among the chief villains in a great dumbing-down. "As long as they have the Walkman on," he bemoaned of the nation's wayward youth, "they cannot hear what the great tradition has to say." (They also had the considerable pleasure of not hearing what Allan Bloom had to say, reason in itself to crank up the volume.) Even more indignant was a history professor who wrote in *Christianity Today* that the Walkman was a menace because it called "into existence still one more competitor to the voice of God." (A fear that would be echoed in November

2005, when Cardinal William Keeler of Baltimore warned parents about iPods because they might be used to store pornography.)

More interesting criticisms focused on the dark side of the features that had made the Walkman compelling to begin with. The music columnist Norman Lebrecht complained that when music originally created for concert halls is packed "to go," the magnificent sound of God's pure language "becomes a utility, undeserving of more attention than drinking water from a tap." (Oddly, he values music more when one can't hear it.) But what really bugged those of priggish bent was the sight of people thumbing their nose at the reality everyone else had to deal with. "The autism of the Walkman listener," wrote Rey Chow, "irritates onlookers precisely because the onlookers find themselves reduced to the activity of looking alone." Nothing could trigger the feeling of exclusion Bob Dylan sings of in "Ballad of a Thin Man" like a gaggle of people absorbed in a Walkman reverie: *Something is happening, and you don't know what it is . . . do you, Mr. Jones?*

Twenty years after the Walkman's introduction, when Akio Morita died of pneumonia at age seventy-eight, critics took note of the way the world had changed—and weren't too happy about it. A *Washington Post* critic once again invoked "the look and sound of the Walkman dead: the head cocked at a slight angle, the mouth gently lolling. . . . The eyes flicker with consciousness but they don't *see*. They're somewhere else."

What is the attitude of Pavel, the uncelebrated revolutionary who was the first headphone dropout, when he notes these attacks? Defiant and decidedly unapologetic. "So what?" he says of people critical of this mass escape from reality. "Do I have to be always responsible? Why do I have to be accountable twenty-four hours a day? If I'm on a boring walk to the bus stop for the hundredth time and want to make it into something interesting, why should other people be concerned with that? I'm not walking on the street to be accountable! The secret theater is annoying to the other guy because you always want to know what other people are doing, and he doesn't have the slightest idea. And number two, he is in the same place where I am and I'm having a good time and he's not! So he's getting a little jealous, isn't he? Folks are getting happier without taking drugs, because it's like an electronic drug. I can't see anything wrong with that."

All of these issues, of course, and more have resurfaced in the Age of the iPod. By the time the iPod came around, a lot of people had put away their Walkmans. Cassettes had been supplanted by compact discs—expensive, awkward to carry around, unwieldy, and totally unsuited for exercise. The personal audio experience needed an upgrade, and while digital music seemed to be the answer, the first efforts fell short. Enter the iPod, an easily navigated portable jukebox that looked like a jewel. And it held your whole music collection! Suddenly the streets, subways, and gyms were full of people wearing white earbuds.

What's more, because the iPod holds so much of one's music and can play the music back with near-infinite variety, the druglike aspects—and the addictiveness—far exceed those of the Walkman. Also, because the iPod is more compact—and became even smaller and more adorable when it shrank with the mini and then the nano—it went more places, more easily, than the Walkman ever could. So the complaints about the Walkman were not only echoed but amplified. The world seemed to be split into two: those locked into iPod reveries and those griping about how they had lost contact with the cooler half of the world.

With all your music at hand, in an enclosure to die for, the personal experience with the iPod goes beyond mere listening. It's almost a relationship. So maybe it's understandable that people often cement the relationship by personalizing the iPod itself. This helps explain the popularity of Apple's program that offers free engraving on iPods bought online at the virtual Apple Store. (Originally it cost $50, but within a few months Apple dropped the fee.) When you compose the two lines of text and send it off to the Apple online store, the company transmits the message to the factory in Taiwan, where a laser engraving machine etches the words on an iPod's stainless steel rear casing within a matter of seconds. No obscenities or offensive language are permitted (though one owner proudly displayed his nano on the Internet with the legend "I rape Japanese schoolgirls," something an Apple spokesperson insists was a fraud or a mistake). People have used the etching to mark special occasions, to express feelings for each other, and even to propose marriage.

Another form of iPod personalization comes from literally dressing the devices, like a doll or a small pampered dog. This can be done by enclosing it in a high-fashion encasement sold by the likes of Coach, Prada, Kate Spade, Louis Vuitton, or Christian Dior. Or you can use special tattoos, Apple-produced "iPod socks," or the fruits of one enterprising company that paints iPods in twenty colors. The most expensive iPod case to date seems to be one displayed at the Chicago International Gem and Jewelry Show in December 2005. Built to house a nano, it has over 580 diamonds (total 10.32 carats) set in 120 grams of white gold. The case is $12,495, but the nano is included. This is not to be confused with the specially built iPod that HP presented to the rapper/producer P. Diddy—a shiny black lacquer model encrusted with a measly 120 diamonds.

The sociologist Michael Bull, who once wrote a book about the behavior of Walkman users, now studies Apple's digital device. He is sometimes referred to as "Dr. iPod," having launched a massive study of hundreds of users. Bull reports that the iPod, even more than the Walkman, privatizes one's space. The Walkman was "an in-between device"—you'd use it in transit—but the iPod, storing days and days of your music, can be a persistent presence, "giving the user the unprecedented ability to weave the disparate threads of the day into one uniform soundtrack." But something else is going on. With the Walkman, it was you who stuck the cassette in and the device simply obeyed your order in playing it back. Similarly, it's up to you to fill up the iPod with music, but from then on, it can be the iPod that does the programming. This makes it less a tool and more of a companion—a socially deft one at that. One interview subject explained to Bull that by her reasoning, the iPod is better than a mobile phone because the phone is only as good as the person you're talking to, while the iPod always makes the perfect noises because it's *your* music.

"People define their own narrative through their music collection," Bull told me in 2004. "It gives almost infinite variety. People say to me, 'It's almost as if my iPod understands me.'"

Years earlier, Bull noticed that Walkman users often wound up playing the same cassette over and over. But with thousands of songs and the ability to program them in playlists, iPod users have a much richer palette and more ways to exert control. In the most prosaic form, they put pulsing songs on their workout playlists and ballads on playlists for mellow moments or lovemaking. But people can also tailor playlists to create moods rather than fit their moods. A playlist for making one's way to work can make the experience a floating ethereal sensation or a grand procession. "It's as though I can part the sea like Moses," a female iPod lover told Bull.

It's not surprising that a new wave of finger-wagging editorialists has lambasted the iPod for isolating its users from human discourse, just as they did with the Walkman. The critic Christine Rosen, in a scathing attack on the iPod, calls it "the technology of the disconnected individual, rocking out to his headphones, lost in his own world." Rosen goes beyond the normal criticisms to warn that the "whole music collection in your pocket" is a dangerous temptation to the dead end of musical solipsism. Many iPod users feel like kids in a candy store—and that, she cries, is the problem. "The iPod, like the Walkman, can be leveling or narrowing as well as freeing," she warns. "It erodes our patience for a more challenging form of listening. The first time a person sits through an opera, patience is tested; they might wonder whether hour after hour of *Die Meistersinger* is really worth it. But with experience and patience comes considerable reward—the disciplined listener eventually achieves a different understanding of the music, when heard as its composer intended. Sampling is the opposite of savoring." It does not seem to occur to her that an ideal way to get through a difficult piece of music might be to upload it to the iPod and spend some time alone with it.

Rosen also wrings her hands about another doomsday vision: What if music lovers, sated by the narcissistic delights of their self-created playlists, decide there is no need to expend the time and ticket prices of live music? This is a rather wacky and unfounded fear. It seems rather obvious that the more music you hear from an artist, the more likely you are to want to see that person or band perform in public—and the high price of concert tickets seems to confirm the suspicion that the iPod has only enhanced the desire to see music live. (Since my own exposure to the iPod, I've roughly quadrupled the number of shows I've attended, ranging from alt-rock bands in uncomfortable clubs to Rolling Stones concerts with ticket prices that cost roughly the same as iPod nanos.)

But the main objections to the iPod seem to hew to the same moralistic lines as those against the Walkman—only more so, because outsiders get almost apoplectic at the near-lustful bond that the iPod inspires in its owner. Some critiques, like Sullivan's over-the-top descriptions of the iPod damned, have an apocalyptic, *Reefer Madness* quality to them. Gabriel Sherman, a writer for *The New York Observer*, after missing his subway stop because he'd been so transfixed by his iPod, concluded that the white earbuds and all they entailed were "like a drug . . . it had come to dominate my daily existence . . . I had grown increasingly numb to my surroundings, often oblivious to the world around me, trapped in a self-imposed bubble."

Another form of attack on the iPod focused on the trademark white buds, specifically in the way they deliver sound directly into the ear canal. In late 2005 and early 2006 a rash of articles appeared on the potential impact of iPods on hearing loss. Specialists in the field profess concern, though they say it's too soon to tell whether iPod users are really self-destructive, especially since no one has studied the effects of "a direct feed of sound into the ear," the otolaryngologist Jennifer Derebery of the House Ear Clinic told *The Wall Street Journal*. The Who's great guitarist, Pete Townshend, who has lost much of his own hearing (in part because of his refusal to die before he got old, a fate he hoped for in "My Generation"), thinks the time for alarm is now. While he admits that he's not sure how much the iPod will cause problems, he writes on his blog, "My intuition tells me there is terrible trouble ahead. The computer is now central to our world . . . The downside may be that on our computers—for privacy, for respect to family and co-workers, and for convenience—we use earphones at almost every stage of interaction with sound." (From personal experience, though, I can attest that no amount of iPod music at top volume compares to the sonic monsoon I experienced at a Who concert at Philadelphia's Electric Factory in 1969. My ears didn't stop ringing until the '80s.)

Someone even filed a class action suit against Apple, equating the potential of ear damage by high volume with a design flaw like the rear gas tank in the Ford Pinto. The alleged flaw is that iPods can pump up to 115 decibels of sound into a budded ear, which is more than a chain saw, though less than a jackhammer. (Oddly, that level of sound is not permitted in France, where the government—which has no problem with people smoking like fireplaces in public—forced Apple to reduce its top output to conform to a law restricting audio devices to 100 decibels.) On the other hand, it's very easy to turn down the volume. And Apple made it easier in March 2006, when it introduced a "volume limit setting" with which people could lower the maximum setting to their choosing and parents could even permanently set Junior's iPod to a level that would preserve his precious eardrums.

If some in the medical community are alarmed by headphone use, others cultishly embrace the experience. In the past few years a nebulous organization has generated a mysterious series of events called the Placard Headphone Festivals. A description of a typical event, held in London, explained, "Listening is via headphones only; upwards of 100 plug-in points are provided throughout the space for listeners who have brought their own headphones." The London performance was slated to last fourteen hours; a Paris-based headphone festival went on for ninety-five days. One participant in a London event extolled the direct connection she had felt during the intimate concert: "In my lifelong experience of witnessing live music, I had never felt so relaxed, comfortable in my surroundings and skin, and reassured by the presence of the musician who, with equal intent, directly plays to your ear canal with no interference from that annoying guy who's trying really hard to get laid."

The image one gets from the Headphone Festival—a live band playing to a widely scattered audience plugged into, above all, themselves—is kind of scary. What's more, it's a perfect embodiment of the fears of the iPod critics, who see the millions of users as a digital archipelago for whom even a communal experience is transformed into a form of aural masturbation. On the other hand, it can be argued that the aggregate of iPod use is indeed a binding movement, one huge global Headphone Festival. Maybe the question isn't whether the iPod cuts us off from society. A better question might be whether it's a society in itself.

There was a time early in iPod history when owners felt a kinship to fellow travelers, making silent eye contact or giving some other sort of high sign to anyone showing those telltale white earbuds. But as many others joined the group—and the demographics of the iPod crowd became broader—there seemed no more reason to feel a bond with another iPodder than there was with someone who, like you, wore a pair of blue jeans. So there was no special bond to sugarcoat the fact that putting on those earbuds made you alone—a "bowling alone" solitude that critics seem to find pathetic.

But that's an aloneness that comes *by choice,* and by that measure it's a quality that should be respected. As one of Bull's interviewees explains, an artificial sonic space is not necessarily antisocial but rather a needed tonic to the pressures of life. Auto commuters take this for granted, but urban travelers on public transit are exposed to all sorts of indignities, intrusions, and, worst of all, energy-draining social obligations when a chance encounter dictates a polite interaction. "Having my iPod on decreases the chance that [my private space] will be invaded so makes me feel calmer," says a Bull subject named "Adam," who recounts the time he peripherally spotted one of his work colleagues on the station platform. Ordinarily Adam would have been compelled to acknowledge the fellow, unhappily yielding his blissful isolation. But with bud in ear, he could stare blankly into space, ignoring his acquaintance. "He's a nice bloke, of course," Adam told Bull, "it's just that commute time is the only real private time I get."

As with the Walkman, wearing an iPod is a particularly handy method for women to fend off pickup artists and other creeps. "I have to admit, it's my crutch for avoiding strangers talking to me," says Katy Carmichael, a recent Ohio University grad who moved to New York City. Not that it's just an excuse: she really *is* wrapped up in her iPod, sometimes so much that she almost misses her stop. "It's gotten to be my baby," she says. "My worst nightmare is having it fall on the subway tracks because I'd probably end up going down and getting it." (In February 2006, a first-person article in *The New York Times* actually described this very scenario. The author, literally risking his life, had jumped onto the tracks to retrieve his mini.)

Unfortunately, for a rare few, the flash of the earbud has proven to be the exact opposite of *leave me alone*. It turns out to be *steal me*. Resting somewhere between the fuzziness of urban legend and the grim reality of city life are many stories of iPod muggings. The perpetrators range from street hoodlums to, in one well-publicized case, the daughter of the actress Dianne Wiest. As portable cocooning with iPods became increasingly popular, law enforcement officials began sounding alarms that zoning out on playlists made you vulnerable not only to 'pod theft but to other crimes, including purse snatching, pickpocketing, and even violent mugging. They even came up with a term for this easy-pickings status: "iPod oblivion," the opposite of vigilance. "When you have [the earbuds] on, you've signed off mentally as to paying attention to anything other than what you're doing . . . walking and listening to music," Boston Transit Police Lieutenant Mark Gillespie lamented to a reporter.

The most sensational iPod crimes are not the results of distraction but violent assaults by crooks bent on obtaining an iPod no matter what evil it takes. A twenty-five-year-old high school teacher, Bryce Wisell, was on his way home to Brooklyn from his classes, delighted that his shuffle mode had arrived at "Scarlet Begonias" by the Grateful Dead, when he saw a group of seven or eight teenagers clustered around a stoop. As he walked past, they surrounded him, one kid holding a lead pipe and another reaching into his shirt, saying something he couldn't make out because of Jerry Garcia's scintillating guitar line. He pulled his earbuds out and asked, "What?" "Give me the fucking iPod," said the kid. Wisell did not want to give up the silver iPod mini, which had been a gift from his mother, but, as he later explained in an e-mail, his attacker "got back in front of me, pulled out his box cutter, extended the blade, and put it to my stomach. I quickly considered my options and handed over the iPod." His father later replaced it—and Wisell now uses black earphones.

You might think from the proliferation of stories like this that hooking up to an iPod is a virtual dare to the criminal element. But it's more likely a case that iPod theft, which has a sexy ring to it, is much more often reported than robberies of less glamorous items. Robbers can snatch a variety of possessions, but if a nano or mini is among them, it's labeled an iPod theft.

The most heartrending iPod crime story involved fifteen-year-old Christopher Rose. The boy's family was concerned about his safety; though they lived in the tough Brooklyn neighborhood of East Flatbush, they sent Chris to school in a rural town in Pennsylvania. It was on his way out of Flatbush one day in July 2006, en route to the Port Authority Bus Terminal to take a bus to his school grounds to watch a fireworks show that a gang of perhaps a dozen teenagers approached Chris and three of his friends, demanding Chris's iPod. The gang beat up the four boys, robbed them—including tennis shoes, a cell phone, and, of course, the iPod—and stabbed Chris to death. This tale reached the ear of Steve Jobs, who called Errol Rose, the boy's father. Jobs did not feel responsible but was disturbed that his product had had a role in the tragedy, and he wanted to express his sorrow directly to the family. Though Errol Rose had never heard of Jobs, he appreciated the call. And, judging from what Rose told a *New York Times* reporter, he was won over by Apple's CEO. "He was so familiar," Rose said. "After every word, he paused, as if each word he said came from the heart." Rose was moved to a sort of poetry himself: "We have the technology that can give us the iPod and everything else, but . . . we have to work on the minds and the hearts."

Ironically, for millions of people the iPod has helped them do just that. To outside observers who can't hear the joyous sounds pulsing through the cables, it's hard to tell. But those people supposedly retreating into a self-directed fantasia *are* engaged, mind and heart—just as Andreas Pavel was, dancing through the snow in Switzerland back in 1972. Having gathered their musical favorites and stored them in a tiny box, iPod lovers are viscerally connecting with the creations of artists and musicians who mean the most to them. If as a by-product they happen to be gleefully transcending physical reality, what's the problem?

Download

❯ "When we first approached the labels, the online music business was a disaster. Nobody had ever sold a song for ninety-nine cents. Nobody ever really sold a *song*. And we walked in and we said, 'We want to sell songs à la carte. We want to sell albums, too, but we want to sell songs individually.' They thought that would be the death of the album."

So goes Steve Jobs's description to me of the task he faced when trying to establish the iTunes Music Store. Many thought that establishing such a store in 2003 was a quixotic misstep, since the competition, file-sharing networks where millions of users downloaded songs from one another, had a seemingly unbeatable price point: zero.

But a year after the store flung open its virtual doors, Steve Jobs was delighted to put in a call to twenty-year-old Kevin Britten of Hays, Kansas, congratulating him for buying the hundred-millionth song sold on iTunes. Less than two years later, Jobs got back on the phone to dial up Alex Ostrovsky of West Bloomfield, Michigan, with the good news that the sixteen-year-old was getting ten iPods, an iMac, a $10,000 music gift certificate, and a scholarship established in his name at the Juilliard School. Ostrovsky's purchase of Coldplay's "Speed of Sound" was Apple's *billionth* downloaded song.

Apple Computer's online emporium lays a plausible claim for itself to be the savior of a music industry that feared that all its revenues would be drained by pirates. In a sense, though, the iTunes store was inevitable, the culmination of a story that began in 1988, when the music world changed forever and didn't know it. Those late-middle 1980s seem fuzzy now and somewhat quaint. The World Wide Web wasn't yet a glimmer in the eye of Tim Berners-Lee. Steve Jobs was trying to sell NeXT computers to educational institutions. The Sony Walkman was still the hottest thing going in personal music. But plenty of computer scientists knew that ultimately computers would be taking center stage in both audio and video. The digitization of everything had begun, and it was time to convert everything analog to the new regime of bits.

It doesn't seem obvious that the film industries (the music labels, ominously, were out of the loop) would entrust the crucial task of digitization to a consortium of two German entities: the Fraunhofer-Institut für Integrierte Schaltungen (Institute for Integrated Circuits, part of a bigger research conglomerate, Fraunhofer Gesellschaft) and the University of Erlangen, named after the small town in southern Germany where it was located. But that's what happened in 1988. An international group of geeks gathered there to create a "codec" (shorthand for code-decode), a standard means of processing recorded music and captured video images into a compressed digital file. The result of their labors was actually three such approaches, or "layers." Two of the layers did the coding and decoding at high speeds and required very heavy technology, while a third did its work in a tempo more suited to personal computers. This last was dubbed with the snooze-inducing appellation Moving Picture Experts Group 1, Layer 3. So everyone called it MP3. In

1992, the International Organization for Standardization bestowed upon the codec the status of an official standard. "Nobody, I promise you, had any idea what this would mean to music," said one engineer on the project.

It wasn't until almost a decade after MP3's creation that some people did begin to get the idea. Things got started when one clever geek discovered the MP3 code on a German server and hacked up a means of playing songs and storing them on a PC. Though the propeller-heads who concocted MP3 had never envisioned its use as a home-brew activity for music fans who wanted to turn their computers into music boxes and swap songs electronically, some people began to do just that. In 1997, a kid from Sedona, Arizona, named Justin Frankel created WinAmp, the first application that could credibly call itself a digital jukebox. He offered it free to anyone who cared to download it. (Eventually, AOL bought his company and another one he'd started, for $400 million.)

The next step was to move MP3s off the computer and into portable devices. In 1998, a small Korean company called Diamond Multimedia released a tiny speakerless device, the Rio PMP300, that would play about an hour's worth of MP3 songs that you could upload from your computer. At this point the record labels stepped in. Their reaction set the tone for the way that the music industry would hereafter deal with the technology that was destined to be its future.

They sued.

The argument of their lobbying and legal arm, the Recording Industry Association of America (RIAA), was that the very *existence* of a digital music player that could make computer copies of the songs they owned was a violation of their copyrights. But a judge refused to block the sales of the device. Thereafter it was clear that if the recording industry could not stop technology, it would

Download

have to come down hard on the digital distribution of music on the Internet.

In retrospect, it would seem that instead of fighting such an idea, the labels might have done better to embrace it. After all, one of the toughest problems faced by the labels was getting the right numbers of CDs to retailers or getting stuck with unwanted goods when overly optimistic sales projections did not pan out. Moving bits instead of discs would solve that problem. Another frustrating challenge was getting new material into the ears of potential buyers. Labels were desperate to expose listeners to new releases, so much so that periodically scandals would erupt when it turned out that the labels were doling out bribes to radio stations to play their songs—a practice that had long ago earned a word of its own, "payola." But "streaming" songs on the Internet—playing them in real time, just like on the radio—would make it easy to give hot new tunes vast worldwide exposure; what's more, the deep-search features of the Internet would ensure that interested listeners could actually find some of the music that might interest them. This wasn't rocket science. By the end of the twentieth century, when virtually every publication in America was screaming like a carnival barker to hawk the wonders of cyberspace and the promise of friction-fee commerce, your fear of change would have had to be very substantial indeed to limit your vision to the Internet's threats and not actively pursue its benefits. Mama, this was a *world-class* fear of change. Blind to the prospects of plenty, the industry chose to circle its wagons and take aim at even the most well-intentioned would-be allies on the Internet.

One of those potential allies, for instance, was Michael Robertson, and his story bears telling. In 1997 Robertson was running an early search engine called Filez, which logged what kinds of information people were looking for on the Internet. One day he noticed an unfamiliar term in search requests: MP3. "I didn't know what that was," he says, "but I thought if people are searching for it, it must be an opportunity." He did some homework and was amazed to discover that there was actually a kind of file—that thing called a codec—that could make your computer sound like a stereo. He tried it himself—a friend sent him an MP3 of Dave Brubeck's "Take Five" (a song that Steve Jobs would include among the disks he sent to the first iPod reviewers). Compared to the fuzzy audio you normally got when you tried to play songs from the Internet, it sounded great.

Robertson created a Web site for people searching for information about MP3 files, figuring he could use it to send traffic to his real business, Filez. He tried to secure the Internet domain name MP3 and found that someone had already registered the address. The owner had never heard of Moving Picture Experts Group 1, Layer 3, or its soon-to-be-famous abbreviation; he'd claimed the name because his initials were MP, and since MP.com had been taken, as well as MP1.com and MP2.com, he'd settled for the next best thing. Robertson paid him a thousand bucks for the domain name. By simply turning on his Web site MP3.com—with nothing yet on the site—Robertson logged 10,000 unique visitors his first day. Apparently, like members of some weird cult, thousands of people had been blindly typing "MP3" into search engines, just waiting for the day a decent result would emerge.

Robertson now had to figure what to put on the site. He first thought that he would publish articles about MP3 music. "I ran out of news stories to aggregate in about four minutes, because there weren't any," he says. So he wrote his own. In researching these articles he learned about Justin Frankel's WinAmp and other developments in the digital music world. But even as the site became a central repository for MP3 information, visitors were frustrated because there was no music. Robertson vowed to change that. He solicited songs from unsigned bands, promising to store all their tunes and let them use MP3.com to promote themselves. In exchange, they would give Robertson a few tracks to give away on a nonexclusive basis. He recalls the reaction: "Everyone in the music industry said, 'You're going to give away free bandwidth and free storage? Well, you're going to go bankrupt.'" But MP3.com thrived. It would eventually accumulate more than a million songs from more than 150,000 bands. A million visitors a day would come to hear songs.

Then Robertson came up with a scheme to let people listen to music from their own collections while they were online. The immediate problem was how to get the songs from the user to Robertson's service. At that time, most people connected to the Internet on slow dial-up connections. They would not tolerate interminable waits to upload their songs to his site so he could stream the songs back to them when they wanted to listen. Robertson's solution was a scheme that would, he believed, follow the law and please the music industry. He called it the "online locker." The first step was to verify that someone legally owned a CD. One did this by putting the disc in his computer, which would scan the disc to verify it and send the verification to MP3.com. From that point, the songs would be registered in that person's account. MP3 would already have its own copy stored online—its servers would store just about any song you could think of, legally purchased—and make it available to you for listening.

Robertson was taking pains not to rip off the labels. He had the data to show that his system actually made money for them, since it encouraged people to listen to and buy more music. And if the industry heavyweights would build on a system like this, they could have fantastic new ways to promote new artists and deepen the connection fans had with the performers they already adored.

What did those industry heavyweights do?

They sued.

Why? "For one thing," says Robertson, "they didn't want to break their track record of suing every new music technology that's ever come out. That's a fifty-year tradition, maybe a *hundred*-year tradition."

Perhaps you can tell that the guy is a little bitter. "People looked at me and said, 'Oh, yeah, you're one of those free-music-for-everyone people, you're getting sued for copyright.' I'm like, 'Hey, I'm not free music for everybody.' This system is *good* for the music industry, because it sells more CDs. And in fact, we did sell more CDs through every online retailer that signed up with us. But the courts considered what are called statutory damage laws, which means [the record companies] didn't have to prove any actual damage. So even though I had evidence that we helped them sell more music, it didn't matter."

These comments came years after the fact, as Robertson and I were finishing a lunch in New York City. He struck me as a guy with a fairly sunny disposition, a blithe surfer-dude type. Those dark days are long gone for Robertson. In fact, the days were never so dark that he went broke—in 2001, at the height of MP3.com's glory and the apex of the Internet bubble, he sold the company for $400 million, pocketing about a third of that. But I got the impression that sometimes his eyes pop open at four A.M. with the painfully recurring questions busting in on him like home invaders: *Why didn't they see? Why did they want to kill something that could make them money?* "They sued me for $150,000 per CD that I had in my index, which was, you know, four trillion dollars," he says. "So I had to settle, and I couldn't appeal."

The rest is history. The way young people would learn about digital music would not be from MP3.com and its almost fanatical contortions to stay on the right side of the copyright law. Instead kids would go bonkers with a music sharing system that sprang out of the mind of an eighteen-year-old college freshman, Napster. It used a system called peer-to-peer file sharing that was a step beyond a digital locker; essentially it threw open the doors to everyone's hard drive. Billions of songs were downloaded. Cumulatively, it created the biggest music store imaginable—one without a cash register.

I was dazzled by Napster the first time I saw it. The interface was crude, almost nonexistent. But when you typed in the name of even the most obscure song you could think of, it would grind away until it found the song on the computer hard drive of some stranger you would never meet. *Someone* always had your song; the system could not be stumped. (The ability of the Internet to expeditiously deliver items that appealed to only a tiny slice of the buying population, to the very few who wanted such goods, would later be dubbed the Long Tail effect.) Then you would begin the process—not always successful—of handshaking with that stranger's computer and downloading a song. Sometimes it took a while, but it was always amazing when the download was finished and you'd play the song. So amazing that the fact that you had gotten the song for free was almost a secondary consideration. A few months after Shawn Fanning, Napster's creator, invited the world to download his program—sort of like introducing an aggressive virus in the wild—millions of people were Napster nuts and the program was consuming more than half the bandwidth on college computer networks nationwide.

In March 1999, I wrote a column for *Newsweek* outlining the threat to the established order it represented, as well as the possibilities for glory if the music industry embraced the model. One of my readers showed the piece to her husband. He was Hank Barry, a copyright lawyer who was also a venture capitalist at Hummer, Winblad, one of the alpha dogs of Sand Hill Road, where Silicon Valley's top VC firms were located. Barry was so intrigued that he not only got Hummer to invest in Napster but became its CEO.

Barry's job was to make Napster legit, first offering, then begging the record labels to help the company shift to selling songs legally. "We're trying to build a bridge to everybody involved in Napster, from music educators and users to record companies," he told me in 2000 after thanking me for cluing him in to the company. (Later, the thank-yous would be bestowed ironically.) He even opened a dialogue with Lars Ulrich, the drummer of Metallica, a heavy-metal band whose outrage at its unwanted presence on the Napster net had become a *cause célèbre*. "It's a weird situation, because we're in the middle of putting him out of business," said Ulrich. But even though Napster was arguably the biggest popularizer of music the world had ever seen and the rewards of using it to let people buy music rather than steal it were unimaginable, the record labels didn't want to give Napster a hug and make it part of the team. They wanted to kill it.

So they sued.

The labels won their suit for copyright infringement, and Napster was no more. I have talked to Hank Barry since and seen the same helpless look that I saw in Michael Robertson's eyes. *Why didn't they work with us?*

Killing Napster was easier than killing the idea of free music. A new generation of file-sharing systems sprang up, using a more cunning means of distribution. Napster had directed its users to songs on other users' computers by means of a central database under its control; this was the smoking gun that made the service legally culpable. But newcomers like Morpheus, Freenet, Kazaa, and Grokster did not have a central database. Their software set up self-sustaining file-sharing networks that lived on their own in cyberspace, like those giant fungi that cover thousands of acres in the northwest. Those networks enabled people to make their stuff available to anyone else on the network and find where the stuff was elsewhere on the Net. What that stuff was and whether it infringed on anyone's copyrights was not the business of Morpheus to worry about, was it?

Another set of lawsuits—MGM (and all the other content owners) versus Grokster, et al. But by then the music industry understood that its problem wasn't just file-sharing systems but file sharers. These were people who loved music—*customers*. They thought that getting music off the Internet was a birthright. And these customers, especially the younger ones, were developing the belief that Internet music, like Internet mail and Internet instant messaging, worked best when you got it free. (To paraphrase the soul singer Luther Ingram, how could anything that feels so right . . . be *wrong?*) To quell this belief, the music industry began a huge educational initiative on the immorality of grabbing songs from the Internet. They paid for MTV-style commercials and took out big ads in periodicals. On the Grammy Awards telecast, the head of the Recording Academy brought festivities to a dead stop as he lectured the nation's youth. This was *stealing,* he insisted, just as larcenous as jimmying the door of someone's big black Cadillac, hot-wiring it, and tire-burning into the night. But of course there was a difference that a twelve-year-old had no problem identifying. Cars are zero-sum. When you drive away someone's Caddy, the owner is faced with an empty parking space and no car. But when you download a song from someone, it's still there. Music downloads are an infinite-sum game, and everybody knew it.

The other problem with the ethics lesson was that record labels were themselves spotty on the morality thing. Their history was an unbroken litany of publishing credits pilfered from artists, unpaid royalties, and envelopes stuffed with illegal payola. Their plea against downloading came across like an etiquette lesson from the Green River Killer.

It would be unfair to say that the music industry was full of stupid executives. Instead, the people at the top were well-paid pashas who lived and died by short-term results. They'd attained their lofty posts by cunning and a gut instinct for what the public wanted. If the glaciers that supported their current business models were to melt, the smart play for an executive was to hope that there would be sufficient ice to support him until retirement. Nonetheless, they could not ignore the howls of criticism coming their way as a result of their refusal to provide a legal means of getting music online. So the music industry reluctantly began its own music services, called Pressplay and MusicNet. They were pathetic, half-hearted efforts. For one thing, the labels could not agree to work together to create a service that sold music from all their catalogs, a requirement met by the most humble mom-and-pop record store in the physical world. Sony and Universal were on Pressplay, Warner and BMG on MusicNet, and only EMI was on both. So it was virtually guaranteed that no one service would have all the songs you wanted. In any case, only a sampling of the catalogs was on either service. Compared to Napster's long tail, this was a short stub.

MusicNet's interface and restrictive rules made it particularly abominable; it asked users to pony up $10 a month to stream up to a hundred songs and download a hundred. But these were so-called tether downloads; after thirty days, the songs would no longer play and to revive them you had to draw on your allotment again. Pressplay was more reasonably designed but still laden with speed bumps and outright roadblocks for music buyers. The mentality of both systems was that copyrighted songs should be released to music lovers only if they were loaded with software time bombs that would prevent their subsequent theft. This put the music industry into the position of asking people to pay for inferior crippled digital files when unprotected versions were readily available on file-sharing services for free. *The Wall Street Journal's* Walt Mossberg wrote, "MusicNet and Pressplay are designed in a way that reflects the false lesson of Napster—all people are thieves—much more than the true lesson, that there's a business in selling downloadable songs for a modest price."

Could anyone crack the code of selling music on the Internet—music that customers would simply buy and then would be free to play thereafter—and getting the record labels to allow him to do it in a way where his customers did not feel like criminals?

Well, yes.

During the whirlwind iPod development process in 2001, the idea of an Apple music store had never come up. You loaded songs onto iTunes one of two ways. The first was very simple: you inserted a CD you owned or had borrowed into the optical media slot of your Mac, and iTunes would launch automatically. If you were connected to the Internet, your computer would, without prompting, venture online to a database that would quickly analyze the characteristics of your disc and, with uncanny accuracy, fill in the titles of the tracks. Then, with a single mouse click, you would "rip" the songs into digital form and your Macintosh would place them in the appropriate place in your iTunes library. This would work, of course, whether the disc you inserted was one you bought or one you borrowed from a friend.

The second method was to bypass the ripping process and import the digital files themselves. In almost every case this involved venturing onto the Internet and getting songs from someone who was willing to collaborate with you on an act of piracy. (Napster or its successors would be your enabler.) You could also send digital music files to your pals via e-mail or even instant messaging, and they could install the songs in their iTunes library for transfer to the iPod. This was technically copyright infringement but felt like a victimless crime.

But Steve Jobs was keenly interested in giving iPod users a legal pipeline to purchase digital music. As with the iPod itself, he felt he could create an experience that would far surpass anything that had come before. This wasn't a high bar. Also, there was a pretty good template for an e-commerce site: the hugely popular Amazon .com. People would go to Amazon and just hang out, as if in a cool shopping mall, because there were fun things to do and discover, like seeing other people's lists of favorite stuff or reading reviews of books you were thinking of buying. Jobs's bigger problem, one that Amazon didn't face, was that his store would have to compete with a widely distributed system that allowed people to download just about any recording ever made—for free.

Nonetheless, by 2002 Jobs felt that Apple could build a music store so delightful to visit, easy to use, complete in its selections, and reliable in its performance that people would happily pay a fair price. After all, he liked to point out, people pay good money for bottled water when a free alternative is the turn of a faucet away. What he could not do was establish the store without the cooperation and permission of all the owners of the music he would sell: the five major record labels, Universal, Warner, EMI, BMG, and Sony. The kind of store Jobs envisioned would require virtually any song that anyone could imagine, and lacking even one of the big players would mean that users would face a second-rate selection. "Second rate" was not in Jobs's vocabulary.

Jobs organized his assault on the labels like a major military campaign. He had many advantages that the trailblazers in the field had not enjoyed. Unlike an upstart founder of some punk Internet start-up or an expatriate Microsoft executive, he was a full equal of, and sometimes held superior status to, the top executives he wooed. Not only would his mug have to be included in any virtual Mount Rushmore of the personal computer industry you'd imagine, but Jobs was a bona fide movie studio head, having built Pixar into a dominant digital animation operation. So when Jobs came to deal, he would not be closeted with the "new media" executives who were two reports down from the CEO.

As someone who had a big footprint in both Hollywood and Silicon Valley, Jobs felt he had a unique perspective on the culture clash between those two worlds and how it had led the record labels to the brink of ruin—and why he was the person to breach it. He believed the reason that the labels had not worked with the likes of MP3.com or Napster was as much a cultural gap as anything else. "People in Hollywood think that technology is just something you buy, and they don't think it's a creative process at all," he says. "All of a sudden the Internet comes along and people start to steal their product. They're shell-shocked by Napster, and they're looking for someone to blame. And they blame the technology industry. Since the technology industry doesn't appreciate how much work goes into making these products, they dismiss these things— 'Well, they have to adapt to a new business model.' Both are dead wrong."

Jobs felt ideally placed to convince the top person at each label that the new Apple online store would provide a way out of the stew. Part of his success would rest on which companies he approached first—and which last. The first two were obvious to Jobs. In the fall of 2002, he met with Roger Ames of Warner Music. At the time, Ames was pitching Jobs on supporting an extrasecure version of the CD, but Jobs used the meeting to talk about his music store. Ames was impressed.

But the key domino was Universal, with the biggest market share of the majors. The label was known as a hardliner in the digital music wars, but was going through a rough time—its parent company, Vivendi, was on the rocks and was openly peddling the label. So Jobs made a beeline for Universal Music's CEO, Doug Morris, to begin the process of nailing down the big prize. Meanwhile, he would woo EMI (known as the most eager to license) and BMG, another company on the block in the turbulent industry (it would soon merge with Sony Music). The one big hurdle then would be Sony, whose own weird politics made it unpredictable; the Japanese giant was often paralyzed by conflicts between its electronics divisions and its artistic holdings. Not to mention that Sony, maker of the Walkman, might not have been willing to kiss up to the guy who was boasting, with excellent reason, that he had created "the Walkman of the twenty-first century."

Here was the m.o. After the initial contact with the big boss, Jobs would invite a team from the label to fly up to Cupertino and there, in the big boardroom on the fourth floor of One Infinite Loop, he would unleash a full-fledged charisma assault in presenting his plan. And if there were any remaining doubts, he would have the executives consider one more thing: the iTunes store would serve only an insignificant sliver of the marketplace—the measly four or five percent market share who had Macintoshes, and within that only the sliver of think-different-ers who had iPods. In 2002, Apple had begun selling Windows versions of iPods, but since iTunes, the basis of the Apple store, did not run on Windows, the vast majority of the recording industry's customers would not be able to utilize the proposed store. "Our smaller market share turned out to be an asset!" Jobs says. "We only convinced them to let us do it on the Mac at first. We said, 'Well, if, you know, if the virus gets out, it's only going to pollute five percent of the garden here.' And that's probably what, in the end, enabled us to get them to come along with us. Doug Morris, who runs Universal, said, when he was arguing with his own team, 'Look, how—I don't understand how Apple could ruin the record business in one year on Mac. Why shouldn't we try this?'"

Going to Universal, which had proven itself a tough sell for digital music efforts, was a great early move for Jobs. "At the end of the day, everything follows Universal," says Sean Ryan, an entrepreneur who had dealt with all the labels in an effort to license their music for his company, Rhapsody, which streamed music rather than sold it. "Sony will fight anything, but the rest of them just follow Universal, the strongest square." Some believe that Jobs's secret weapon with Universal was a rumor at the time that Apple might be interested in merging with a music company. Howard Stringer, then CEO of Sony USA and now in charge of all of Sony, puts it bluntly: "Steve Jobs was able to fool Universal into believing he was going to buy it—that was quite smart." The facts are a little more complicated. After Jobs had a good talk with Doug Morris, the Universal CEO contacted the head of the most powerful label in the Universal family, Jimmy Iovine of Interscope. Iovine was a music industry icon. In the seventies, he had engineered Bruce Springsteen's records. Now he was the head of several of his own powerful labels in

Universal's camp, including the key hip-hop imprint. He had the ear, and the respect, of everyone from 50 Cent to Sheryl Crow.

As a guy who knew the purpose of every solenoid on a studio soundboard, Iovine was not scared of technology. But by the time he headed to Cupertino, he was distraught at technology's impact on his industry. "I realized we had a problem between content owners and technology users. It's a very attractive thing to buy an album, make ten copies, and give it away or sell it, whatever's attractive." He had made it a point to connect with people in Silicon Valley who were devising schemes for the future of music and had been shocked at what he had found. One incident in particular stuck out in his mind. Iovine was visiting Intel, the company that makes the lion's share of processors, the electronic brains inside computers. Iovine was describing the concerns of the music industry to a top executive at the semiconductor giant, and the man looked right at Iovine and commented, "You know, not every industry is meant to last forever." It was such an insulting viewpoint—a flipped-off observation that what Iovine had done all his life had no economic future—that Iovine just laughed. But it bugged him plenty. That's why he was eager to hear something new when he headed to Cupertino.

What impressed him right off the bat was not only the well-developed scheme that Apple had cooked up but Jobs's attitude. "We just hit it off, what can I say?" Iovine recalls. "Every other company was telling us, 'Give us your licenses and we'll build you a system.' He had a complete thought."

Was there also a tempting possibility that Apple might merge with Universal? It did cross Iovine's mind. "I would've loved for that to happen," he says. "We are not a technological industry, and we needed a relationship with a technology company to fix our

Download

problem. So I brought it up." Iovine, however, insists that the possibility wasn't the reason he got on board with Apple. "That's not why I did it," he says. "I fell in love with [Apple's system] and thought it was fantastic."

Iovine not only became a loud voice urging Universal's support but, after the deal was done, would wind up putting Jobs together with his artist Sheryl Crow for a *Fortune* magazine cover shoot.

But before that happened, there were huge obstacles to overcome. The stickiest part of making the deal was determining what rights would be given to and what rights withheld from those buying songs on the system. The songs sold on the iTunes store would be saddled with a layer of protection known as digital rights management, or DRM. Unlike files in the MP3 format, which are completely unfettered and can be copied infinitely without degradation, Apple's downloads would have a layer of protection laid on top. The exact rules of copying would be crucial in determining how users would view the iTunes store. An overly restrictive set of rules would kill the whole project. Instead of adopting someone else's technology for protecting music, Apple decided to start from scratch and build its own system. The idea was to strike the happy but as yet elusive medium where labels would feel their intellectual property was protected and consumers would be able to make use of the music without feeling as if they purchased disabled product. At that point no one was sure that this zone existed.

"We told them that to compete with Kazaa, we had to offer users broad personal-use rights," says Jobs. "Like being able to burn as many CDs as you want. And being able to put your music on as many iPods as you want, being able to put it on more than one computer. They were not in that mind-set when we first talked."

Jobs found this out pretty explicitly in one of his presentations with music executives. As part of his spiel, he would outline the details of the iTunes store. But at one session, each time he'd write down an element of his rights scheme—how many burns a user was allowed, how many computers could have access to a music library—a guy from the record company would jump up, erase the figure, and put in a more restrictive number. "Jobs wasn't used to someone else writing on his whiteboard," recalls one participant at that meeting, highly amused.

But Jobs understood that allowing users the maximum level of freedom would be essential. There was no way in hell that he would allow a system with the Apple imprimatur if it felt as though it had been designed by lawyers. The only way the system would work would be if people rarely, if ever, ran into antipiracy restrictions. And when they did run into them, they should be more like speed bumps than barriers. This philosophy was reflected in the name that he used for his DRM software: FairPlay.

Eventually he was able to get all of the labels to agree to the following rules: downloaded songs could be retained forever, just as CDs are. Since people commonly own more than one computer, or expect music they purchase to be available to everyone in their immediate family, the songs would be playable on as many as three "authorized" computers. (The iTunes Web site would keep track of those, and if you got rid of a computer, you could decommission it and add another to the approved list. A year after the store opened, this number was increased to five.) You could burn a song to a CD as many times as you wanted, but you could not make limitless CDs of the same collection of tunes. (In other words, FairPlay would not let you make endless copies of the new Black Eyed Peas record.) Ten burns of a playlist was the original limit, later adjusted to seven.

Eddy Cue, the Apple executive in charge of the store, admitted that the process of corralling all the labels was frustrating. "It's not a secret that the negotiations were painful in the sense that we were trying to move some of them faster than they wanted to move," he says. But the labels also knew that the public was losing patience with them. Everybody was worried about a lost generation that saw nothing at all wrong with grabbing music off the Internet for free. The court cases against Napster had been won, and the subsequent case against the post-Napster sites was heading to the Supreme Court, with good prospects. But that was lousy publicity, and the RIAA's next step was even worse—a set of lawsuits against actual music fans whose identities had been traced through the files they had shared online. While music executives rode around in limousines and mugged on the red carpet with their divas *du jour,* they were slapping their future customers—sometimes blue-collar kids barely making college tuition—with settlement demands of five to fifteen thousand dollars. If they were seen as publicly rejecting their best shot yet to actually sell songs online, who would not feel justified by grabbing what he could? On the other hand, Apple was promising to make *not* stealing . . . cool. And promising to jam the airwaves with irresistible commercials, in pulsing hot pinks and yellows, to hype the fun things about buying music. (Quite a change from the music industry's don't-steal-or-you'll-go-to-jail-or-Hell campaign.) The contract the labels signed with Apple specified a multimillion-dollar marketing commitment, and Apple indeed spent tens of millions on its ads. "These were smart guys," says Jobs. "They basically in the end trusted us, and we negotiated a landmark deal."

BMG and EMI fell into place. The last domino to fall was, as expected, Sony. Sir Howard Stringer, the recently knighted former CBS News executive, was personally frustrated that Sony hadn't created such a store first. "It's our fault," he said, explaining that several years earlier Sony had been working with IBM to create a similar operation. "We were well ahead," he moaned, "but we tried to write the perfect legitimate download experience and got bogged down." He believed that Apple's solution—which he called "security light" because of the relatively simple ways people could get around the iPod's restrictions—was an inadequate shortcut, but he also understood that Jobs had backed his company into a corner. Ultimately, Stringer recognized that since there was no short-term solution to the industry's problems, being the lone holdout to Apple's store just wouldn't play. He told his bosses in Tokyo that Sony should join the others.

The iTunes Music Store launched on April 28, 2003, with 200,000 songs. (Also on that day, Apple introduced the third-generation version of the iPod, a slightly slimmer model with the four control buttons beneath the display screen.) The intention was to cajole the labels—both the majors and smaller indie concerns—to submit many more songs to Apple. (Indeed, by 2006, the store listed more than two million tunes.) For the bulk of the songs that would fill the infinite rack space, it was just a matter of logistics: finding the masters and digitizing the tunes. But some superstars (or their managers) just didn't want their songs online. Jobs had gone to a few performers he knew, like Mick Jagger, to make a personal appeal. Apparently he could not convince the big-lipped sexagenarian to license the songs, because the Rolling Stones were missing in action. (A year later, they came on board.) Another omission was the Beatles, despite the buddy-buddy status Jobs claimed with Sir Paul McCartney. This situation was particularly complicated, since the Beatles' record company has the same name as Steve Jobs's computer company. Years ago, when Apple Computer created software to let its users play CDs, the Beatles sued, claiming that the Cupertino company had violated an earlier agreement not to venture into the music business. Apple paid $26

Download

million to settle the case in 1991. But the appearance of an Apple iTunes store led the Beatles to claim that Jobs was going beyond the terms of the settlement, which didn't specify that Apple could start its own music store. "It'll get resolved, it's not a big deal," Jobs told me after the other Apple filed suit in London. "It's unfortunate because we love the Beatles. I'd do anything for those guys." (The English judge hearing the case began proceedings by confessing that he was an avid iPod user. No one thought it a conflict. *Everybody* has an iPod. The judge ruled for Apple Computer.)

In the first week, users bought more than a million songs on the iTunes Music Store, more than had been legally downloaded in all of history. And remember, that was from only the percentage of Macintosh users who had iPods and took the trouble to download from the iTunes store on the Internet.

What made the store so good? One key reason was that the store is not a Web site but an actual component of the iTunes software that iPod users already adored. According to Jobs, this was partially a consequence of the systems Apple had set up long ago on its online store. "We had a lot of the pieces in place," he says. "The store runs on top of our internal systems, which uses SAP [a customer transaction management software], so it's very rigorous in terms of its controls and its transaction processing and all that stuff, so that saved a lot. And we already had a lot of expertise in sending bits all over the planet, because we're the number one movie trailer download site in the world."

More important, this approach made it immeasurably easier to buy songs. To venture onto the store, one did not have to fire up a browser, punch in a Web address, and tap in a password, the virtual equivalent of putting on one's boots and driving five miles to Tower Records. All you had to do was click the mouse on the "Music Store" option, and the store would appear almost as if it had been on your own hard disk all along. Since Apple kept your credit card information, there was no barrier to making a buy, no series of menus asking you to fill in your name, address, e-mail address, credit card number, and the security code of your credit card. (Apple would eventually accumulate a stockpile of tens of millions of live credit card numbers, a treasure second only to Amazon's in the online world.) And when you did buy, the download would be quick and the song would go straight into your iTunes library. For iPod owners, this process was immeasurably easier than seeking out tunes on some file-sharing network, where the download might or might not work, and then taking the steps to load it into iTunes. And since most people didn't bang their heads against the restrictions of the FairPlay DRM, the iTunes store felt like an *Apple* experience—as opposed to the lawyer-designed Bleak House feel of the previous efforts.

The next step was obvious: Apple began making a version that would run on Windows computers, too. Jobs returned to the record labels to explain that the small experiment involving 5 percent of the computer-buying population was now about to cover everyone. "We were able to convince them after six months to let us expand it to Windows," says Jobs. Not that the labels had much of a choice; it would be a public relations debacle if the music industry shut down the one place where people actually bought online music legally.

The record labels professed delight at the store's success. Finally, people were paying for music and liking it. "The iPod and the iTunes Store are shining light at a very bleak time in the industry," said RIAA President Cary Sherman. But the good feelings were mixed with more than a little consternation at the not-so-subtle shift online buying represented for their business model. Downloading music a song at a time is not just an alternative means of distributing and acquiring the musical products otherwise found at Tower Records and Wal-Mart but one of those fundamental shifts in the way people consume music and, ultimately, the way people will go about making music. Fifty years ago, the advent of 45-rpm "singles" changed the fundamental nature of the business and created not only a marketplace but an entire culture based on the frenzied three minutes a hit song would last. In the sixties, around the time that the Beatles arrived, this was supplemented and ultimately surpassed by the dinner plate–sized slab of vinyl known as the long playing (LP) 33-rpm record, on which music was distributed in two helpings of roughly twenty minutes each. That restriction became a ground rule, like the rhyming scheme of a sonnet, and the great rock artists of the 1960s and '70s shaped their creations to the vinyl clock. (Think *Sgt. Pepper, Ziggy Stardust,* and *Dark Side of the Moon.*) In the 1990s, the CD ripped the needle across the surface of the LP age, and suddenly artists had a full hour to fill, with no natural breaking point when you flipped over the record. That hour exceeded the available time and attention span of most listeners, and in any case all too often a singer-songwriter, band, or hip-hop crew didn't have enough good stuff to fill the space. So they filled it with their second-rate offerings. "People are making a lot of shit," Stephan Jenkins of the rock group Third Eye Blind told me. "They have a couple good songs and then the rest of the album isn't very good. People aren't trying to make whole albums good. They're just trying to get that royalty rate for all twelve tracks."

Nevertheless, the CD was still a *package.* Buying music song by song hadn't been the norm since the days when bobby-soxers parceled their pennies for the latest single from their favorite heartthrob teen idol. In the interim, pop music had gained the status of art. Messing with the work—the song selection, even the sequence—was frowned upon. "If you reprogram the order of cuts in a pop album, you dissolve the album, at least as the album was once conceived—as a story the artist wanted to tell," wrote *New Yorker* critic David Denby. "Played as a selection of favorites, 'Sgt. Pepper's Lonely Hearts Club Band', disintegrates into a random collection of eccentrically charming songs—not the end of the world, of course, but not what John Lennon and Paul McCartney intended, either." Denby's tirade was written as a criticism of compact discs (because they could in theory be reprogrammed), but the album's integrity really didn't come under serious attack until the iPod and Apple's alluring store.

From the music industry's perspective, of course, keeping the package whole wasn't an artistic consideration but a commercial one. Listeners had been griping for years that all too often a CD would have only two or three songs worth listening to—or even just one great song and fifty minutes of junk. Now they could do something about it. Listen to Heather McNeil, a Boston-based Virgin Megastore employee in her early twenties. She'll still buy a CD—hey, she works in a store full of them—but prefers buying songs off iTunes. "I think what record companies charge for a CD is ridiculous," she says, "so I go and get the three songs I like and pay three dollars instead of twenty dollars." She might be surprised to hear that plenty of her favorite artists think she's doing the right thing. "Eighteen dollars for a CD is a lot of money," the singer Sarah McLachlan told me after performing a few songs at the launch of the Windows iTunes Store in October 2003. In contrast, buying on Apple's store comes closer to her belief that "music should be like air." Plus, she added, "I just love the five A.M. availability."

Not coincidentally, the cherry-picking method reflects the way people now *listen* to music . . . shuffling it on their iPods. "The linear experience is gone," says the rock musician John Mayer.

"There's a new digital etiquette. The iPod scroll bar has changed the chemistry of listening, and we're now a skip-forward generation."

The experience is even changing the dynamics of fandom. Instead of staying loyal to a band and dropping a bundle on its CD, people can spread the love, snaring a song a friend liked or one they heard on Internet radio. It's a looser, more adventuresome way to consume music. Reviewing the 2005 version of the independent Coachella rock festival in the desert town of Indio, California, *New York Times* writer Kelefa Sanneh wrote that the satisfying diversity of the festival was a direct result of the iPod. "The promise of Coachella, like the promise of an iPod shuffle, is that it will let you hear your favorite music in a totally different context," he wrote. "Narrow obsession has come to seem less appealing than broad familiarity [of the] scrupulously eclectic world of . . . iPod shuffle owners, all of them finding ways to make chaos part of their listening experience."

As the iTunes store evolved, it began taking advantage of this flexibility, offering artists a chance to come up with new ways to package music, often in less formal and more vital formats. In 2004, for instance, the iTunes store began selling a package of three songs recorded live by Liz Phair, at an impromptu concert in the Apple Store in Chicago. "If you were to sell only 50,000 of these in the real world, you wouldn't do it," the iTunes store manager, Eddy Cue, explained to me. "Here you do it, because the formula changes completely. I don't have to do a print run, decide how many CDs to press. I don't have to worry about distribution and which stores I'm going to put them in. I can be very instantaneous, make changes, do what works, and stop doing what doesn't work. As the business of music changes, the economies may change with it. That's just the reality. Over time they will change, and we think we'll be in a great position."

iTunes *already* seemed in a great position, grabbing and maintaining almost three fourths of all legal music downloads. Had Cue been thinking of opportunities that could come if Apple held on to a significant share of those sales as the percentage of music that is sold online climbed above the current two or three?

He had. "We'd be Wal-Mart," he says.

Sweet. But not even Wal-Mart has Apple's 85 percent market share, a number that didn't budge as the music industry granted licenses to more and more competitors. Online buyers could now buy downloads from Microsoft, Yahoo!, Napster (not the original file-sharing crew but some company that bought the name at a bankruptcy fire sale), and, uh, Wal-Mart. (Oddly absent was Amazon.com; as late as 2004, CEO Jeff Bezos assured me that his company would join in, but only when it figured out some innovative twists.) Didn't matter how many or who . . . iTunes ruled.

That dominance began to make record executives more than a little nervous. They voiced two complaints in particular. One was that Apple was scooping up too much money. Not from running the store—two thirds of the revenues went straight to the record labels, a much better cut than they got from bricks-and-mortar record stores, and with no outlays in materials, no returns, and no having to chip in for Apple's massive promotional efforts on billboards and TV ads. (At best the iTunes store made a tiny profit.) What bugged them was that Apple was making money on *iPods*. Howard Stringer complained to me that since the iPod wouldn't exist without the songs sold by labels like Sony, Apple should share its iPod profits with the recording industry. (An interesting argument coming from a company that sold 340 million Walkman players—and as far as I know, had never volunteered to kick back revenues to Warner Music or EMI.) When I reported this conversation to Jobs, he went a little nuts. "That's a fantasy!" he howled.

"Howard must be flying too much between New York and Tokyo. Of course it's absurd—let them go invent something themselves."

The other gripe was that with Jobs's insistence on holding the song tariff at ninety-nine cents, he was subverting the labels' God-given right to set their own prices. Of course, they wanted to charge more. After Warner Music head Edgar Bronfman, Jr., went public with this complaint, Jobs struck back at a Paris news conference in September 2005. "If they want to raise prices, it means that they are getting greedy," he said. "If the price goes up, [the consumers] will go back to piracy and everybody loses." A few weeks later he explained his comment to me. "I didn't call anybody greedy," he said, "except those who would choose to extract more money out of the consumer."

It's a given that those moguls are greedy. That's why they're *moguls.* But they're also wrong in their belief that charging more for online songs will fatten their bank accounts. Digital economics indicate that the wise course is charging *less.* Look what happened when Rob Glaser, the CEO of RealNetworks (which had purchased the Rhapsody subscription service and online store), tried an experiment during a campaign to sign up new users. In the summer of 2004 he cut the prices of his song downloads from 99 cents to 49 cents. (The labels, of course, made sure that Glaser ate the difference, paying *them* as if the tunes sold for full price.) What Glaser found was startling: his users bought *six times* as many tracks. So by cutting the price in half, Glaser tripled his revenue. It's fair to conclude that 99 cents is a low enough price for people to purchase the songs they want, but when the price goes down to 49 cents, customers are likely to grab tunes on a hunch or a whim. You would think that the labels would sit up and take note—after all, someone who buys six songs instead of one is not only forking out more money but getting more intensely involved in music, being more

daring in sampling new bands, and generally becoming a more devoted customer. But—are you surprised by now?—the music executives *hated* the idea. They felt that it sent a signal that their music
wasn't worth very much.

Is it any wonder that music lovers hate record labels and love
the iPod? This dichotomy played out vividly on March 29, 2005,
the day the Supreme Court considered *Metro-Goldwyn-Mayer Studios, Inc. et al. v. Grokster, Ltd., et al.* This was to be the final deter-
mination of the lawsuit the labels had instituted against the
post-Napster file-sharing services, which claimed that they were
not responsible for any infringement that might be occurring on
their networks. Clearly the Groksters of the world looked to be operating on the wrong side of the law—anyone whose IQ was in the
black could see that just about the *only* thing people used those
networks for was stealing songs. But should a service—or a technological device—be outlawed because people generally used it in
an illegal manner?

Some people worried that the Supreme Court might rule too
broadly in striking down the file-sharing networks. Specifically,
they feared the decision might negate the Sony Betamax decision, a
previous Supreme Court ruling that had preserved a consumer's
right to dub copyrighted works for personal use. The most dire scenario would be to allow people who create content—movies, books,
songs—a veto over new consumer electronics products because
the products were too user-friendly in the way they permitted you
to make copies of their DVDs and CDs. In that case, it wouldn't be
just the Electronic Frontier Foundation crowd, the Intellectual
Property academics, and the street geeks bent out of joint—the
entire electronics industry would be at risk. So said amicus briefs
by the likes of Intel and the Consumer Electronics Association.

All of these arguments were rather esoteric, but it turns out there was a succinct way to put it so that anyone—the guy next to you on the subway, or that gal in black robes who's an associate justice—could get it. *What about the iPod?* The scariest nightmare of all would be if the ruling had pulled the plug on the next great gadget coming out of Apple. On the day of the argument people stood outside the building with signs like SAVE THE IPOD. And once the argument began, Justice Stephen Breyer nailed the MGM lawyer with the question of the day: If Hollywood prevailed, could he "recommend to the iPod inventor that he could go ahead and have his iPod, or, for that matter, Gutenberg his press?" Even before the lawyer could respond, Breyer barked at him, "What's your answer?" Yes, the lawyer insisted, Jobs could have his iPod and Gutenberg his printing press. But the justices weren't satisfied. A couple of minutes later, Justice David Souter took up the cause. "How is that clear in the iPod case?" he wanted to know. Before he got an answer, the associate justice launched a loving description of how one could get music on the iPod either legally or illegally and wondered if that variation was something that "the guy sitting in the garage figuring out whether to invent the iPod" should have to worry about. It couldn't be clearer that Souter knew his iPod inside and out. So it was no surprise that while the June 2005 decision went against the file-sharing services, the justices emphatically reaffirmed the principle of allowing individuals to copy music—to keep the iPod safe.

Good thing, because the era of digital music is just beginning. In a 2004 interview Jobs shared the big picture with me. "I'm one hundred percent clear that we will all listen to music on devices like an iPod," he said. "They may take different forms, but they'll all be devices like this, that hold a thousand or more songs. And we will all buy our music off an online music store. The Internet was *built* to deliver music."

What about physical media?

"It'll all go away. Eventually. I think burning CDs is passé already. Why would you burn a CD anymore? Just plug your iPod into your car! And I think the transition from portable CD players and all that stuff to iPods is going to happen in the next three to five years. The majority of the music in this country to be bought online will happen over the next six to eight years."

Thanks, in no small part, to iPod.

It's not so hard to see why the music industry so desperately clings to its business model. But once the CDs are discarded into history's dustbin, the labels will have to endure the transformation that was inevitable from the day MP3s hit the Internet. What's the sense of maintaining the illusion of a CD-size package when there are no CDs? And how can the labels keep their lock on the artists they sign when rock bands and classical orchestras can bypass the entire process of signing with a label and go straight to iTunes and other online stores? What's the point of a record label then?

Apple itself never set out to change the music business. The idea was always to sell iPods. But the principle that guided Apple was one that the music industry, with its overpriced CDs; its focus on blockbuster acts of boy bands, pop tarts, and American idols; and its lawsuits against its most ardent fans, seemed to have lost track of. The best way to sell music is for the seller to keep in touch with that part of him or herself that simply loves the songs. The people at Apple are proud of their passion for music. They talk about it at every opportunity. When it comes to business plans they are businesspeople, and when it comes to negotiating they can be hardliners. But their success has come largely because of their ability to ask themselves as potential customers, What's the way *I* would want to use this product? And when the tunes start playing, they are perfectly capable of being starstruck, if not fawning, fans.

Download

That includes the CEO. One of Steve Jobs's greatest days at Apple came on October 26, 2004, when Apple announced the U2 iPod, a digital boxed set of the band's entire catalog, and a new iPod commercial featuring the Irish band, at the utter top of the music heap at that moment, singing their new tune, "Vertigo." (That was also the day Apple announced the first iPod with a color screen, the iPod photo. Though the tiny display wasn't ideal for passing around shots of bridal showers and landscapes, the high-contrast output made text more readable, and it was immediately evident that soon all iPods would be color.) The day almost certainly had special significance for Jobs, because it marked his return to the public eye after his cancer surgery a couple of months before. In the newly restored California Theatre in San Jose, Bono and guitarist The Edge performed a couple of tunes after Jobs made his announcements. Tentative at first, Bono quickly gained his footing and was soon projecting his persona through the modest former vaudeville house as if it were a football stadium.

The U2 iPod was a landmark for Jobs and Apple. Other bands had done deals with digital music, releasing previously unavailable cuts or songs from live shows. But the U2 event was truly strength meeting strength, a meeting of equals. And that was reflected in a small press roundtable after the show, with Steve Jobs flanked by Bono and the Edge. Bono, who at an earlier Apple event via satellite connection had joked that he was "there to kiss the corporate ass," was still kissing, contending that Apple was less a corporate entity than a creative one. "They're like a band," said the Irish icon.

"I guess we're a big corporation, but it doesn't feel that way to us," said Jobs.

Bono proceeded to debunk the music industry's complaint that piracy was killing them. "Don't believe those people," he said. "*Crap music* is hurting music. Give people what they want when they want it. The CD is not a fair fight with the download." His solution? "We want to stop running away from the future, like the music business has. We want to walk up to it and give it a big kiss."

After that meeting, I got to talk to Jobs in private. He was in a sentimental mood. In fact, he was getting a bit *verklempt*. It reminded me of the time we had talked after the iTunes Store for Windows was launched. The music he had played when people entered the hall was a haunting rendition of the Beatles' song "In My Life" by Johnny Cash, who had died a month earlier. I asked him who'd chosen the tune. "I did," he said. "When he died, I went on the site and I looked at all the Johnny Cash stuff and was listening to that. I'd never heard that, that old Beatles song, and it's beautiful. That was one of the last recordings he made. And you could imagine him singing that to his wife. Here's a guy who's done what he's done in his life, who he's been, what he's been through, and he's singing that song and you know he's thinking about his wife, who's recently departed. It doesn't get any richer than that. So to me it's just one of those reminders of how powerful music can be in your life."

Now Jobs was reflective again. "The iPod is three years old next month," he told me. "When we started this, nobody really knew what it was, and people that did really didn't believe it would be a big hit. And when we were trying to do the iTunes Music Store, it was"—he paused, groping for the phrase—"such an uphill battle. Everybody in the industry [thought it wouldn't work]. It was almost impossible. And to see it blossom into what it's become, and to see U2 performing at our event, it was just—" He stopped, and an extremely rare moment passed when Steve Jobs was at a loss for what to say next. "I'm trying to think of the word," he finally said. Another long silence. "I don't have a word," he concluded, obviously moved, giving an Academy Award level performance, or both. He gave a long sigh. "When they were on," he continued, "I was sitting next to one of my close colleagues at Apple and I socked him on the leg *really hard* and said, 'We're going to remember this for the rest of our lives.' That's how I felt. It was really great."

Similarly, the music industry will remember the iPod for the rest of *its* life. However long that is.

Shuffle

❯My first iPod loved Steely Dan.

So do I. But not as much as my iPod did. By 2003, among the three thousand songs or so on my iTunes library I had about fifty Steely Dan tunes, mostly ripped from the boxed set *Citizen*, which I bought as a CD replacement of my vinyl collection of the terse, jazzy, and sometimes lyrically incomprehensible Donald Fagen/Walter Becker collaboration. Yet every time I shuffled my entire music collection to "randomly" mix the tunes, it seemed that the Dan was weirdly overrepresented. Only two or three songs after "Rikki Don't Lose That Number," I'd hear "Kid Charlemagne." Then, twenty minutes later, there would be "Pretzel Logic." Where was the logic in this? I didn't keep track of every song that played every time I shuffled my tunes, but after a while I would keep a sharp ear out for what I came to call the LTBSD (Length of Time Before Steely Dan) Factor. The LTBSD Factor was always perplexingly short. It seemed that I was perpetually destined, while waiting on the platform of the Union Square subway stop, my Shure buds jabbed snugly in my ears, to hear that tight drumbeat and those opaque yet unforgettable turns of phrase, like "Guadalajara won't do."

Meanwhile it began to dawn on me that there were songs, and even entire *artists,* that my iPod had taken a *dislike* to, if not a formal boycott. Where was Van Morrison? His work was in abundance in my iTunes library, but in my iPod's marathon rock fest, the Belfast Cowboy was perpetually waiting in the wings. Another puzzle: one of the first songs I downloaded from the iTunes Music Store was the garage classic "Wild Thing." My iPod avoided it like bird flu. What did a hunk of plastic and silicon have against the Troggs?

This Steely Dan thing baffled me. Was it a conspiracy, perhaps engineered by Jeff "Skunk" Baxter, the spectacular guitarist on songs like "My Old School" who is now, improbably, a leading consultant to the Pentagon on superspook terrorism issues? Or was it simply an anomaly? Or—and here is the nub of an issue that would consume me for over a year—was the shuffle function, meant to mix up my music collection in a random fashion, *actually not random at all?*

The LTBSD Factor is important because it cuts to the heart of an amazingly appealing and, in terms of people's listening habits, perhaps the most revolutionary aspect of the iPod: the shuffle.

I grew up in the era of LP records, where the assumption was that God decreed that music should be delivered to humans in two sets of about twenty minutes each, labeled Side A and Side B. Whether the result of weeks of a perfectionist's painstaking cogitation or an off-the-cuff distribution by some stoner in the studio, the unvarying order of the songs on an album became burned into our consciousness with repeated playings. Even now, decades after my turntable has been retired, when I hear a tune from those days, my mind anticipates what used to come next on that banded vinyl plate.

When compact discs appeared, there was suddenly the possibility of overthrowing the established order. After all, it's no problem to instantly direct the laser beam to any point on the disc with no time lag. Much easier than futzing with a needle. So manufacturers included a function in their CD players that let you mix up the songs. Few took advantage of it.

When MP3s and jukebox software came along, shuffle became something quite different from resequencing an hour's worth of music from the same album—shuffling could mix up your whole music collection. The packets of bits that make up computer files are infinitely fungible, making it a natural leap to regard entire hours and days' worth of music, gathered over a period of years from various sources, as a rich reservoir ready for tapping. But it wasn't until the iPod that people began to stumble on this possibility en masse. Even the people at Apple originally underestimated the impact of being able to reorder your library. By exposing all your music, stuff you'd forgotten about would spontaneously leap into your head, old friends coming to visit. Your whole record collection was like a giant radio station, or an endless night in Clubland where your deejay doppelgänger played nothing but your favorites. You could revel in constant novelty from the building blocks of your own song passions.

What's more, shuffle turns out to be the *techna franca* of the digital era—not just a feature on a gadget but an entire way of viewing the world, representing the power that comes from aggregating content from a variety of sources and playing it back in an order that renders irrelevant the intended ordering by those who produced or first distributed the content. Google shuffles the Web, and iPod shuffles the music.

Part of shuffle's mystique, however, is its claim that only chance does the programming—that is the key to, as one blogger put it, "the white-knuckle ride of random listening." But now I was wondering whether something odd was afoot. Had Apple screwed up the randomization algorithm, or, worse, were its programmers secretly tilting the playing field in favor of their own favorite crooners? The integrity of shuffle was at issue, and I vowed to get to the bottom of it.

I first became emboldened to pursue this issue while interviewing Steve Jobs at the January 2004 Macworld Conference & Expo in San Francisco. We had finished talking about GarageBand, the music-making software for the Macintosh he'd just introduced, and were into the random-question phase of the conversation. "Steve," I began, a little abashed at driving this nail in, "I have a situation with my iPod. The shuffle function just doesn't seem random. Some artists come up way too much and some don't come up at all."

Jobs expressed surprise, as if he were hearing this for the first time. I elaborated and, drawing from a bit of my experience researching the world of cryptography, wondered if the randomizing algorithm in iTunes—the mathematical voodoo that is supposed to distribute the tunes without fear or favor—was really sound. He told me it was.

"Are you sure?" I asked.

"Well, let's talk to the people who did the software," he said. He instructed someone to call Cupertino, and within five minutes I was on the phone to an engineer (Jobs wouldn't say whom) who double-honest-really-I-mean-it assured me that random was random.

This Steely Dan thing? It was in my head.

Well, not just in *my* head. My perceptions were far from unique. Over the next few months, I made it a point to ask iPod owners if their beloved little units were judicious in distributing the songs among various artists or whether they played favorites. People would generally respond with a sigh of relief. *Yes! Someone else has noticed!* From the results of this admittedly nonscientific survey, it appeared that nearly *everybody's* iPod seemed to have a favorite artist, or two, or three. Or, they believed, when their iPod performed a shuffle, the iPod, despite being the inanimate object that it was, would *decide* which artist it was in the mood for and then flood the listening session with that performer's works. After I wrote about the Steely Dan problem in *Newsweek,* my in-box was flooded with e-mails from people who said yes yes yes, their iPods played favorites, too. A few of them even reported that their 'pods shared my own device's preference for Steely Dan! Others said that their computers had a fondness for Linkin Park, the Beatles, the Beach Boys, or John Cale. Or that their iPods just decided who they liked that day and played the hell out of that music. Typically, the notes read like this one:

"I have experienced the phenomenon of hearing two Chicago songs in a row, Randy Newman's 'Short People,' and then two more Chicago. What makes it even more interesting is that I only have nine Chicago songs on my iPod."

I took two things from these responses. One was that using shuffle on the iPod had become incredibly important to people. In a subtle way, the iPod had become a standard-bearer for one of the big effects of the digital era, where the fungibility of bits encourages previously unthinkable mixing and remixing. A new way of listening to music had suddenly become possible. Free at last from the bounds of physical media, our musical selections could no longer be reliably stored in pigeonholes, and people were falling in love with this freedom the instant they tasted it.

The second thing was that almost no one believed that random shuffle was random. iPod owners were taking very serious note of what happens in shuffle, and virtually all of them seemed to think that something funny was happening. A lot of them felt compelled to report their theories to me.

Some people assumed that their iPods not only played favorites but drew on mystical powers to choose their songs. "My iPod is my crystal ball," wrote Paul Toennis of Billings, Montana. "Although I am still a beginner cryptologist, I do know for a fact that two songs from any artist is a danger signal. I learned this the hard way a couple of years ago—just prior to getting popped off my road bike by a red pickup truck, a second Bare Naked Ladies song in a row began to play from my white oracle box." Mr. Toennis was not alone in considering that the iPod was telepathic. "Over the last couple of days that I've been [putting my entire library on shuffle], I may think of a certain song or band, and lo and behold, that winds up being the next song or band played on my iPod," writes a blogger named Kapgar. "It's like some sort of symbiotic relationship." Kapgar also reported another instance where he was working out and his iPod played seven great songs in a row that were perfect for cardio. Another time when he was on the way to work, "every single song that was played was absolutely spectacular. And just what I wanted to hear at the moment."

I was becoming the clearinghouse for the X-Files of iPod shuffle. A fellow named Gary Baker noted that he has the entire Beatles collection on his iPod, and while playing the shuffle function, he has heard "Get Back" eighteen times, while eight other Beatle tunes have been played only once. "Plus, it has moods," he added, "Sunday and Monday nights, bluesy. Rocks at night during the week. Does folk on Monday and Wednesday mornings. Bluegrass on Thursday mornings and Sunday afternoons." Furthermore, he claimed that every time his girlfriend was in the car it began playing Bob Dylan at a rate of every other song. She complained about it, and the next time she was in the car, it played a preponderance of Bob Dylan songs—done by other people. "And it seldom plays Dylan otherwise," Baker informed me.

Brian Verhaaren of Salt Lake City portrayed his iPod as an annoying contrarian: "Most glaring," he wrote me, "is how irritating it is that my iPod only seems to play Christmas music in the summer and never around Christmas."

One person even suggested that it was not the iPod that was telepathic—I was. "Have you considered that maybe *you* are the 'wildcard' factor in your iPod's 'random shuffle' and are influencing it to play a particular song that has a high emotional value for you?" asked one correspondent. (This particular woman also informed me that "as a person with a high ESP level," she routinely knows what song is going to be played next on the radio.)

Even assuming that there's a tongue-in-cheek aspect to these reports, there seems to be a deep-seated belief that the results of shuffle are just not random. The issue became even more pressing in January 2005, when Apple introduced a junior model of the iPod at the price of ninety-nine dollars. Its name? The iPod shuffle.

According to Steve Jobs, the impetus for this new member of the iPod family was to open up the world of digital music to the budget-minded. Yes, other companies were offering similar MP3 players for as low as $50, but in Jobs's mind these fell so far below the bar of coolness as not to exist. A year earlier, Apple had introduced the iPod mini, which was smaller and held fewer tunes than the full-size iPod. But that cost $249. So there was an entire segment of the market that Apple wasn't reaching—and those people weren't using iTunes. As Jobs put it to me, "We wanted to make something great at $99, so that people who can't afford a mini have a way into the digital music revolution without buying the [competing] pieces of crap that're out there."

But in designing an iPod to sell at that price, Apple had to overcome some problems. The basics of the iPod—the screen, the scroll wheel, the hard drive—were just too costly. The lower end of the entire universe of digital players, in fact, didn't have a disk drive and stored many fewer songs on a chip that used "flash memory." These memory chips also had the advantage of taking up less space and consuming less energy than a disk drive. Apple decided to adopt flash memory for its low-cost player, too.

But how would you solve the problem of screen display on a device too small to sport a screen and too cheap even to attempt it? Most low-cost players had a one-line display that scrolled like the text "zipper" across the bottom of your television during a news show. This articulated the single song you were listening to pretty effectively, but no one had figured out how to make an interface with this type of display that let you control even the fifty to one hundred songs you might have on your flash player. After "noodling" around (Jobs's term), with this idea for a few months, the CEO, as he tells it, experienced a sort of epiphany. Apple had come to understand that almost everybody who had an iPod fell in love with the shuffle function, and most wound up using it as their default method of listening to music. Responding to the popular impulse, Apple had changed the software on the iPod in the summer of 2004 (along with the introduction of the fourth-generation iPod), promoting the shuffle function to the top menu so people could initiate a completely new play mix with a single thumb-click. Doing so made shuffle even more of a phenomenon.

"So," Jobs explained to me, "I came in one day and said, 'Hey, I've got a crazy idea. What if this [low-end iPod] was really based on shuffle. What if that was what it *was?*' And I was almost thrown out of the room for a second. It took me a while to get people think-ing. And after a while, they said, 'That's a really good idea.' "

From Apple's point of view, the beauty of this idea is that peo-ple wouldn't need a way to navigate through the songs on their device—so there was no need to install a precision scroll wheel. That eliminated another pricey part, the screen. You only have to tell the shuffle when to start shuffling. "An iPod is an easy thing to use," he crowed, "but this is even easier!"

Only Steve Jobs could convince people that taking away much of what makes an iPod great (the display, the storage space, the wheel, and the menu-driven interface) can make an even greater iPod. So much was lost, in fact, that it seemed blasphemous to call the shuffle a "true" iPod. Now we had an ontological issue: What makes an iPod an iPod? A scroll wheel? A whole music library in your pocket? Shiny metallic back? Connection to iTunes? The fact that Apple says it is? I asked Jobs the question directly. "An iPod," he said, "is just a great digital music player."

You had to admire the guy. He was declaring that the lack of a simple way to choose a song on your device—or even know what song is playing—*isn't a problem.* It's a fantastic, defining *feature.* When you use this device, you go directly into shuffle. What the iPod was *really* about, the move implied, was jumbling up all your songs and feeding them back to you in unexpected ways. This is so great a feature, in fact, that *we're naming the device after it.* Apple's advertising campaign for the shuffle was a celebration of a limita-tion: the potential bummer that, using this music player, you were unable to choose which song came next, even if your life depended on it. This was *good.* "Embrace Uncertainty," read the ads. This im-plied that people who demanded order from their music devices were hopeless control freaks who needed to loosen up, sort of like stiff-backed, bespectacled wonks in screwball comedies who desperately required the wacky life force of a singin'-in-the-rain, embarrass-the-boss heroine. Like Barbra Streisand in *What's Up, Doc?*, the iPod would fulfill that life-affirming role.

Then there was another slogan: "Life is random."

This was particularly fascinating because at the time Jobs was introducing the shuffle, he was only six months past a horrible, life-threatening cancer scare. In late July 2004, Jobs had gone to the doctor and gotten the shock of his life. Here's how he told it a year later, in a speech to the Stanford University graduating class of 2005:

About a year ago I was diagnosed with cancer. I had a scan at 7:30 in the morning, and it clearly showed a tumor on my pancreas. I didn't even know what a pancreas was. The doctors told me this was almost certainly a type of cancer that is incurable, and that I should expect to live no longer than three to six months. My doctor advised me to go home and get my affairs in order, which is doctor's code for prepare to die. It means to try to tell your kids everything you thought you'd have the next 10 years to tell them in just a few months. It means to make sure everything is buttoned up so that it will be as easy as possible for your family. It means to say your goodbyes.

I lived with that diagnosis all day. Later that evening I had a biopsy, where they stuck an endoscope down my throat, through my stomach and into my intestines, put a needle into my pancreas and got a few cells from the tumor. I was sedated, but my wife, who was there, told me that when they viewed the cells under a microscope the doctors started crying because it turned out to be a very rare form of pancreatic cancer that is curable with surgery. I had the surgery and I'm fine now.

That speech would become widely circulated throughout the Internet. It was Jobs's most complete and certainly his most candid public statement on his cancer. But the January 2005 shuffle introduction took place months before he made that solitary statement. The previous November, in his first public appearance since the surgery (the U2 event in San Jose), he'd brushed off health queries from well-wishers with a quick thanks. Clearly, although he did not want to appear unappreciative of the good feelings offered to him, his brush with mortality was something he had not been eager to discuss, and in January 2005, when introducing the shuffle, Jobs wasn't making statements about it, either. Nonetheless, by coincidence or not, the slogan concocted by his ad agency to promote this new device blatantly celebrated the quirky randomness of life's unpredictably spinning mandala. At the end of our conversation I mentioned this to him, indicating that the circumstances of his own life might have cast this campaign in a different light. He acknowledged the irony. Yes, he had learned that life can be random. And sometimes dark. But when you have a shuffle, the surprises that come from randomness aren't like divorce or totaling your car or, heaven forbid, cancer. The worst that can happen is that your iPod plays a song you don't want to hear. And how often does that happen, since you put all the songs on it yourself?

Still, there remains the knotty question of iTunes and *its* alleged randomness. Life can be messy, but software shouldn't be. I used the new device to test out my suspicions.

As soon as I got my iPod shuffle—a lovely white plastic stick slightly bigger than a pack of gum, with buttons arranged similarly to the scroll wheel—I performed an experiment to see if I could detect a flaw in the shuffling. Apple had come up with a way to fill up the device with a supposedly chance selection of songs from your iTunes library. This feature was named Autofill. It required but a single click to perform an act equivalent (we were to assume) to a spin of a virtual roulette wheel, reshuffling your songs and selecting a group of them to load up your shuffle with just the right amount. All done randomly, at least in theory. In my test I performed a number of Autofills and printed out my results.

My results were interesting. The Autofill function didn't particularly favor Steely Dan—the band was represented about as much as you'd expect, one or two songs per run. But Autofill seemed to like—*really* like—Bruce Springsteen. On one memorable run, nine out of the 118 songs jammed into the shuffle were Boss tunes, even though I had only about 50 Springsteen selections in a library of more than 3,200 songs.

It was not just Springsteen who proved out of whack. On *every* run some artists seemed strangely overrepresented. On one Autofill, for instance, the Tex-Mex band of Valerio Longoria, represented by only a single CD in the library, had three songs. Weird. Surely not random.

Right?

Wrong, said Apple, when I asked for more answers. "Look, I go through the same thing as you," said iPod marketing director Greg Joswiak (also known as Joz, a predictable diminutive for someone working for a company whose cofounder was named Wozniak and was nicknamed Woz). "But I've checked with the engineers again, and it's essentially random. They have checked and rechecked it."

Apple hasn't released the code (and never will, I'm sure), but it is possible to bring some technical analysis to the matter. Let's look at the way shuffle works. First of all, note what it doesn't do—it's not like mixing all the songs in the equivalent of a big bucket of lottery balls and picking out the next one. Instead, as the name implies, it shuffles the entire library so as to reorder them, just as a blackjack dealer shuffles a deck of cards. If you listen to the entire library all through, you will hear every song once and only once. What's important, then, is not whether a song is included but how evenly an artist's songs are distributed throughout the list. When we say that Steely Dan is overrepresented, it means that the band's songs show up early in the run—it would be like a blackjack dealer whose first hand had aces in it. (No one ever listens to a complete run, which could take as much as a week or so of constant playing; long before then, you'd do another shuffle and remix the deck.)

One assumes that the iPod, when reordering, mixes the songs up thoroughly, so that the beginning of the newly shuffled library won't have a preponderance of any artist. Beginning with the very first version of iTunes, predating the iPod, a shuffle feature was provided, and a key part of the software was a mathematical randomization function. Apple insists there's no computational flaw in its execution. "It is completely random. It is absolutely, unequivocally random," says Jeff Robbin, who was one of the original authors of iTunes and later became head of the iTunes development team. Just as a thoroughly shuffled deck of cards will change the order of a factory-sealed deck to an unpredictable jumble, so does (according to Apple) iTunes reorder the songs so that the chance of any one unplayed song coming up next is equal to that of any other remaining song appearing. "We've many times proved to ourselves that it is truly random, because every now and again, at least once a year we get the 'Is this really random?' question, or someone asks if you guys have just some sort of bug," says Robbin. "No, no, no, it's truly random."

Robbin is talking randomness in terms that software can reasonably produce, which is not perfect randomness. True randomness, it turns out, is very difficult to produce. This is well known to cryptographers. A well-funded, sophisticated cryptanalyst will seize on any variation from a random distribution as a means of attacking a code. This subject was most famously examined by Claude Shannon, arguably the Father of Randomness. Shannon himself expressed some random behavior: the MIT math professor was known for his eccentric habits, which included riding a unicycle. But his papers on information theory are rock solid. Basically, he defined randomness as a question of unpredictability. If a series of numbers is truly random, you have no possible way of guessing what comes next. If something isn't random (as in the case of what letter might follow another in a message written in English), you have a better chance of figuring out what comes next. That's why it's so crucial to remove the natural redundancy of language from an encoded message and make the coded text look random.

But perfect randomness is an elusive ideal. For instance, if you're flipping a coin, a minuscule weight imbalance might, over the course of millions of tosses, make heads come up slightly more than tails. If you're randomizing on a computer, you have to introduce a "seed," which is a starting point for the algorithm that mixes up the selections. The seed must draw on some unpredictable input of time that begins outside the computer. Otherwise, the results would be the same over and over again. Even then, a peculiarity in the computer hardware may prevent you from attaining absolutely pure randomness. In certain cryptosystems, the search for the most unpredictable seed relies on quantum behavior of atomic particles. (Talk about nanos!)

"Apple doesn't need iTunes to be random to the degree that you need randomness for cryptography," says Paul Kocher, the CEO of Cryptography Research. The consequences of less-than-perfect randomness on an iPod aren't as dire as a broken national security cipher. So for purposes of mixing up songs, you don't really need to draw on quantum disintegration, just a reasonably strong pseudo-randomizing function in your shuffle, which Apple insists it has.

Kocher concludes that Apple's claims of a high degree of randomness are almost certainly valid. Another expert I consulted, John Allen Paulos, a Temple University mathematician whose works for the lay reader *(Innumeracy)* have made him perhaps the premier ambassador from the world of numbers, agreed. He wasn't surprised, though, that iPod users were questioning whether the shuffle was random. "We often interpret and impose patterns on events that are random," he says. "Especially with something like songs. Songs evoke emotion, and some stick in our minds more than others."

In other words, we think the shuffle is flawed, but the problem is actually in our heads. Even if we know something about math, cryptography, and statistics, we still can't deal with randomness when it comes up at the spin of a click wheel. Steven D. Levitt, the self-described "rogue economist" who cowrote the best-selling *Freakonomics,* also fell into the trap. Writing on his blog, he professed constant surprise at how often his iPod shuffle "plays two, three, or even four songs by the same artist, even though I have songs by dozens of different artists on it. On a number of occasions, I've even become mistakenly convinced I don't have the iPod on shuffle, but rather, I'm playing all the songs by one artist." But as a statistics maven, he understood that the bottom line is that "the human mind does badly with randomness."

Indeed, says Paul Kocher, "Our brains aren't wired to understand randomness—there's even a huge industry that takes advantage of people's inability to deal with random distributions. It's called gambling."

So why does Autofill produce nine Bruce Springsteen songs out of 188? Because that's what almost *always* happens in normal distributions of items from databases. Clusters of something are to be expected. Here's a classic math trick: Gather forty people in a room, and have everyone write down the day he or she was born. What are the odds that two people will have the same birthday? Nearly 100 percent. It sounds like a coincidence, like two Steely Dan songs in a set of four. But mathematicians will tell you that it's much more unusual for there to be *no* such clusters.

We perceive trends when there are none. Poker players invariably believe that they can lock into streaks where God will make sure that their cards are winners—or the Devil will deal them losers. Backgammon champions swear that dice can go hot or cold, a concept that is regarded as beyond dispute by crapshooters. Mathematicians consider this an illusion. Likewise, longtime baseball observers swear by the phenomenon of the clutch hitter, whose performance improves with men on base or the game on the line. Sabermetricians—those who analyze the national pastime from the geeky perspective of statistics—insist that the whole idea of clutch ability is a myth, unsupported by the hard evidence. What happens, they say, is that clutch situations, because they are so important, stand out in our minds. We remember when Derek Jeter hits a triple late in a World Series game, and we don't forget when Alex Rodriguez hits into a double play in the deciding game of divisional playoffs.

Likewise, this explains why people think they can cosmically predict what song will come next on their shuffle. The blogger Kapgar, who claimed this power, remembers vividly the times when he predicted a song and the iPod amazingly delivered it. Like a Derek Jeter clutch hit, it stood out. But there may have been a thousand times when his iPod played songs that he didn't guess— nonmemorable circumstances that, not surprisingly, didn't make an impression. Likewise, is it really so astounding that his iPod played a run of what he considers great songs? Dude—*he's loaded the iPod with his favorite tunes.* You know what would be really freaky? If his iPod came up with a run of tunes that he absolutely *despised.*

The more I thought about it, the more it seemed utterly clear that Kocher and Paulos were right: the nonrandomness was not in our iPods, but in ourselves. And after my column appeared I heard from Jan Melin, a reporter for *Ny Teknik,* a Swedish technology magazine "read by most engineers in Sweden." Melin had been inspired by the column to do an experiment on his own to test whether the shuffle function indeed favored songs. It is much too convoluted to explain here. Since his magazine was not interested in his experiment, he sent me the results—a fantastically complicated series of spreadsheets, charts, and distribution graphs. The bottom line? A pretty random distribution. "My study is not a scientific proof," Melin wrote, "but my results are so obvious that I think it is good enough to convince anyone (at least me) that 'shuffle' is random."

A few months later I got wind of another experiment, this one conducted by a self-proclaimed math geek named Brian Hansen, who posted his results on a Web site called OmniNerd. This is the way he broke it down: the "patterns" people claim to perceive from their psychic, or temperamental, iPods are generally cases where multiple songs from the same artist come up in clusters. "Think of it this way," he wrote. "If you have 2000 songs and 40 of them are from the same artist, there is always a 2% chance of hearing them next with random play." But if that artist is, say, the Kinks, you don't have to hear "A Well Respected Man" just after "Waterloo Sunset" to sense that something funny is happening: hearing just a few Kinks tunes within an hour of shuffling will trigger your suspicions. Hansen calculated that with the figures in the hypothetical case he cites above, your odds of hearing a second Kinks song within the next thirty-five selections is 50 percent. And there is a 64 percent chance you'll hear one in the next fifty selections. It was one more confirmation of something counterintuitive but increasingly indisputable: what we perceive as shuffle favoritism is well within expected mathematical bounds.

All of this seemed conclusive enough to shut the book on the LTBSD question. My original iPod's fixation with Steely Dan turned out to be *my* fixation—shared with all iPod users if not all of humanity when trying to deal with randomness.

But the nonrandomness illusion was so prevalent that ultimately Apple felt compelled to address it. In the version of iTunes rolled out in September 2005, there appeared a new feature: smart shuffle. It presents iPodders with a scroll bar that "allows you to control how likely you are to hear multiple songs in a row by the same artists or on the same album." If you pull the lever to the right, the iPod will mess with its usual distribution pattern, intentionally spacing out songs by a given artist. (You can also cluster your favorites by moving the lever to the left—that way, all your Todd Rundgrens and Eminems will come in bunches.) As Jobs explained it in his presentation the day the new iTunes rolled out, he gave what he hoped would be the last word on the Great iPod Randomness Controversy: "We're making it *less* random to make it feel *more* random." After the event, he summed it all up to me: "When we talk to people, they say, 'There's two Bob Dylan songs right after another, how could it be random?' You explain to them it could happen, it often does. What they really want is to make sure that *doesn't* happen. So we're making sure it doesn't happen. Or [if they want], making sure it *does* happen. Rather than argue whether it's random or not, we can give them the outcome they want."

At another event a couple weeks later, Joz came up to me and asked if I was finally satisfied. (I had become the leading crusader on this arcane issue: if you typed "iPod randomness" in Google, the top link was the column I had written about iPods playing favorites.) To be honest, I *wasn't* satisfied. I was, in fact, a bit let down. I had already come to terms with the idea that the iPod version of shuffling creates a sufficiently unbiased distribution to earn the casual appellation of "random." What was bothering me was now something even deeper. Yes, the bothersome clusters of certain artists are within the bounds of randomness. But that made me realize that the seemingly magical effects of the shuffle function—a spooky just-rightness, even brilliance, that comes from great song juxtapositions—were *also* consequences of randomness.

And in its own way that was much more disturbing.

Here's an example of what I'm talking about. I start a shuffle with a song by the Mendoza Line, a Brooklyn-based indie rock group named after the notoriously low batting average of a shortstop named Mario Mendoza. Amazingly, iTunes finds a song to follow it that also has a baseball theme: Ry Cooder's "3rd Base, Dodger Stadium." This subtle link makes the two very disparate songs illuminate each other and adds a weird excitement to the listening process, almost as if the selection itself were a kind of performance.

When iTunes/iPod makes a connection like this, I am reminded of the famous "Hand of God" move in the May 1997 match between Garry Kasparov and IBM's Deep Blue Supercomputer. The human champion had won the first game against the digital challenger and was slugging it out fairly evenly in game two. But at the thirty-sixth move, Deep Blue rejected what seemed like an obvious path to a draw (which seemed inevitable at the time) and instead made an incredibly subtle pawn capture, with devastating long-term consequences. This was the kind of move that chess computers, no matter how powerful, were supposedly not capable of making. Ultimately, that brilliant feint set the stage for Deep Blue's victory in the game—and the match. Kasparov became convinced that this move could only have been the result of a human intelligence. He accused the IBM team of cooking the computational books. He was so wigged out that his game fell apart and he became the first human chess champion to lose to a machine. To this day, Kasparov does not accept that it was a computer that moved that pawn. He has compared the move to the notorious 1986 World Cup soccer match when the Argentine star Diego Maradona scored a key goal against England. Replays clearly showed it was a handball, but the player described the force as "the Hand of God."

Similarly, some transitions from one song to another in shuffle are so breathtakingly perfect that it is difficult to accept them as the fruits of a computer algorithm, even though intellectually I know this is the case. Is there a Hand of God factor at work here? Is that what caused my iPod on one sunny day to follow Ike and Tina Turner's "So Fine" with Creedence Clearwater Revival's "Proud Mary," a brilliant segue not only because the songs flowed so smoothly, but because of the implicit recognition that "Proud Mary" is the song that was arguably Ike and (particularly) Tina's breakthrough in the mainstream? Hey, I knew that. But my iPod didn't.

This was something that my e-mail correspondents (still mystified by iPod doesn't-seem-random behavior) had wondered about as well: "Why," asked one, "did my iPod decide to play Neil Young's 'The Loner' followed by Bruce Cockburn's 'Loner' yesterday?" Yes, I know that the correct answer is that the iPod didn't "decide" anything, that the software just got lucky. But that seems an unsatisfying resolution.

I am old enough to remember the glory days of free-form FM radio. In Philadelphia, where I grew up, there was a stone-cold maestro of the segue, a deejay named Michael Tearson. He held the night shift at the city's hippest station, WMMR, which not only was the city's key source for "progressive music" but was the glue for the burgeoning social/political/cultural movement lapping even at our urban backwater. My friends and I had an unforgiving enforcement of taste when it came to our music. Only the great stuff (in our opinion) was worthy of attention. We had Dylan lyrics memorized; we could argue for hours about the relative contributions of the members of the Buffalo Springfield, talking about them as if they were part of our own circle. And anytime "In-A-Gadda-Da-Vida" was played in our presence, no matter where we were, we would immediately leave the room. We sensed that Tearson understood all this. He was on our wavelength not only literally but cosmically. He would hit the air around ten o'clock and weave an intricate series of song sets, each one as perfectly constructed as a Raymond Carver short story. No duds, no Iron Butterfly. We hung on each segue with the tension of a Saturday-morning movie serial; the end of a song was a cliffhanger that always paid off with an edifying, and sometimes astonishing, transition to the next selection. We were convinced he was sending us messages simply by what song followed another.

What a cruel joke if this magic could be duplicated by software inside a plastic box. Yet I had to admit it—I was getting the same excitement from the juxtapositions of the iPod's shuffle function as I did from the truly great DJ. Apparently, millions of others were, too, with their own iPods. No wonder the radio industry was

Shuffle

throwing fits over the iPod phenomenon. Years ago, radio had abandoned the idea of providing variety to listeners and instead concentrated on putting just a few well-tested songs on "heavy rotation" so the most popular tunes at the moment (generally the lowest artistic common denominator, catchy and forgettable stuff) would dominate the airwaves. Who could tolerate such unimaginative programming when there were iPods, which could shuffle thousands of songs that had passed the ultimate focus group—you, the sole listener, endorsing every cut because you consciously ripped it into the system?

Radio industry consultants, explicitly pandering to the millions of people perpetually zoned into the permanent shuffle of their own music collections, have tried to answer this challenge with the first major new broadcast format in years. It is dubbed "Jack." The name comes from the buddy-buddy moniker assigned to the occasional voice-over interspersed between tunes—though some stations call their voices Bob or Hank or Dave or Max. Instead of sticking to a playlist of a couple of dozen carefully chosen songs, a Jack station draws on a selection of hundreds, spanning several decades and multiple genres. The unofficial motto of Jack is, *If you can't beat 'em, join 'em.* "The almost anything-goes eclecticism of the format, sometimes called adult hits, seems to appeal to listeners accustomed to scanning through thousands of MP3s at a time," explains a *New York Times* reporter. WCBS, the New York City station that adopted the format, puts it more blatantly in one of its promos: "It's like an iPod, only the batteries never run out."

But why accept someone else's version of your iPod when you have the real thing?

I wondered what Michael Tearson himself might say about all this. I hadn't encountered him on the radio for almost thirty years but had heard about the trajectory of his career, which unfortunately had been downward. At one point not long after I left Philadelphia, he had left WMMR. Though still a local icon, he had found fewer places to practice his craft as one by one the Philadelphia progressive stations became regressive. The last one switched format in 2004; a few of its deejays went onto the Internet in hopes that listeners still hungry for Interpol and Arcade Fire would find them there. This reflected the desperation all over the country at alternative or modern rock stations; at Miami's WZTA, a program director, looking for ways to keep listeners, heard a pitch from his supervisor that the station should run a contest with a prize of an iPod filled with songs. The PD nixed that idea, explaining that people with iPods "don't need to listen to [us] any more." Not long after that Clear Channel, the huge corporation that runs more than 1,200 radio stations, pulled the plug on WZTA.

In this hostile climate, Michael Tearson was no longer employed full-time. He was getting by with several gigs on stations on the far left of the FM dial, like one called "Psychedelic Supper" for the Burlington County College station, filling a void for aging heads who listen to 88.9. In recent years, he'd suffered some other setbacks, including the death of his wife and ailments of his own. So, after e-mailing him a request to visit him to talk about the iPod, I wasn't sure what to expect when I went to see him at his small house in South Jersey.

A harried man with the same unforgettable pixie-ish voice answered the door and almost sprinted away to the back room. He was on the phone to a computer support person, he yelled at me, and had to finish the call. Tearson's PC was apparently on the fritz, and from the back room I heard anguished cries as he got the news that it would cost a hundred dollars just to have it looked at. When he got off the phone and ushered me past mounds of clothing, books, and other detritus of an un-picked-up house, to a bedroom converted to a studio, he was clearly in distress. He was preparing a weekly show for Sirius Satellite Radio—and couldn't proceed without the computer. I didn't mention to him how the scene struck me as symbolic: the master of analog music, laid low by the digital foe.

He brightened when I asked him how he had managed to craft his brilliant sets back in the good old days. "I just developed the knack of being able to take music and make more of it than A plus B," he said. It was, he emphasized, all about storytelling. Tearson tried to give the songs formerly imprisoned by their placement on LPs "entirely different shadings" by recontextualizing them in unexpected pairings. "The songs took on completely different meanings and impact than they could have either by themselves or in the context of the album they came from," he said. Since he worked later at night, he just hung around during the day concocting set concepts and jotting down segues. "There was something about the radio then that would surprise you constantly. You would put me on at night to take a ride."

He never kept any logs of what he played, but as we talked he was able to recall some of his sequencing triumphs, like the time he played three different versions of "I Am the Walrus"—the Beatles', Spooky Tooth's, and that of "an eccentric Englishman named Lol Coxhill, an avant garde sax player who had schoolkids sing what they thought were the lyrics to the song, and he [mixed] that with atonal flute and piano." What iPod could serve up *that* trifecta?

Tearson, though, is an iPod fan. "The one thing the iPod does is make that listener an active participant in the music again. You create your own universe of music," he says. But when I began to explain that my iPod can sometimes deliver the same wonderful connections that his show did, he didn't seem to understand. I tried to explain what I meant, using as an example the Ike and Tina/Creedence segue that had recently struck me. But though Tearson certainly understood the connection between those songs, he would not accept that the iPod was doing what he did. "It's nothing other than a random sequence program," he sniffed. "I was working on creating with the listener these flows of mental imagery, and the progressions of growth and the evolution of ideas. And that simply doesn't happen [with the iPod]."

Well, it doesn't happen *intentionally*. But sometimes it feels as though it does. And what's more, there is the promise that in the future we're going to see a new kind of software that will make the magic happen more often. Programs will analyze the actual music file, assess the lyrics, data-mine the Internet buzz about the musicians, and sync all this information with your personal preferences to deliver you Robo-Tearsons who almost always get things cosmically right. I can see why free-form deejays feel embattled, like the one who wrote an online article that complained that because of the iPod shuffle mode, "the art of the set and the segue is in imminent danger of dying." But I wonder whether it's just the opposite—whether the set and the segue are entering a new golden age. Only this time, the programmers are algorithmic.

Working largely under the radar so far, there is already a thriving cottage industry of small companies devoted to the classification and study of digital music. The ultimate goal is perfect delivery of digital music to your ears, in perfect order, blending the comfort of familiarity with a steady diversity.

There are generally two approaches to the way these enterprises classify music. The first is by hand. Companies typically hire up to a few dozen so-called musicologists—aficionados of a microgenre like blues, post-punk, or alt-country, who know their little corner of sonic geography down to the inch—and, sitting in cubicles or working from their cluttered homes, methodically listen to and catalog every single piece of music in their designated realm. Once things are codified and put into databases, then the algorithms can step in, using those microcategories to deliver just the right song at the right time.

The second method is a mathematical analysis of the song file itself. This sounds like a process doomed to miss the point—isn't music largely made of emotion and other unquantifiable intangibles? But electronic musicologists insist otherwise, and a great race is under way to untangle the dense thicket of binary code inside a digital song file and discover the inner truth of the music within. This will allow the automatic construction of playlists that flow with the trippy wisdom of free-form radio, as interpreted by someone high on Panama Red.

So we have companies like Pandora, seeking to, as its founder, Tim Westergren, puts it, "understand the DNA of music." His company, which now contracts with Barnes & Noble, Best Buy, AOL, and Tower Records to make music recommendations for their customers, employs thirty "music analysts" with a minimum requirement of a four-year degree in music theory. Every time a song arrives in this musical DNA shop, an analyst will devote twenty to thirty minutes of intense concentration to identifying as many as four hundred distinct variables, or "genes." Just to capture the emotional metrics of the singing voice, there are thirty-two variables—things like timbre, vibrato, pitch, and range. "Any voice can be understood as the combination of these genes," says Westergren. When this system is applied to all the instruments as well as the traits of the song—tempo, amplitude, etc.—the analyst produces a précis. If done right, says Westergren, another analyst can look at and virtually play the whole song in his or her head. More to the point, using this Music Genome Project, you can automate what a disk jockey does to customize a set according to your tastes.

Another company, Predixis, sells a program called MusicMagic

Mixer that will painstakingly analyze your entire iTunes library—isolating 255 attributes, including mood, tempo, and lyrical quality—to discern the musical "fingerprints" and generate a playlist from a single song you pick to establish the mood—sort of a Michael Tearson on command. "We can reach deep into your music collection," says the system's architect, Wendell Hicken. Is the system better than a DJ? "It depends on what you expect," says Hicken. "A local DJ you find on the street? We can do better than that." (Hicken, by the way, has two iPods and 67,000 songs in his iTunes library, a collection he considers "medium size.")

Year by year, the electronic music analysts are getting closer to understanding how to classify and organize music without human intervention, working toward a goal of something way beyond a smart shuffle . . . call it an omniscient shuffle. One of the most startling papers in this new field is called "Automatic Record Reviews." As the title implies, the coauthors, Brian Whitman of the MIT Media Laboratory and Daniel P. W. Ellis of Columbia University's DeRosa Lab believe that by computer-analyzing the digital files of a song, in conjunction with an electronic survey of Internet chatter, it is possible to generate actual record reviews without having a human being ever listen to the songs or albums under discussion. Such a process has the advantage of being totally free of the noisy, sometimes intentionally provocative biases of flesh-and-blood rock critics, as well as avoiding bizarre personal associations (referred to in the paper as "extraneous nonmusical discussion") that make record reviews fun to read but often not sufficiently useful as guides to music that fits your taste. Automatic reviews cut to the chase and can also provide "maximal semantic value for future retrieval tasks."

Pioneers like Westergren, Hicken, and Whitman and Ellis are paving the way for the next turn of the sequencing wheel, when it won't be just a near-random shuffle process that determines what comes next on your high-capacity Wi-Fi-connected iPod. Instead the sequence will probably be a machine-directed set of dream transitions, capitalizing on lyrical coincidences, genealogical connections between bands, and seamless musical transitions to make every segue a momentary burst of joy. It will weave in the latest efforts from your favorite artists, or songs from bands you've never heard of, that fit perfectly into your collection. When you start exercising, the iPod might even pick up your increased heartbeat and begin feeding you songs from an ideal workout playlist.

Can Michael Tearson, or anyone like him, ever compete with that? Like Garry Kasparov, haunted by a chess move that could be explained only by the Hand of God, he and the other great radio sequencers are the John Henrys of the digital age, creating artisanal effects that powerful chips can calculate by the billions. (Tearson, by the way, got a more prominent gig at Sirius not long after my visit.) The iPod Nation will continue shuffling, obsessed with what comes up next and often thrilled at the result. And if we don't like it, or don't think it's sufficiently random-sounding, there's always the "forward" button on the right side of the click wheel.

Apple

❯May 1998, a sunny day in Silicon Valley. In less than twenty-four hours, Steve Jobs would unveil the first fruits of what would be a historic effort to salvage Apple Computer. Less than a year earlier, in July 1997, he had retaken control of the company he had cofounded—and been fired from. After a dozen years in the wilderness he was back, running Apple as its undisputed leader for the first time. Most people thought it was a hopeless case. Just before Jobs took over, *The Wall Street Journal* had actually written a eulogy on the company. And weeks after Jobs's return, Michael Dell, whose eponymous company sold more computers than any other, took a question in an industry conference about what he would do if he were in Jobs's shoes. The PC mogul offered the following advice: "I'd shut [Apple] down," he said, "and give the money back to the shareholders."

Now Steve Jobs was rehearsing the launch of his first major project since he had taken over at Apple, the computer that would kick off a new era of innovation and start to shut up the critics and reenergize the faithful. It had been an intense time. In the first months after Jobs had taken control—in a board of directors coup that had the previous CEO squealing that he had been ousted by a

Machiavellian poseur—Jobs had thrown himself into nonstop meetings to figure out a strategy, "from eight in the morning till eight at night," he said. The result of this was a commitment to new kinds of products. The first of which, the weird-looking but utterly charming iMac, would now be revealed at a private event near Apple's campus.

On the stage of the auditorium that would hold the event, Jobs stood back and watched as his television production crew screened a video to be shown after he introduced the iMac. Marketing mini-documentaries were commonplace in the tech business: lots of product shots from flattering angles, edgy Greek chorus–like close-ups of talking-head executives and industry analysts singing the praises of the new product. Jobs watched with an eagle eye as the sharply edited vignettes ran on the large screen. One of the highlights was a playful reference to the retro-futuristic look of the egg-shaped, lollipop blue machine, which looked like something from the 1960s animated television series *The Jetsons.* As homage, the video included a five-second clip from the actual series. Though it would be over almost as soon as the crowd recognized it, the clip would be sure to delight the geeky audience.

Then one of the production guys gingerly approached Jobs and warned him of a problem. It seemed that Hanna-Barbera, the animation house that owned the rights to *The Jetsons,* had yet to sign off. The permission was still stalled with the lawyers. If the issue isn't resolved before tomorrow, the nervous media specialist told Jobs, the clip will have to go.

Jobs's face turned to steel. "Keep it in," he said.

"Ummmm, Steve, we can't do that," said the production guy. He began to explain what Jobs certainly knew from his other job as majority shareholder of the Pixar studio and thereby the owner of some of the animation world's most valuable intellectual property:

using the clip without permission could incur huge liabilities. Jobs abruptly cut him off. "I don't care!" he shouted. "We're using it."

The clip stayed in the picture. (Presumably the permission was subsequently secured.) And the iMac, a beneficiary of that perfectionism, did indeed initiate a string of Apple products that made the company one of the most admired corporations on the face of the earth.

The Jetsons moment, while in a sense unsettling, is also illustrative of some of the attributes behind Jobs's success: his unwavering focus, his insistence on excellence, and his belief in his own vision. These were all in play when Apple developed the iPod. Jobs did not invent the device, but he created the conditions that made it possible and focused on ensuring that the end result would meet his exacting standards. It may not be accurate to say that only under the leadership of Jobs and the culture he created could the iPod have been devised and only under Jobs could it have further evolved into its current dominance—but there is the undeniable fact that no one else did it.

There have been five biographies of Steve Jobs to date, and every single one feasts on his dark side and tries to reapportion the credit for his successes. By and large, their tone is condescending. One book, called *Accidental Millionaire,* concludes with an account of his 1985 ouster from the company, flatly stating that Apple "was facing a brighter future without him." Randall Stross's *Steve Jobs and the NeXT Big Thing,* an account of Jobs's venture between his two terms at Apple, takes delight in the failure of the NeXT computer—a flop later mitigated by the computer's significant impact. (The NeXT legacy can be seen not only in the current Macintosh operating system but in the World Wide Web itself, which was created on a NeXT box.) In *The Second Coming of Steve Jobs,* Alan Deutschman paints him as an intolerable schmuck and awful manager who makes the boss in the television series *The Office* look like Peter Drucker; reading the book, you could only conclude that no company could succeed with Jobs at the helm. Oddly, the fairly bland *iCon* was the one book that so angered Jobs that he took vengeance on the publisher, Wiley, ordering the firm's instructional books to be removed from the shelves of the Apple store.

It's not as though Jobs doesn't get respect; in the business mags he is the equivalent of Princess Diana as a cover subject. (Jobs considers cover stories his birthright and often grants exclusive access in exchange for getting Apple's new products on the cover.) But only recently, with the dual success of the iPod and Pixar, have people come to realize that Jobs is building a historical legacy. This is a guy who has pulled off *four* accomplishments that rocked the world. With the Apple II, he was instrumental in introducing the concept of a personal computer to the world. With the Macintosh, he popularized what was to become the dominant—and friendliest—means of using a computer. As the CEO of Pixar, he helped usher in the era of computer-animated feature films. And now there is the iPod.

Jobs himself looks back to the Macintosh effort as a peak. Other people involved in the effort look back to that period with a Camelot-type nostalgia. But at the time, it was a jagged fever chart of highs and lows—and it vividly illustrated why Jobs is not your normal leader. Those were the days when his employees created the term "Reality Distortion Field," which stuck with Jobs as a description of how his own beliefs—often at odds with conventional wisdom and, at times, at odds with the facts—were irresistibly contagious to those within earshot. On one hand, the term reflected the frustration of the Mac workers; Jobs would get things into his head, and that would be it. Only a repeated assault by actual reality (when things just didn't work) would change his mind.

But the term was not strictly pejorative. For one thing, Jobs was often right, and only his unwillingness to compromise would convince others that taking an untrodden path was correct. More to the point, people who were in range of the reality distortion field often came to believe they could actually accomplish what seemed impossible. And they wound up exceeding their own wildest expectations, simply because they knew that nothing less was expected. Even when Jobs's criticism went overboard, his tantrums would often have a beneficial effect. Think about it: How often does *anyone* do a job so well that it cannot be improved upon? People on the Mac team would go berserk when Jobs looked at a task they had completed pretty well and dismissed it with a vulgarism. But they would bite their tongues and often make something better. (Other times, to be sure, they'd just stay out of his way for a while, and the next time he saw the work, he'd call it genius.) "My best contribution to the group is not settling for anything but really good stuff," a twenty-nine-year-old Jobs explained to me a few weeks before the original Macintosh came out. "A lot of times, people don't do great things because great things really aren't expected of them, and nobody ever really demands that they try, and nobody says, 'Hey, that's the culture here.' If you set that up, people will do things that are greater than they ever thought they could be. Really some great work that will go down in history."

Indeed, the people who worked on Macintosh now look back and can't believe what they did. I have kept up with many who worked on the original Macintosh—some have become close friends—and to the last person, they describe that time as the most bruising period in their professional lives—and by a long shot, the most satisfying. Reality distortion field or not, they believed they were working on one of the most important products in the history of technology. This could be described as a mass delusion except for the fact that the Macintosh *was* one of the most important projects in the history of technology. In Steve Jobs's case, the emperor had clothes.

On the Mac's twentieth anniversary in January 2004—basking in the success of the iPod—Jobs told me, "I love what we're doing at Apple now, I think it's the best work that Apple's ever done. But I think all of us on the Mac team point to that as the high point of our careers. It's like [the Beatles] playing Shea Stadium. We were really working fourteen-to-eighteen-hour days, seven days a week. For, like, two years. Three years. That was our life. But we loved it, we were young, and we could do it."

(It's no accident that the younger people who worked on the iPod were intimately familiar with the legends of the Mac team. At a party held at the Macworld Conference & Expo in 2004 to celebrate the publication of Mac pioneer Andy Hertzfeld's account of the machine's beginnings, one prominent iPod designer collected the Mac team's autographs on the book with the excitement of a kid getting signatures of the winning World Series squad on a baseball.)

Jobs's mania for excellence has persisted in his current reign at Apple. "He makes me do things I would never do on my own, because I would never be that aggressive. He's always raising the bar on me," says Jon Rubinstein, who was with Jobs for fifteen years. On the other hand, adds Rubinstein, if Jobs's demands are actually impossible, he will eventually ease off on them. But not without insisting on another try. "If things are not possible, I can sit down with him and I go, 'Look, here's the facts, here's the trade-offs, here's the issues, here's my recommendation.' And most of the time, he'll take my recommendation. If it's really important, he'll go, 'Okay, I understand all that, but do me a favor, try to go do this.' And if it's really impossible, I'll go, 'I can't, sorry.' But most of the time I'll go, 'Okay.' And then I'll make an effort."

Jobs can be capricious, but the persistent application of a standard of excellence—excellence that, at a minimum, must surpass all previous efforts—is a powerful tactic for any commercial or creative enterprise. The path of least resistance is accepting work that is, well, acceptable. But what if a company considers merely acceptable work as unacceptable? What if good excuses for not pulling off a tough task are rejected? What do you get when even people's A-minus projects are curtly tossed back in their faces, with the implication that if they don't deliver A-plus maybe they would be happier somewhere else?

You get Apple.

In 1997, when Steve Jobs returned to the company, he insisted that his stay was only temporary. It was like, he said, finding an old girlfriend who had fallen on bad times and needed a bit of help to straighten out. And they were really bad times; Jobs once told me Apple had been ninety days away from bankruptcy. "I'll just continue until I can hand the baton off to someone else," he told me that summer, a few days after he assumed the post on an interim basis.

"You will absolutely not be the CEO?" I asked.

"I think we should go out and recruit a really great CEO. I am the CEO of Pixar, and I really love my job," he said.

"So the answer is yes, you won't be CEO?"

"My hat is not in the ring to be CEO."

But he immediately began an ambitious plan to resurrect the company, not just as a viable concern but as a symbol of what a great corporation could be. Years earlier, when he had been in his earlier phase at Apple and working on the Macintosh, I had asked him what he wanted for Apple. "I want us," he said, "to be a ten-billion-dollar company that doesn't lose its soul." Now Apple's revenues had fallen from a high of eight billion dollars to barely five billion. And Jobs would be the first to tell you that the soul level had fallen from Solomon Burke heights to the Lawrence Welk abyss.

"I think the world is a slightly better place with Apple Computer," he told me then. "If Apple could return to its roots as an innovator, then the whole industry would benefit from that. When you really look at it, there are two things about Apple that are remarkable. One, Apple owns one of the two high-volume operating systems in the world. Second, Apple is the only company left that makes the whole widget. Apple is the only company left that can bet the company on things that involve hardware and software and marketing. All together. So there's tremendous opportunity for innovation."

Jobs began Apple's comeback in May 1998, when he sent out an invitation for the aforementioned iMac event with little more information than the silhouetted fruit-with-a-bite-out-of-it logo. No one knew it, but he was stamping out a template for all Apple launches thereafter. In the future, his stealth would be a huge tease, and there would be as much suspense in whether his secret would be preserved as in the mystery of what he was introducing. But at this point there was very little speculation because, frankly, people didn't expect much from the company anymore.

I'd come to Cupertino a few days early to get a close look at the new product—and the new Apple. Jobs wasn't just introducing the iMac but unveiling his grand strategy for fixing Apple. Many pundits had been opining that the only way for Apple to survive would be to give up its long-time strategy of producing both the computers (the hardware) and the operating system (the software); the "whole widget" approach Jobs had trumpeted seemed to be doomed in the world of the Microsoft monopoly. Jobs bristled at that charge. "That's not our destiny." Instead, he explained, he would revive Apple by a regimen of innovation, at a level competitors were unable or unwilling to sustain.

I followed him around for a while on the fourth-floor executive offices at One Infinite Loop, a quadrant of buildings off Interstate 280 in Cupertino. Though the buildings postdated his previous tenure at Apple, the area was rich in Apple's history, as well as Jobs's own life. He had grown up in this town and had led the Macintosh team in offices just across the street from these tall modern structures, in a three-floor office-park-style building called Bandley Three. Now he was bivouacking in digs that seemed a little overstated for his tastes. He nodded to a huge corner office that used to belong to his predecessor, Gil Amelio. "I never go in there," he said. "Do you know that he wanted to install a private men's room here that would cost a half-million dollars?" The office Jobs was working from then was relatively tiny, a sliver that would be appropriate for a junior executive. There was a small round table stacked with books, videos, and advertising awards. Facing a wall was his desk, on top of which sat both Mac and Wintel laptops. I listened in as he took some calls. One was from Pixar regarding *Toy Story 2,* another from Jerry Seinfeld regarding an Apple television ad that would highlight a clip from Seinfeld's first appearance on Johnny Carson's show.

But when Jobs got to the boardroom, dominated by a long table, he was all about Apple's product plans. He worked the whiteboard as if beginning a lecture. "When I got here," he said, *"these* were all the computers we were selling or working on." He wrote down a long list, ten of them PowerBook or Macintosh models delineated only by numbers, and a few more products that were named: Newton, eMac, and Pippin. "Now," he said, "we're selling none of these."

He wrote down the following grid on the whiteboard:

	consumer	pro
desktop	iMac	G3
portable	1999 1st half	PB G3

That was his plan: four great products, two high-end and two consumer-priced. At the end of this presentation, Jobs pulled back a sheet that had covered an elliptical object on the conference table. The first new product on his grid: the iMac. It was a weird, egg-shaped beast but disarmingly attractive. Like all great Steve Jobs products, it had a human feel to it. You wanted to touch it. Its plastic case was a feel-good shade of fruity blue. During its development the informal code names for the project had been the names of Columbus's ships: *Niña, Pinta, Santa María.* Why? "A new world," he explained. After putting the machine through its paces, he bore down on me. "Isn't that just *great?*" he asked, with the pride of a very pushy parent. Yes, I agreed, it's really neat. "It's not just 'neat,'" he corrected me. "It's fucking *fantastic.*"

Over the next couple years I would be summoned back to Cupertino to see how Jobs filled out his grid. A year later I was in the same boardroom to see the iBook, "an iMac to go." That day, Jobs also introduced me to another new technology that Apple had decided to embrace: the wireless Internet standard called Wi-Fi. Apple was building it into its machines and offering an easy-to-hook-up home wireless router, which looked like a flying saucer, called the AirPort. "The technology has been around, but nobody uses it," Jobs explained. "It hasn't been cheap enough. Two, somebody makes the wireless card, somebody makes the computer, and somebody makes the software, and they're three different companies. If you go to Microsoft and say, 'Wireless is the most important thing,' they'll go, 'Hey, get in line, maybe in two years we'll talk to you.' If you go to Dell and say, 'Wireless is important,' they'll say, 'No, it's not.' So when we decided to do it, we said, 'Wireless networking is one of our major initiatives at Apple. We're going to make our hardware work with it, make our OS operate with it, bring it to the marketplace.' " Sure enough, Apple's decision was instrumental in making Wi-Fi a ubiquitous technology that changed the way people connected to the Internet.

Jobs officially removed the "interim" from his title in 2000. By then the Apple turnaround was shaping up as one of the great business stories of all time. "I sort of think of it like there was this really beautiful Porsche speedster that had been sitting out in a field," he said. "And it got really dirty, covered with mud. You couldn't even see the speedster any more; it just looked like this muddy thing. And we've taken it through a car wash in the last two years. And now it's this really beautiful speedster and we're polishing it up constantly and putting on new tires."

But 2000 was the year the tech industry hit the skids. Apple's business wasn't as damaged as the dot-com companies were, but as befits an enterprise that prefixes its products with an "i"—as in Internet—its financials took a big hit. In October 2001, the week before the iPod came out, the company reported its quarterly results. Both profits and revenues were down compared to the previous year. In the fiscal year 2001, which had just ended, the company had logged a net loss of $25 million on revenues of just $5.36 billion. The previous year, the company had taken in almost $8 billion for a profit of $786 million. "It was a challenging year for us and our industry," said Jobs, sounding very much like a traditional CEO trying to downplay a crummy performance.

Still, Apple was in decent shape, sitting on more than a billion dollars in cash and solidifying the base of fanatic Mac users. The big problem was that no matter how impressive its products were, Apple seemed doomed to low market share. Apple was blowing everyone away with its cool designs and its innovative new operating system, but it seemed stuck at around 4 percent of the domestic computer share, and even less worldwide. Since the world buys lots of computers, it's possible to be profitable at that rate, and there was always a good chance of grabbing a point or two more. But this really didn't seem like a triumphant fate for one of the world's best brands.

Nonetheless, Jobs felt deeply that Apple's best days were ahead. So when the tech world went bust, Jobs did not cut back like everyone else; he *boosted* investment. "We doubled down," recalls Apple executive Greg Joswiak.

Then came iPod.

The success of the diminutive music player changed the very nature of Apple. No longer was the company a niche leader, producing fine products revered by a loyal cultlike following. Suddenly it was the overwhelming market leader in a key category. So dominant was Apple in the portable digital music player field that only one word could be used to generically describe such devices: iPod.

Obviously, this could have happened only once the iPod became available to all the world, not just the sliver of the public who used Macintoshes. This was not always in the cards. During iPod's whirlwind development process, the device was always thought of as part of Apple's Digital Hub strategy: just one more enhancement in the suite of features created to make Macintosh the computer of choice for think-different consumers who wanted to use the exciting new media technologies. Jobs's strategy was to encourage "switchers": PC users who would escape the Evil Empire and embrace the trippy world of Apple, where productivity, great design, and fun are in a constant group hug. Jobs hoped that the exclusive ability to hook up an iPod to a Mac might drive music fans to Apple's door.

But even before the launch in October 2001, some people on the iPod team were pushing for Windows compatibility so that instead of a potential market of 25 million or so Mac owners, more than 500 million PC users would potentially be iPod buyers. In press interviews at the time, Jobs was equivocal about giving up iPod's status as a sweetener for potential switchers. But in private he was adamant. "I remember that day," says one Apple executive. "He said, 'I'm never taking this to the PC!'" Over the next few months, though, it became increasingly clear that the iPod was a business in itself. "We realized that we're going to be in the music business," says Apple's Phil Schiller. The company did a marketing study that concluded that there was little downside to going on Windows. Schiller took the results to Jobs, who finally agreed.

"We really had a debate whether to take the iPod to Windows or not," Jobs later admitted to me. "The answer that we came out with unanimously inside the senior team of the company was 'This is such an incredible opportunity we have to redefine the music business that we're not going to keep this just as a lure to sell more Macs.' Now we will have the added advantage of putting an Apple product in people's hands. If they love it, they'll want to see the rest of the Apple products. But even putting that aside, we felt this opportunity was so big that we were going to go for it." So in early 2002, Jobs okayed a deal with MusicMatch, a company that made a jukebox application for PCs, to provide the software to allow iPods to work on the Windows platform. In July 2002, Apple began selling the first iPods that worked with Windows.

But MusicMatch didn't sync with the iPod nearly as well as iTunes did. Also, because the link between iPods and computers exploited the FireWire technology—included on all Macintoshes but relatively few PCs—Windows users often had to purchase extra hardware to add FireWire to their computers. Above all, using iPods with Windows wasn't an Apple experience. An Apple experience meant you just plugged the little bugger in and everything worked perfectly.

Even worse, iPod Windows users couldn't go to Apple's legal download emporium introduced in 2003, because the store's software was a part of iTunes. Obviously, Apple needed to write iTunes for Windows. This would require the company to produce from scratch a full-fledged Windows application that would not only work seamlessly with iPods but accomplish what the Cupertino crowd had previously considered impossible: they would have to make a Windows application that was as cool as a Mac app.

"We had a few design goals up front," says Jeff Robbin, the original iTunes designer, who headed the project. "We wanted the iTunes for Windows and the iTunes for Mac to be very, very similar. We wanted the feature sets to be the same, the music source to be the same, the simplicity and ease of use to be the same. Things generally aren't done that way. When you have one and the other, each of them takes the flavor of that particular operating system. But in this one, the Mac version looked great. The challenge for us, that I think we just nailed dead-on, was building a Windows app that Windows users would feel comfortable with but had Apple exceptional user interface and ease of use."

In an uncharacteristic preannouncement of a product, early in 2003 Apple revealed its plans for a Windows version of iTunes, promising its release by the end of the year. There is one constant in the history of software development: projects are always late. Worse, Apple was venturing into the foreign realm of Windows-land—where, all too often, plans for easy-to-use programs go to die. Plenty of skeptics predicted that delivery would come at a later date, maybe the end of the year *after*. But at an Apple event in October, Jobs projected the screen output of a computer running iTunes on the giant display. The translation was so visually faithful to the Mac version, and the way it worked was so similar, that almost nobody noticed that the program was running on a Windows PC. When he announced what was in front of their eyes, even the Mac fans in the room exploded with applause. (Never big on understatement, Jobs called this iTunes the best Windows application ever written.)

That October 2003 event proved a turning point for iPod sales. Less than four months earlier, Apple had announced that it had sold the millionth iPod. After almost two years on the market, this was nice, but nothing to write home about. The iPod had garnered a lot of press, and its users loved it with a passion. But a lot of people reacted as Bill Gates did when I first showed him the iPod. *It's only for Mac?* Now it was for everybody. The new Windows version of the iPod was even free of the FireWire problem, using a lightning-quick version 2.0 of the previously pokey original USB (Universal Serial Bus) standard.

Microsoft professed indifference. "Steve's been good in the minor leagues," Dave Fester, the general manager for Windows Digital Media, told me. "In the major leagues, it's a different game."

Actually, Apple was stepping up to kick Microsoft's butt—and that of everyone else who tried to compete with the iPod—in a way it had never been kicked before. Two years after launch, the iPod market was poised to explode. And helping matters considerably was the fact that no credible competitor had emerged to challenge Apple in the MP3 market. Certainly plenty of companies were trying. Almost all were allied with Apple's archrival in operating systems, Microsoft. The software giant, one of the world's richest companies, was used to winning such long battles by steady improvement and attrition. Its strategy was to exploit the fact that the iPod did not play songs that were encoded in Microsoft's proprietary Windows Media format. The motto it suggested for its confederation of competitors was "PlaysForSure." Considering that the players that displayed that logo were guaranteed *not* to play songs purchased from the Internet store that sold well over two thirds of all legal downloads in the world, this was a rather strange approach.

It is true that Microsoft's task was made more difficult by Steve Jobs's refusal to license the FairPlay digital rights management system. iPods could not play music downloaded from music sites like Rhapsody, Napster, Sony Connect, and Wal-Mart. And MP3 players sold by Creative, Dell, iRiver, Sony, and everyone else could not play the song files downloaded from the iTunes Music Store. Yes, it is possible to work around this limitation—intentionally meant to be a speed bump rather than a firm barrier to copying— but it's a pain in the neck and a time-consuming operation that one shouldn't have to endure when simply wanting to exercise the right to listen to music one paid for, on the device of one's choice.

Jobs has always been unapologetic about this incompatibility, insisting that Apple should not make iPods interoperable with competitors until its customers demand it. I once tried to get him to admit that the limitation was unfriendly to consumers, but he would not budge. He challenged me to provide an example where Apple's actions could harm a listener. Finally I came up with something. "You love Bob Dylan, Steve," I said. "He records with Sony, your competitor in selling music. What if Sony sold a really great, previously unreleased Dylan song on its music store? None of your iTunes customers could download it and listen to it on their computers or iPods. Isn't that a disadvantage?"

"Bob Dylan *loves* us," said Jobs. "He'd never do that."

I thought that was a fairly lame comeback. But a few months later, Dylan did okay the release of two fantastic outtakes from the legendary *Blood on the Tracks* sessions for online sale—on the iTunes store, not his own label Sony's store.

iPod's other competition falls into several camps. First are the Asian electronics firms, spearheaded by Creative, which is headquartered in Singapore, though it has research and development labs in Silicon Valley. Its founder, a heavily caffeinated businessman named Sim Wong Hoo, had an attitude toward Apple that is common among the Asian MP3 makers who have been thoroughly trounced by the Cupertino juggernaut: grudging admiration, heavily mixed with festering resentment and more than a bit of denial. "I think Steve Jobs is a personality we all have to reckon with," said Sim when I spoke with him in early 2005. "The way he deals with the media and all these things is legendary. But he was not the first to come out with an MP3. We started way back, in 1999, when the players were thirty-two megabytes [barely enough for an album's worth of songs] and had to plug into the printer port. So we paid our school fees in the early days, and those fees were well spent."

What Sim and his compatriots don't get is that the iPod is more than just a hunk of electronics, not just an MP3 player but an elusive mix of style, performance, and status. When companies like Creative think of improvements to their products, they figure out how to put more capacity in them, extend battery life, make more colors, add in FM radios. But they don't make iPods, and people know it.

The other rivals include PC companies. Because digital music players are actually tiny computers, it is no surprise that the firms that make Windows machines felt they could produce models that would outsell Apple just as Windows outsells Macintosh. The most prominent of these challengers was Dell Computer, whose CEO had kindly suggested to Steve Jobs in 1997 that he disband the company and return any cash left over to the losers who held shares in it. Dell had enjoyed a spectacular success in the PC business by keeping its margins down to sell well-made, fairly generic computers at prices its competitors couldn't match. The same thinking lay behind Dell's music strategy. The Dell DJ might look like a cigarette-box-sized version of its yawnworthy computer boxes—it was designed and produced offshore by some nameless electronics house—but when it played "Hey Ya!" it sounded just like the iPod playing "Hey Ya!" So the fact that the Dell DJ held as much music as iPods for a lower cost, had a longer battery life, and worked with Windows machines indicated to Dell's executives that they had a shot at slowing down the iPod juggernaut. Dell's marketing geniuses concocted a campaign that asked Apple users to send Dell their iPods in exchange for a $100 rebate on a Dell DJ. "We think they'll be willing to forgo the color pink for a battery that lasts," said Dell spokesperson Colleen Ryan. "Style is nice, but function and value are what ultimately matter to consumers."

What mattered to consumers was iPod. Dell put the hard-disk-based DJ out of its misery in early 2006.

Another potential competitor, Hewlett-Packard, didn't bother going through the stages of denial. At the January 2004 Consumer Electronics Show, HP's CEO and corporate diva, Carly Fiorina, announced with much fanfare that since in her judgment even a tremendously innovative company like her own could not beat the iPod, it would *join* the iPod; in fact, HP had cut a deal with Apple to sell iPods under its own brand name. I spoke to her in a quiet room off the bustling show floor just after HP went public with the deal. According to Fiorina—a tightly wound but impeccably prepared interview subject—it was part of a strategy called "focused innovation." As best I could tell, this translated to strategic withdrawal when someone beats you to the punch. It would have been interesting to hear her comments on the irony of yielding in a category that her company had actually invented, but Fiorina appeared to have no idea that the actual innovation of the "music library in your pocket" MP3 player had been created in 1998 by the Compaq corporation, which HP had recently taken over—or that she owned the rights to the ill-fated Personal Jukebox along with some patents that might have given her extra leverage with Apple. Instead, she said, "We looked at the music world and said that this is the best device out there. What we can do is bring it to the mass market."

I got a glimpse into the star-crossed nature of the relationship between Apple and HP on the very day the companies announced the deal. When I'd asked Fiorina who would decide the color of the, um, hPod, she'd responded instantly, "We do." In fact, she promised that HP would sell a *blue* iPod, which was quite a departure from the shocking neutrality that Apple's design guru Jony Ive had established as a trademark look for the device. But a few hours after my conversation with Fiorina at the Las Vegas Convention Center, I was on the phone with Steve Jobs. Steve, I asked, does this deal allow HP to determine the color of the iPods it'll sell? "We'll see," he said with the gravity of an executioner. When the HP iPod came out half a year later, it was the same bright white as the Apple version.

Fiorina had assumed that HP would be able to do what Apple could not: distribute the iPod widely, through its relationship with

10,000 retail outlets, including Radio Shack stores. But as the iPod became more popular, the big electronics chains like Circuit City and Best Buy needed iPods for coolness cred, so they dealt with Apple directly. At its peak the hPod accounted for only about 10 percent of iPod sales. In early 2005, Fiorina was gone, and later that year HP announced the end of its iPod deal.

What about Sony? If any company could have been expected to launch a challenge to the iPod's dominance, it was the elite, stylish Tokyo electronics giant. The Sony stylists had invented personal audio, and they even owned one of the major music labels! So why wasn't the Walkman of the twenty-first century created by the company that invented the Walkman of the twentieth century?

Sadly, Sony in 2000 was far from the nimble enterprise run by its visionary cofounders. Its divisions operated separately; its best software people had nothing to do with the electronics division, which in turn had nothing to do with the entertainment divisions. Sony's leader Howard Stringer contemptuously called these divisions "silos" and charged that they drained the company's energies and thwarted innovation. In short, Sony entered the battle for digital dominance as a weak, conflicted giant. When the iPod appeared, the company really didn't get what had hit it. After much delay, it finally produced a digital Walkman, but it was so hard to get music on it that the device was almost unusable. Because of Sony's fears of piracy, it didn't even play songs in the most popular format, MP3— an MP3 player that couldn't play MP3s! Stringer himself used the word "crisis" to describe what happened when the weaknesses of Sony's digital music player were exposed by the iPod. But Stringer, after assuming the CEO post in 2005, tried to remain hopeful, even as Apple was selling the bulk of the world's MP3 players, and Sony's market share scraped along in single digits. "We don't quite give up on the iPod," he told me. But when I asked him whether it might be too late to gain against iPod by simply improving Sony's digital Walkman products, he couldn't maintain that charade. "I don't know," he said with a sigh that implied that he did know—all too well.

Even Apple's executives can't quite believe their good fortune at the pratfalls and shortcomings of their competitors. "When we came out with the iPod," says Jon Rubinstein, "we thought we would have a year lead on Sony and everyone else. We didn't figure it was going to be five years. That was *never* in our thinking. It was always 'Okay, we own *this* Christmas, but next year they're coming after us.' And so we always acted as if the competition were right there and ready to overtake us. As the years went on, it's like, 'Okay, we've got *another* Christmas behind us.' "

It seems that Apple's main competition was itself. Every time it announced a new generation of iPod, those who had recently purchased the previous model would curse themselves for poor timing. A lot of spouses, nephews, nieces, and old college buddies found themselves recipients of slightly used iPods when lustful owners rushed to buy the new models.

Sometimes, though, people were compelled to buy a new one because the old models simply broke down. Though Apple was diligent about replacing broken iPods during the one-year warranty period, plenty of people became furious when their units came up lame just after expiration. The economics of silicon often made repairing an iPod more expensive than buying a new one. (Some people who have been through a number of models over the past few years call this "the iPod tax." Apple, however, has always insisted that its products' breakdown rate is no worse than similar products'.) The touchiest problem had to do with the battery. Not long after the warranty period of the first wave of iPods ended, a lot of people seemed to be unhappy with what they claimed was too short a period before the battery had to be recharged.

"Lithium ion batteries have time cycle limits, and they degrade over time," says Jon Rubinstein, Apple's hardware leader, who became the head of a new iPod division of the company in 2004. "The battery should last for years if you use it in a rational fashion." Apple maintains that iPod batteries will lose 20 percent of their charge after four hundred charges.

It turned out the problem for some people was a software glitch that made iPods behave as if their batteries had prematurely run out of juice. Before Apple sent out a patch to fix the problem, thousands of people attempted to perform a rough kind of surgery on their iPods that required cracking open the case. Others may simply have had a faulty battery.

It's unclear exactly what the problem was with filmmaker Casey Neistat's battery, but this glitch was one that wound up biting Apple back. Neistat had owned his iPod for a year and a half and was frustrated because he was getting less than an hour of use before the 'pod went dead. "I called Apple and asked them to replace the battery," he said. "They told me, don't replace it, get a new [iPod]." Neistat was so outraged that he and his filmmaking partner, his brother Van, decided to make a protest movie about Apple's intransigence—sort of a geeky *Fahrenheit 9/11* about the iPod's battery life. Just before Christmas 2003, the brightly colored posters of silhouetted iPod users dancing madly to the music piped into their heads were all over New York City. Working on a budget of about forty dollars, the Neistats filmed *The iPod's Dirty Secret*. The short film began with a taped call to Apple support, where Casey outlined his problem and the Apple rep could be heard saying it would cost $255 plus handling charges to refurbish the iPod, "but at that price you may as well get a new one." The rest of the film showed Casey Neistat defacing iPod posters with graffiti, a stencil reading IPOD'S UNREPLACEABLE BATTERY LASTS ONLY 18 MONTHS, all to the tune of a catchy hip-hop song. At the end of the movie, the filmmakers noted that the film had been edited with Apple's iMovie program.

The Neistats finished in mid-November 2003. "I posted it on a Sunday, and I got really excited when it got up to a hundred downloads," says Casey Neistat. "By the end of the day it was up to, like, three hundred, and I was like, 'Wow, that's amazing.' And the following day when I woke up, it was up to 40,000." Soon news organizations—ever anxious to document anything to do with iPod—began to pick up on the phenomenon, and the Neistats were on CBS and Fox, and in *Rolling Stone* and *The Washington Post*. Eventually the movie was downloaded more than a million times.

Within a few days after *Dirty Secret* was eating up bandwidth on the Net, Apple announced its new policy about batteries and warranties: users could send iPods back to Apple to replace the battery for a charge of $99. (It was later reduced to $59, plus a $6.95 shipping fee.) Also, iPod buyers could extend their warranties for another year for $59. Apple claims that the new policy had been in the works for a while. Van Neistat, however, might be right when he says, "I think we sped them up." On December 23, Casey Neistat e-mailed Jobs and asked him if he thought Apple had made a mistake with its original policy. Jobs's complete reply:

> *Nope, I don't think Apple made a mistake.*
> *Steve.*

Later, some lawyers in California organized a class action suit over the battery life; Apple settled, making a bundle for the lawyers and providing a $50 discount coupon for early iPod owners who bothered to fill out some complicated forms. Between that settlement and the new replacement policy, the battery flap burned itself out.

None of those controversies slowed down the iPod craze in the least. By 2004, iPods had attained a rare sort of ubiquity. Apple's "whole widget" strategy had paid off, as the iPod was now a solid three-pronged system of player, software, and online store. New models like the iPod mini and fourth-generation iPod, with a click wheel that embedded the buttons on the circular control, were so exciting that a lot of people who owned earlier iPods bought the spiffy new versions. Apple had created a Windows version of the iPod that was as easy to use as the Mac version. The iTunes Music Store was the hottest place for digital music. And with Apple's Day-Glo marketing, the incessant free publicity of a media gone mad with iPod fever, and the fierce word of mouth from ecstatically satisfied customers, it was like the mother of all tipping points. Sometime that year, the iPod moved from a cool thing owned by someone you knew to something that you had to own yourself.

The momentum was such that even the cottage industry of people making accessories for iPods—not only skins and cases but electronic add-ons like radios, microphones, and devices where you plugged the iPod into something with speakers—was outgrowing any imaginable cottage. Though small players still tried to turn a buck with products like the waterproof iPod case (in case you couldn't live without your playlists while scuba diving on the Great Barrier Reef), big companies like Bose were jumping in. Even BMW got in the game, as one of the first auto manufacturers offering customized iPod interfaces to its stereo systems. (By 2005, a third of all auto manufacturers would provide iPod interfaces in their cars.) Kolcraft made an iPod baby stroller. Hearing aid manufacturers changed course by offering $1,000 in-ear iPod head-phones. The industry of add-ons came to be a billion-dollar-plus enterprise that some called "the iPod Economy."

All of this was becoming clear by the spring of 2004. Jobs himself noticed the shift one day in New York City. "It was on Fifty-seventh Street, or maybe it was on Madison. On every block there were one or two people wearing white headphones. And I thought, 'Oh, my God, it's really starting to happen.' "

Hard numbers backed up the impression. In the holiday season of 2003, Apple sold 730,000 iPods. The expectation was that during the following few months, the sales would be flat at best, since, after all, people were no longer buying Christmas presents for family and friends. But in the next quarter sales went *up*—people bought 807,000 iPods in the dreary winter months of January, February, and March 2004. And they kept buying, until the holidays came around again—and Apple sold four and a half million iPods in the last three months of that year. What happened after that seasonal buying orgy? *Another* gain during the so-called dead months—more than five million iPods sold. The iPod's momentum was such that *every* quarter was Christmas.

You would think that a run like that would pause to take a breath, and certainly a willingness by the company to ride with the most successful versions of the iPod. But that was not what Jobs had in mind. Jobs has instituted a periodic meeting of what he calls the Apple 100. Ever the elitist, he describes those invited as not the highest-ranking executives on the organizational charts but the *really key* people, the people, he says, who you'd take on the life raft with you when the ship was sinking (presumably everyone else would go down in the drink). "I usually get up in the beginning," Jobs says, "and say something like 'Our revenues have doubled in the last two years. And our stock price is high and our shareholders are happy. And a lot of people think it's really great, we've got a lot to lose, let's play it safe. *That's the most dangerous thing we can do.* We have to get *bolder,* because we have world-class competitors now and we just can't stand still.' "

Then Steve Jobs told the hundred what he intended to do. Even though Apple had created one of the most successful consumer electronic products in history and the most popular of those was the tiny iPod mini, he was going to pull the plug on it—and make something *better.* "We are going to redefine the whole industry," he told his people. "By coming up with a player that's a full-featured iPod, color display, a click wheel, dock connector, photos, everything—at a size that completely changes the rules."

The opportunity he saw was to replace the iPod mini's hard drive with chips that used a technology called "flash memory." Unlike the random access memory (RAM) that temporarily holds data in a computer, flash memory retains the information stored on it even when the device is turned off. In that respect, it works just like a hard drive, but it has the advantage of taking up less space and using less energy (no moving parts). It was a fairly expensive technology, but in the manner of all digital devices, its cost was coming down dramatically, making possible, for instance, new products like those cunning little "thumb drives" that you can jack into your computer to load up with files for backup or sharing. The iPod shuffle used flash memory, and those chips were the main cost to Apple, the reason why Apple charged $99 for a player that stored only 240 songs. Now Jobs felt that he could get a price for flash memory to stuff an iPod with enough chips to store a *thousand* songs, the same number that the original iPod held. He envisioned a player that would have all the great features of its bigger brothers—a sharp color screen, a click wheel, built-in games, the capability to program a playlist on the go. And Jobs—ever the fetishist for miniaturization—wanted to make the tiniest jewel of a player ever. "We *might* be able to do it," he says, reconstructing his thought process. "There *might* be enough flash in the world. We *might* be able to design a click wheel that thin. There *might* be the engineering to do this." He cut a deal with the Korean electronics giant Samsung to buy billions of dollars' worth of flash memory, locking up the bulk of its output until 2008. He retooled his factories to stop making minis and to begin making the new iPod . . . so small it was called the nano. (The prefix "nano" means one billionth.) "We call this a heart transplant—stop one production line and start another."

The iPod nano was so beautiful that it seemed to have dropped down from some vastly advanced alien civilization. It had the breathtaking compactness of a lustrous Oriental artifact. It wasn't really much bigger than a large mint left on your pillow at a fine hotel. Measured sideways, it was .27 inch, slimmer than a pencil. But it was a full-featured iPod that stored as much music as the original. Jonathan Ive had enveloped it in a shiny shell—ebony or ivory—and the tiny, full-color screen glowed like a gemstone. "I remember going over the model with Jon," says Jobs. "We were giddy. People had told us it was impossible when we showed them the layouts. This was not easy, but we pulled it off." Even though the nano held fewer songs than the mini, the thousand songs it did hold were plenty enough for most people. And at $249 (only $199 for a version that held five hundred songs), it was ideally priced as an impulse buy or a gift. Reports came in of kids getting six or seven nanos at bar mitzvahs—and not complaining.

Jobs was exultant. "I don't think there was another company in the world that could have pulled this off," he said at the launch, which featured a performance by Kanye West.

A month later, Jobs introduced the fifth generation of the

full-size iPod, the first to display video. So Apple entered the final quarter of 2005 with a totally revamped roster of iPods, essentially owning the exploding category of digital music devices. Analysts went wild trying to guess how many Apple might sell during the Christmas shopping season. Was it possible that Apple could sell 10 million during those three months?

Earlier in the year, Apple's top executives had been heatedly discussing that very matter. It was betting time; the company had to put in the orders that would determine how many millions of iPods the factories in Asia would produce. For instance, the flash memory chips inside the nano had to be ordered six months in advance. How optimistic could Apple dare to be, knowing that ordering too much would result in an inventory disaster, while ordering too few would mean only that some money was left on the table.

"I was one of the more aggressive folks in the room," Jobs explained. "We had already made a decision to revamp most of our iPod product line right before the holidays. Those were actually even bigger decisions, because if something had gone wrong and we couldn't have ramped them, it would have been zero—we would have had a lot of sets of parts sitting around. Given the attempt to do that, my feeling was, if we were a little too aggressive [in ordering for the holidays], they would still sell. They were the best products we ever made. So we sat around and had some meaningful discussions about what that number should be, and we ended up picking the highest of the numbers. I was willing to be pretty aggressive."

How aggressive? Apple ordered enough to supply its stores and retailers with *14 million* iPods. "You've got to admit," he told me, "picking 14 million in the spring of 2005, when the most you've ever sold in a quarter was four and a half million, was a pretty big bet. I was very happy with that number. But it turned out that that number was too low. *It wasn't big enough.*"

Yes, Apple sold 14 million iPods during the last three months of 2005. Forty-two million iPods had been sold by the end of that year. (The number would reach 58 million by mid-2006.)

Of $5 billion in revenues Apple garnered in the final quarter, less than 40 percent came from the Macintosh business. Thanks to the iPod, 61 percent came from Apple's music business. This was Jobs's legacy: in his first four years back, he had transformed Apple from a marginal player capitalizing on its past glories into the premier innovator in a personal computer industry that had lost its way. In his next four years, he had transmogrified the firm from a niche player in the computer world to a dominant force in consumer electronics—a company that made most of its revenues from music.

Jobs is still committed to the Macintosh, and he takes particular delight in the fact that its operating system consistently out-innovates Microsoft's. He is not shy in claiming that Apple is the only company taking big risks and accomplishing some magic in the personal computer world. He thinks he knows why. "I think back to Detroit in the seventies, when cars were so bad," he says. "Why? The people running the companies then didn't love cars. One of the things wrong with the PC industry today is that most of the people running the companies don't love PCs. Does Steve Ballmer [Microsoft] love PCs? Does Craig Barrett [Intel] love PCs? Does Michael Dell love PCs? If [Michael Dell] wasn't selling PCs he'd be selling something else. These people don't love what they create." Jobs paused for effect. "And people here do."

For the record, none of those three guys has anything but good feelings about PCs. But only Apple's products look as though they were conceived out of love.

On January 13, 2006, something interesting came to Jobs's attention. At Wall Street's close on that Friday afternoon, Apple's market capitalization had reached $72.13 billion. What made it a milestone to Jobs was that the cap of Dell Computers at that moment was $71.97 billion—almost a million dollars less. Recalling Dell's advice almost a decade earlier, the Apple CEO was moved to send out a companywide e-mail. "Team," he wrote his employees, "it turned out that Michael Dell wasn't perfect at predicting the future."

Podcast

❯Early in my career, I wrote a cover story for *The Philadelphia Inquirer*'s Sunday magazine about citizens band radio. Believe it or not, for a little while in the mid-1970s, a lot of people thought that CB radio was going to be a disruptive technology that would democratize aural media and otherwise change the way we work, play, and amuse ourselves.

For those who don't remember—or weren't born yet—let me explain. For years, many long-haul truck drivers had limited-range two-way radios in their cabs. They operated in a zone of the radio spectrum that was not licensed to Big Broadcasting but reserved for the casual use of travelers—thus the name "citizens band." Mostly the conversations were prosaic exchanges involving the amenities of upcoming truck stops, the location of active state troopers, and, on occasion, the availability of hookers. At most, when two or three drivers were moving roughly in sync along some interstate, they would conduct a desultory conversation as they roared along the predawn highways.

In the mid-seventies, nontruckers began installing CB radios in their cars and started conversing in the distinctive CB jargon, a mix of cop argot and redneck slang. In 1976, the government lifted the requirement that operators needed a license to use CB (millions of people were ignoring the rule, anyway). Suddenly CB was everywhere. Two-way radios dominated the Consumer Electronics Show that year. And as the fad caught fire—complete with hit records and Hollywood movies extolling the phenomenon—people began to speculate that the CB could go beyond the highway and actually become a broadcast medium of some sort . . . a *people's* medium. Everyone would be a minibroadcaster, beaming messages and making friends of strangers in the nearby geographic vicinity—on CB. Ten-four, good buddy!

This was a lovely vision, but there were only forty channels on the CB band, which meant that it really couldn't scale to mass use. Also, there was no way to tell whether you might be interested in what was going on at any time or on any channel of CB. You never knew when anything interesting was occurring, and most of the time you scanned the channels all you heard was the lame drawl of suburbanites trying to pass themselves off as truckers. (You also heard a lot of static.) My own article, thank God, avoided the impulse to embrace CB as the next big thing, and, as we all know now, citizens band radio turned out to be a passing fad. In a few years, just about all of the millions of CB radios that had been sold were pitched into Dumpsters. Every so often one appears—a wallflower at the garage sale—and once again I recall that madness-of-crowds moment. But the impulse that lurked behind the excitement was a profound one: Wouldn't it be great to have a medium where anyone could have the reach of a broadcaster?

Twenty years later, the Internet became the communications trend *du jour,* and even wilder predictions were made about its future. We know now that every optimistic prognostication made during the early nineties about the Internet, no matter how outlandish, underestimated what actually happened. No one back then dared to claim that within a decade a billion people would be connected, that many times more e-mails than letters would be sent, that the biggest stores in the world would have no walls, that your grandmother would routinely swap digital photos with your children, that the most popular way to find a mate would be online, or that if you wanted to find even the most obscure fact in the history of civilization—something that an Indiana Jones of information sciences would previously have had to dig through the dusty stacks of all the libraries of the world to find—all you needed to do was type your query into a blank line and in four tenths of a second the answer would appear. You couldn't *imagine* stuff like that back then. Instead, supposedly wide-eyed oracles like myself would be sitting on a panel, taking a deep breath before we pronounced that one day maybe *a hundred million* people would be on the Net, and, yes, one day every person in this audience might have an e-mail address! Invariably someone would smirk at such lunacy—a fad, they'd say, millennial pap! Remember CB radio?

Obviously, the Internet did what CB radio could not and is no more a fad than were language, musical instruments, and indoor plumbing. But as the twenty-first century began, the Internet had not yet fulfilled the dream of CB radio: a people's form of broadcasting. Publishing of the *written* word, yes—it was easy to start a Web site, and the nascent blogging movement made it possible to distribute one's prose worldwide with a single mouse click. But when it came to empowering potential Edward R. Murrows or Howard Sterns, nothing was happening.

Until the iPod.

Early in its brief history, the iPod proved itself a worthy vehicle for spoken-word applications. A New Jersey company called Audible, which at the time included Microsoft as a minority owner, cut a deal with Apple to handle audiobooks. The deal saved the small company (founded by a talented nonfiction writer jaded by lousy book sales!), which had been struggling to distribute MP3-style files of popular literature. The iPod was a brilliant fit for that medium. It had plenty of room to store the digital files (which could reach monstrous proportions on, say, one of those forty-eight-hour recordings of a Harry Potter book), and the iPod's screen could tell you very clearly which chapter you were on, as well as provide a means to pause the narrative for those beginning to doze off in the middle of Bill Clinton's autobiography. Apple also provided some software enhancements that would resume the performance at the point where you'd previously abandoned it. (A subsequent innovation of iTunes allowed you to speed up the reading without changing the pitch in the speaker's voice—so that Bill Clinton's autobiography would zip by 20 percent less lugubriously.)

Other folks had exploited the iPod for spoken-word uses without any need for Apple's cooperation. Museums found that visitors loved to wander the galleries with iPods preloaded with a running commentary on the displays. Companies catering to travelers began preparing iPod-based tour commentaries so people could walk around strange cities, or parts of their own cities made stranger by weird sound tracks synced to places they wouldn't ordinarily wander, with a savvy guide providing the sotto voce skinny on their locations. A Paris tour, recorded in a Pepe Le Pew French accent, actually gave the code to unlock a private courtyard where you could snoop on the residences within. A Civil War tour of Boston put you in the role of an escaped slave; if you could block out all those people wearing Red Sox caps, the shouts and whip cracks of pursuers would transport you back to the Underground Railway. And what stroll in New York City's meatpacking district would be complete without the woolly sounds of a rough-trade S&M bar?

One of the more audacious spoken-word ventures was the ShasPod. This was a caper hatched by Yehuda Shmidman and Uri Miller, two merchandisers who had gotten rich by licensing rock-and-roll band logos on T-shirts, sold at a huge premium at rock concerts. As former yeshiva boys, the two businessmen knew of a massive event in Orthodox Jewry called Siyum HaShas, a celebration of the completion of the seven-and-a-half-year Daf Yomi (one page a day) cycle, the time it takes to read the sacred Talmud, the extensive commentaries on the Torah that provide a detailed guide to life. The event draws thousands in person (and many more on simulcast around the world), and in 2005 it was coming to New York's Madison Square Garden. "Uri and I were thinking, 'How can we leverage that power?' and thought, 'Hey, what else is powerful in the world? The iPod,' " says Shmidman. He and his partner knew about a set of lectures covering the entire Daf Yomi cycle that had been recorded by a learned rabbi and converted to MP3—more than two thousand hours of commentary—and immediately secured permission to load them onto five hundred iPods that Shmidman was able to buy from an Apple-authorized reseller. They priced a fully loaded iPod for a hundred bucks more than a virgin iPod. They printed brochures (with pictures of a bearded, dark-hatted Orthodox Jew adorned with white earbuds) and secured the use of a newsstand a block away from the venue. The units sold briskly and kept selling after the event on the Internet, especially when the ShasPod was spoofed on *Saturday Night Live* as the "OyPod." "The thing took off," says Shmidman. "It's tremendous access to everyone in the world to study the next Daf Yomi. But the iPod, period, is a draw."

But selling copy-protected audiobooks on the iTunes store, as Audible does, or preloading an iPod with Talmudic content is not quite the same as a broadcasting revolution over the Internet. That distinction would be reserved for a phenomenon whose name says volumes about the power of the device to capture not only digital sound but our imaginations: "podcasting." That word has come to stand for the fulfillment of the promise never made good by CB radio—a wide-open global channel for radio-style content unburdened by high expenses, license requirements, or the Federal Communications Commission.

The term is a bit controversial, because, frankly, the iPod's claim to an Internet-based vocal upheaval is somewhat tenuous. Long before the iPod—years before the existence of any digital music player—*someone* was using the Internet as if it were a mixture of broadcasting and the VCR. This was Carl Malamud, an itinerant tech writer working in Washington, D.C. He was an early Internet proselytizer who in 1992 had just returned from going around the world—three times—to research a book about people involved in building the Net. He would routinely go off to Internet Engineering Task Force meetings, where the pioneers of the global grid would deal in the deep gnarly realm of standards and protocols. At one of these meetings, he now recalls, "I was just looking around and I just thought to myself, there's a lot of really good information at these meetings, and a lot of these guys are really smart—maybe I should just sit down and, like, interview them." His brainstorm was a weekly show where he'd use audio equipment to interview a single Internet figure, whom he would dub "The Geek of the Week." And he'd distribute the show on the Internet itself.

This provided a particular challenge. Very few Internet users at that time had access to the high-powered computer workstations and high-bandwidth data capacity that were required to handle a multimedia file like a radio-style interview. Fortunately, those who did were the target audience for "Geek of the Week": advanced engineers or UNIX system administrators at universities or high-tech companies who sat all day behind powerful Sun workstations. In short, geeks. Convinced that this would be a decent base for his digital broadcasts, Malamud got a $500 digital tape recorder, dropped another couple hundred on a nice stereo condenser microphone, and bought some high-end editing software, all the basic tools to create a digital facsimile of an NPR show's professional sheen. Then he figured out how to compress the interviews into thirty-megabyte files to be loaded to a server. From that point those who had the power and the know-how (the geeks) could download the show using an Internet method called FTP (File Transfer Protocol). Using what was then a very fast connection, it would take two hours or so to download the thirty-minute show.

On the first show, on April Fool's Day 1993, Malamud interviewed an Internet infrastructure wizard named Marshall Rose. There was enough time after the interview for Malamud to include a brief restaurant review.

From the get-go, Malamud had what later podcasters would kill for—a couple of big sponsors. Sun Microsystems and the tech publisher Tim O'Reilly each paid him $10,000 for the first year, and Sun threw in a workstation. Everything went so well that Malamud became ambitious and started to record the lunch programs at the National Press Club. In addition to making them available by FTP, he offered the ability to listen to the speeches live over the Internet—streaming the event as it occurred. The first speaker he captured on those netcasts was, appropriately enough, Vice President Al Gore (who at least never claimed to have invented podcasts). Only Internet sites with the most direct access to the "backbone" (the main connections between big nodes on the Net) and the most sophisticated equipment could get a live feed, and when an Associated Press reporter covering this unusual setup asked Malamud how many people were listening, he checked the logs for a precise answer.

"Six," he admitted. "But they're in four countries."

But the downloads were something else. Malamud estimated that each "Geek of the Week" was heard by between 20,000 and 30,000 people. He essentially transformed his operation into an Internet talk-radio station, streaming live and taped events twenty-four hours a day. Eventually Malamud pulled the plug; people were doing too many other things on the Internet.

But Internet broadcasting—not streaming radio shows in real time (that's Webcasting, dude) but a system that combined radio with VCR-style recording (what we now know as TiVo)—was still a great idea waiting for a revival in the age of Net ubiquity. The idea had even occurred to the researchers at Digital Equipment Corporation who had created the first hard-drive MP3 player, the Personal Jukebox, two years before the iPod. They envisioned a follow-up product to the Personal Jukebox called the Pocket DJ, which would load up on content while the machine was recharging. (One thing that the machine might download would be a set of songs selected according to mood and situation.) One of the Personal Jukebox creators from Digital, Dave Redell, gave a presentation to Compaq executives in 2000. According to Redell, the vice president in charge of division said, "That's like radio. Nobody listens to radio anymore."

That statement might have sounded pretty funny to Adam Curry, who at the time was trying to figure out how to merge radio and the Internet on his own. With chiseled looks and pipes that just oozed the smooth cadences of FM, Curry came off like a former MTV veejay—which he was. He was also a huge fan of the Net and an early enthusiast of the World Wide Web; he even took it upon himself to register the then-available mtv.com domain name. His bosses told him to keep it, as they couldn't imagine a use for it. (Later, of course, they threatened to sue him unless he turned it over.) Curry says that from the day he first saw a modem—it was on a tiny Sinclair ZX80, vintage 1970s—he was excited about the possibilities. "From that point on, whenever I saw a modem, I was always thinking broadcast."

It wasn't until 2000 or so that the chips were powerful enough and the Internet connections fast enough for him to imagine how a radio show could be loaded onto a computer or even a portable device for playback at the listener's leisure. What he settled on was similar to what Malamud and the Personal Jukebox team had envisioned. "If the computer is always on and connected, why don't we drip stuff in as fast as we can get it?" he recalls asking himself. "It will be relatively slow and not fast enough for real-time streaming experience, but if you don't know you're waiting, it doesn't hurt. When it's there, bing! You have something new, and then you can open up a five-hundred-megabyte file, and the radio experience is going to be there."

Curry was nowhere near skilled enough a programmer to set up something like that. It turned out he'd met the perfect guy not long before, at an America Online party: a well-known software designer—a Silicon Valley legend, actually—named Dave Winer.

Winer himself had been a phenom in the early days of personal computing, the creator of the first outlining program. He'd started several companies and now was plumbing the vast resources of the Web to bring about the same kind of personal empowerment that he'd seen in the early days of the PC industry. Make that a *bigger* kind of personal empowerment, because while personal computers bulked up our writing, page-layout, and number-crunching muscles, that was nothing compared to the instant and persistent connections with friends, associates, and undifferentiated masses that the Internet provided. A few years earlier Winer had sent out an e-mail journal to hundreds of people and been amazed at how easy it had been to infect the minds of smart and influential people like Bill Gates (who was on the list and once even replied to Winer) with a low-cost (*no*-cost), simple act. He eventually moved the journal to a Web page, laying claim to the first weblog, or blog, of millions that would follow in a paradigm-shifting personal publishing revolution.

Winer got really turned on by tools and really turned off by behavior that he judged inconsiderate to the community. He was particularly sensitive to historical accounts of software development that shortchanged his contributions. His online dispatches could veer from an ecstatic account of an experience he had had that was made possible by the Web to a profane insult of someone who failed to invite him to speak at a conference. But he deeply believed in the constructive value of collaboration, so when Curry asked to meet him at a New York City hotel one day to discuss a new kind of Internet broadcasting—a mix between blogging and radio—Winer agreed. "He had a simple idea but a very good one, about time shifting," says Winer. "He'd been talking about it to other programmers, but the fact is, since he was like a movie star, they didn't think he knew what the hell he was talking about." But Winer had been working on a Web technology that fit right in with Curry's idea. It was called Really Simple Syndication, or RSS. It allowed people to subscribe to "feeds," digital file deliveries, just as they would subscribe to a magazine. It was like a TiVo for radio shows—except that TiVo hadn't even been let loose yet. "I had the raw materials and could see how to do it," says Winer. "The whole thing was about time shifting, downloading in the middle of the night."

In less than a month, Winer had hacked up a system that could include audio files as "enclosures" into feeds. This would allow people to subscribe to and enjoy MP3 audio files that others might post to their Web sites. But though he put the feature into his company's blogging product—in early 2001 he proved it worked by enclosing a Grateful Dead song in a feed from his own weblog—it wasn't widely noticed. Meanwhile, blogging itself was beginning a wild ride up the S curve of massive adoption. Over the next few years millions of people would take advantage of tools that made it easy to create their own weblogs. They would begin posting endlessly on politics, media criticism, tech arcana, and what their cats were up to. But audio wasn't yet a part of that revolution.

In 2003, however, Curry realized that the missing piece of the puzzle was literally in hand. Curry had gotten an iPod. Suddenly, the idea he had developed with Winer was ready for prime time. The new way to think of this enclosure thing was to regard the entire Web as a decentralized iTunes store, with an unlimited number of Web sites delivering the equivalent of iTunes songs. You could set up your system to automatically download audio files from someone's blog or Web page and have them transferred directly to iTunes. Then the next time you plugged your iPod into the computer, the file would load automatically.

"We had this transport mechanism that worked—and here's the iPod," Curry says. "That was really the big wow factor, when the process was end to end. Someone publishes, and it shows up on my iPod. It's magic."

There was a sense of inevitability to this. Blogging and iPods were a great match, two innovations that had enjoyed a parallel run to glory in the early 2000s. Many people blogged about their iPods—what they were listening to on the 'pod, what color they had chosen for their boyfriend, how they slept with the iPod under their pillow, and how pissed they were that they had bought a new iPod just before Apple released a newer, cooler iteration. ("iPod" was, in fact, the most popular "tag," or category, in the massive blog search engine Technorati.)

Among Apple fans and tech watchers, blogs were often the launching pad for strange iPod-related multimedia expression: miniessays, love letters, and borderline psychotic object worship. People would design exotic "fantasy" iPods. In the days before a Steve Jobs presentation, the blogosphere would be abuzz with swooning speculations about what he might be unveiling. Though cynics sometimes debunked the phenomenon by charging that Apple actually seeded this rumor mill itself to crank up the buzz level to full blast, there is every indication that Steve Jobs wasn't happy about these speculations, especially when the predictions— in some cases, apparently arrived at with the connivance of inside leakers—came close to the mark. He actually sued the college student in charge of the Think Secret Web site for overly prescient prognostications leading up to the launch of the Mac mini computer in January 2005. (In this case, Apple found itself on the wrong side of the free speech divide, its lawyers actually claiming that bloggers "are not legitimate members of the press," and should not be accorded First Amendment rights. A judge rejected that claim. Seems that, in this case, Jobs and his minions were "thinking different" from the Founding Fathers.)

So in a way it made sense that Curry and Winer's scheme for audio distribution should adopt the iPod, the blogosphere's obsession, as the chosen destination for the files. But the big bang came months after Curry first started using the iPod in his scheme, when the plan became *linguistically* linked to the iPod. Once this genre of personal broadcast was called a "podcast," the idea instantly reached escape velocity. How did that name come about? The way Curry remembers it, it happened in September 2004. He had been brainstorming with another radio guy, named Dave Slusher, whose blog was called Evil Genius Chronicles ("a journal of geekery, music and joy"). "We'd been going back and forth, without even speaking to each other directly, but he'd say something on his show, and I'd say something on my show, about what are we gonna call this?" says Curry. "We had 'audio blogs,' 'audio shows,' 'bundles of passion,' all kinds of bad marketing stuff." They learned that a blogger named Danny Gregoire had registered some Internet domain names with variations on the word "podcast." (Dedicated historians of this subject—and there are an alarming number of them—have tracked down the original utterance of the word to a British journalist the previous February.) When Curry learned about this, he says, "I went, like, 'Yeah! That's it, *podcast.*' And of course, you know, the debate immediately began that all this was about MP3s and you didn't have to use iPods. But the term had already caught fire. It was a sexy word, it was the right thing, and it just took off."

That's something of an understatement.

By the time podcasting got its name in September 2004, Winer, Curry, and a few others were going full blast with the system. Almost every day Curry would do a podcast he called "Daily Source Code." It would last anywhere from a few minutes to more than an hour. He would share details of his life, play interesting mash-ups he'd heard on the Internet, and spend a lot of time talking about the new medium he was trying out, tracking its progress as other people tried it, too. (Podcasting is no exception to the rule stipulating that the content of any new medium suffers from a preponderance of discussion about the medium itself.) Sometimes he'd go for a walk, taking his microphone and digital tape recorder with him, capturing the actual sounds of his perambulations, and ad-libbing riffs on the sights he encountered, as if channeling Geraldine Chaplin's logorrheic BBC reporter in *Nashville.* He called these "shadowcasts." Meanwhile, Dave Winer had already been doing his own podcast, "Morning Coffee Notes." Dictated in ultra-informal style, it was a window flung open into Winer's mind, full of explanations of various Internet protocols and development tools he was working on, as well as incendiary commentary on the tech world. Many of the shows were recorded behind the wheel of a car, as Winer, who seemed to be running his company while on an endless cross-country trek, kept listeners informed about the traffic jams and tollbooths he encountered, often shutting down his rambling monologue when he pulled into a Denny's for breakfast.

To bloggers, particularly a loose group of "alpha bloggers" whose commentary provided a consistent barometer to the tech world, podcasting was a stunning realization of the democratization of media that the Internet represented. Bloggers had already been feeling their oats by increasingly frequent forays into "fact-checking the media's ass" as well as pounding away at hot buttons the media was ignoring—until the din from cyberspace infected the national conversation. The blogosphere's wide belt sported notches for the takedowns of big targets like Senator Trent Lott and Dan Rather. Now here was a chance to take credit for spreading an entire *medium*. The alpha bloggers not only spewed out podcasts, but they promoted one another's podcasts and yakked incessantly about the promise of podcasting. And then they began keeping score at how quickly the news spread. Remember, before the summer of 2004, the word "podcast" didn't exist. Just after the autumnal equinox a Google search on the word "podcast" yielded exactly twenty-four hits. But alpha blogger Doc Searls knew that would change. "Podcasting will shift much of our time away from an old medium where we wait for what we *might* want to hear to a new medium where we choose *what* we want to hear, *when* we want to hear it, and *how* we want to give everybody else the option to listen to it as well," he wrote in his blog on September 28. While Searls noted that at the time he was writing his post, the Google search brought only two dozen links, he predicted, "A year from now, it will pull up hundreds of thousands, or perhaps even millions."

Searls and his fellow bloggers kept talking about podcasts, tracking their viral spread, and obsessively pinging Google to see how many links would be associated with the word at that moment. By early October, there were 2,700 results. Within a couple of weeks, the numbers hit six figures, and by the end of the year, the word "podcast" was on millions of Web pages. I plugged it into Google in March 2006 and pulled up 215 million search results.

During this amazing run-up, Apple itself had remained silent on the issue, and podcasters were wondering how the phenomenon was regarded in Cupertino. Before I went to talk to Steve Jobs in January 2005 for our usual Macworld Conference & Expo postkeynote discussion, Steve Gillmor, the host of a popular techrelated podcast, begged me to ask what the Apple leader thought of the subject. The question had already been on my punch sheet. *What do you think of podcasting, Steve?* "I think it's cool," said Jobs. "As long as people aren't sharing stolen music, I think it's great. I don't listen to them routinely, but I download some now and then. It's basically turning people into radio stations, which is wonderful."

Jobs would listen to a lot more over the next few months, as podcasting grew even bigger, adopted more and more by mainstream media. The iTunes team began to work on a new version of iTunes and the iTunes store to accommodate the phenomenon. At *The Wall Street Journal's* "D" (All Things Digital) Conference that June, Jobs introduced a new version of iTunes that handled podcasts, distributed via the iTunes store. Anyone could submit a podcast to Apple, which would perform minimal screening before listing it. As usual, Apple had made it easier for people to perform what had previously been a gnarly task. With a single button you could subscribe to a podcast, and from then on, every time you opened up iTunes, the new shows would automatically be downloaded and sent directly into iTunes. The next time you hooked up your iPod, the podcasts would be quickly transported over. Podcast old-timers might gripe that all this stuff could have been done before by simply going to Web sites and enlisting to receive RSS feeds, but the fact is that for millions of people that process is hopelessly complicated. In fact, the very idea of parsing the concept of an RSS feed is so inherently geeky that it's ridiculous to assume that the mass market will attempt it. The proof of this was in podcasting numbers before and after Apple's easy-to-use entry got into the game.

The version of iTunes that included podcasting came out on June 28, 2005. By the first of July, users had downloaded a million podcasts. "We really do see this as the next generation of radio," Apple's Greg Joswiak gushed to me. "That said, a million podcasts in two days really staggered us." Professional tech prognosticators were bullish on podcasts: a Diffusion Group digiswami proclaimed that by 2010, 57 million people would be downloading podcasts. (A Forrester Research analyst weighed in with a more modest estimate of 30 million.)

In the first wave of Apple's hosting, some obscure podcasts got sudden exposure. For instance, I was browsing among the selections when I came across the podcasts of a rabid Philadelphia Eagles fan in Seattle, Washington, who put together a weekly show under the Philadelphia Eagles Podcast Network. (The NFL, not quite knowing what to make of this, initially sent him a cease-and-desist letter, charging that he was violating their trademark. He was compelled to run elaborate disclaimers confirming that he was not part of the professional football machine—a concession *The Philadelphia Inquirer* has never had to make.) If in some barroom I'd overheard this schmoe's endless musings on Terrell Owens's misbehavior and the depth problem on the defensive line, I'd have dismissed him as just another guy who needs a life. But for a couple of weeks I became hooked on his podcasts, which I usually played while enduring the congestion on a crowded airplane. Clearly he had spent hours attempting as slick a production as an amateur could muster, but because he was not a reporter and had no inside access to players or coaches, or even any particular expertise at gridiron analysis, he had very little in the way of illuminating information to impart. Yet as a fellow expatriate who hoped the best from a hometown franchise—and knew in his heart of hearts that a return to the Super Bowl was as likely as finding a decent cheese steak joint in Seattle—there was a melancholy that I connected with, and I devoured his increasingly panicked (as the training camp situation deteriorated) dispatches.

The progress of podcasts followed the earlier evolutionary path of Web sites from fringe to mainstream, this time at a rate so accelerated that it was almost a blur. One day the most popular podcasts were quirky homegrown productions like "Dawn and Drew," by a wacky postpunk married couple living in a Wisconsin farmhouse, and "Madge Goldberg," a broadly performed transvestite parody of a home show. (Curry and Winer apparently didn't get the joke and, when they were told about it, did a podcast themselves that attacked Madge for insufficient comedic disclosure.) On what seemed like the very next day, people were downloading podcasts from *The New York Times*, National Public Radio, and Major League Baseball. It was almost if every media outlet had to have a podcast, right away. But more important, it also seemed as though everyone wanted to be a media outlet—and could be, too. Farmers could download "DTN Week in Review," a thirty-minute summary of agricultural news stories. The former vice presidential candidate John Edwards and his wife, Elizabeth, began a podcast to discuss politics and family issues.

One might have expected the new, more professional podcasts to overwhelm the upstarts. But a funny thing happened: while the NPR podcasts dominated the popularity lists, the Dawn and Drews of the world were also well represented. When performers like Liz Phair began podcasting their backstage ramblings (along with a sloppily rendered song or two), that didn't drive out the more obscure musical podcasting pioneers like the Lascivious Biddies, a show-tune-style singing contingent who let would-be fans eavesdrop on the tour bus and share gossip about the group. It really was possible for someone to grab some podcasting software, make a radio show, and find a niche audience among the millions of people scrounging for something new to hear on their iPods.

No new technology would be complete, of course, without a thriving porn component, and podcasting didn't disappoint on this front. A woman named Violet Blue hosted "Open Source Sex," reading ear-blistering erotica in her podcasts; a former phone-sex operator answered e-mailed sex questions in "MXL (Maximum Libido) Podcast." Apple labeled some of these "explicit," as it does with filthy-mouth songs sold on iTunes; others were removed altogether. But *The Wall Street Journal* reported that of six thousand podcasts listed on iTunes in July 2005, "Open Source Sex" was the twenty-first most subscribed to, beating ESPN, ABC News, and my employer, *Newsweek*. Even Dawn and Drew did a podcast where the couple simulated conjugal relations.

Podcasting also gave an infusion of energy to a trend that had begun a year earlier: integrating iPods into education. In the fall of

2004, with much fanfare, Duke University provided a new 4G pod to every incoming freshman. The idea was that instructors would tailor their curriculum in ways that would exploit the iPod as a sort of minicoursebook and scheduler. Few did. After podcasting caught on, though, it suddenly dawned on academia that iPods could be a valuable out-of-the-classroom tool, a handy means to play back lectures without the stigma of wonkiness that usually accrues to those apple-polishers who make sure they absorb every word the professor utters. Dozens of universities, including Stanford and the University of Missouri, posted podcasts of hundreds of classroom lectures to a new part of the Apple Web site, "iTunes U," which allowed for a controlled distribution (you can limit access to students enrolled in the course, all matriculating students, an extended community including alumni, or anyone who wants to hear a Flaubert critique or undergo a virtual calculus boot camp). It also provided technical support for novice 'pod users, a blessing to overwhelmed campus IT troops.

The prime use of edu-'pods was in time-shifting, essentially allowing students to blow off a class (or relive it) as if it were a TV show to be TiVo'ed. Some institutions, like the University of Michigan's School of Dentistry, quickly got it down to a science. Explains Michigan's director of dental informatics, Lynn Johnson, "A student starts a script at the beginning of the class, and the lecture is automatically recorded through the PA system and fed to the mixer. At the end of the lecture, the student enters the metadata—the name of the class and instructor—and the file is immediately uploaded to the school's area, on iTunes. Four minutes after the class is over, the file is ready for downloading to the students' iPods."

Little-known Georgia College and State University, with only five thousand students on its Milledgeville campus, a hundred miles south of Atlanta, became an unlikely leader in putting podcasting at the center of its educational efforts. One professor (nick-named "the podfather" for his geeky mastery) packed in hours of relevant information for a student trip abroad—undergrads would wander the Prado in Madrid with his lecture as their sound track. A psychology professor made a podcast of the week's most asked questions about the subject material. Another psych professor made weekly podcasts of postings to a blog that commented on the course work. Eventually a third of the faculty wound up incorporating iPods into their class activities.

Schools made use of iPods beyond their pedagogy as well; a small college, Mansfield University in Pennsylvania, made self-promoting podcasts to distribute to potential recruits. Corporations also liked the idea of using podcasting to disseminate company news (and generally do some cheerleading) to employees. National Semiconductor, for instance, decided in 2006 to bestow 30-gig fifth-generation iPods on all 8,500 of its workers. "We're looking for new and more effective ways to communicate with our employees," said Brian Halla, CEO of National. "The iPods will help us do both."

Like blogging, podcasting found itself cast in the role of a democratizing agent in politically oppressed countries—not just as a means of broadcasting dissent but as a subtly empowering baby step toward free expression that begins with the ability to share one's personal and professional interests with potentially huge audiences. In 2005 *New York Times* columnist Thomas Friedman reported that a Shanghai-based Web site, www.toodou.com, was letting a thousand podcasts bloom—with hopes, said its founder, Gary Wang, a U.S.-educated Chinese engineer, of "hundreds of thousands of different channels, maintained by average people." (*Toodou,* by the way, means "potato" in Chinese.) "We all want to be seen and heard and be able to create stuff we like and share it," Wang told Friedman.

Even the Vatican got into the act, as its radio station produced a series of regular religious podcasts, some of which were preloaded on an iPod nano presented to the pope. By then, hundreds of pastors, priests, and rabbis were routinely distributing their sermons via iTunes in a phenomenon someone dubbed "godcasting."

And on August 7, 2005, the astronaut Steve Robinson, on the space shuttle *Discovery*, did the first podcast from outer space. It was a day after he stepped into the void to check out damage on the shuttle's skin. "We sure didn't expect that big piece of foam to come off of the tank," he said in his podcast. "Fortunately, it missed us."

By October 2005, audio podcasts were well integrated into the media food chain, an astounding rise for a technology that had barely been named a year before. But Steve Jobs had scheduled another launch. It was an unusually short time before the previous big day for Apple—just a month earlier, Jobs had unveiled the iPod nano, an irresistible waferlike device that could fit inside your palm yet held as many songs as the original iPod. That had been a big deal, yet here he was again. Web sites were buzzing with speculation that this event would announce the launch of an upgrade to the full-size flagship 'pod—possibly even something that would play video.

Indeed, Jobs rolled out the fifth-generation iPod that day. (Should I list all the generations of iPods here? This *is* a book about iPods, so here goes. First there was iPod classic, with a mechanical wheel that moved when your thumb moved. The second gen had Windows compatibility and a digital scroll wheel that didn't move but sensed when you did. The third gen had an awkward series of four buttons on the front that all too often were triggered when you didn't mean them to be. Maybe the interface guys had a bad day. The fourth generation introduced the click wheel, restoring sense to the button world. And now this.) The new iPod had a few noticeable differences from its predecessors. It was a little thinner. The basic unit had a thirty-gigabyte hard drive, with space for 7,500 songs. But the most noticeable difference was a slightly larger screen: two and a half inches measured diagonally instead of two inches. This was important because the 5G, indeed, could work as a little television set. The 5G Pod was accompanied by a new, video-friendly software release, iTunes 6.0 (thus making obsolete the previous version, which had been launched only a month earlier). It's a testament to both Apple and the pace of technological change that in four years, the company had managed to shrink its standard model from 6.4 ounces to 4.8 ounces, hold six times as many songs, add a color video screen, and add four hours to the time required before charging the battery. And the cost was a hundred dollars less. (If you wanted to spend the same $399 price as the original, you got a 5G iPod with double that storage—15,000 songs' worth, though some of that might well be apportioned to TV shows—and six hours extra battery time.)

What's more, Jobs announced that Apple would begin distributing videos on the iTunes store. There would be three forms of these programs. The first would be music videos, sold for $1.99. To record label executives (who at that point had been increasingly unhappy with Jobs for hogging the legal download business), this was a historic act. They regarded the day in the early 1980s when they had allowed a young cable television network called MTV to air their music videos for free as the Munich Agreement battle of the music business. Though eventually they had been able to negotiate a rights fee on MTV, by and large music videos were troublesome expenses that seldom justified their lofty costs, either in sales or in the headaches generated by vain artists who would settle for nothing less than Martin Scorsese and a four-million-dollar budget. Now Steve Jobs was offering a way for the labels to turn a drain into a profit center.

The second option would be video versions of the podcasts Apple was already offering. Like the podcasts, these would be free. Now bloggers or just about anyone could distribute video through the world's most popular online media store.

But it was the third option that Jobs saved until the notorious "one more thing . . ." finale of his presentation: TV shows. Beginning immediately, the iTunes store would offer commercial-free episodes of television shows. The first wave would be shows originally broadcast by properties of the Walt Disney Company, including ABC television and the Disney Channel. These included the ABC shows that almost always wound up at the top of the Nielsen ratings, beloved by cult followings and viewed by millions more: *Desperate Housewives* and *Lost* (along with three more from Disney's cable networks). All the previous episodes would be available for download, and new ones would go online at eight A.M. following the prime-time broadcast. The price? The same $1.99 Apple was charging for a music video.

This explained the presence of Disney Chief Executive Robert Iger at the launch event. Jobs had despised Iger's predecessor, Michael Eisner. This was a crucial relationship because Disney was half owner of Pixar's movies, and with the contract coming to an end, everything was up for grabs again. Once I was pressing Jobs for details on this relationship, and Jobs confirmed that at one point Eisner had flown up to Cupertino hoping for a bonding experience. They had gone to an Indian restaurant Jobs liked. But breaking nan bread with Eisner did nothing for Jobs. When I asked him if the experience had helped the relationship, all he would answer was "We ate together." I asked him again and got the same answer.

With Iger, Jobs finally seemed comfortable with Disney deal-making. Once he had the idea for distributing TV shows on iTunes, the first and only company he went to for the initial programming was Disney. "We know from the music side of things that negotiating things with four companies at once is difficult," he told me. "When we realized we could get the number one and number two television show from one company, that made it pretty clear." Some months earlier, Jobs himself had flown down to southern California and showed a video iPod prototype to Iger and the head of Disney's new-media business, Anne Sweeney. "Imagine *Desperate Housewives* on this," he said. Iger and Sweeney were impressed, but the idea was put on the back burner until just a few weeks before the launch, when Apple made a push to lock in the deal. I suspected then that the other shoe to this relationship would be the resolution of the Pixar situation, and indeed it was only a couple of months later that Disney agreed to buy Pixar, lock, stock, and rendering software, for an astonishing $7.4 billion. (Half of that went directly to Jobs, who was also given a place on the Disney board.)

But that was for another day. Here in October 2005, Jobs was making history. With a single swoop, he'd changed the nature of television shows. Before his presentation that day, TV shows were basically network-bound presentations that ran in a designated time slot. Now they were no longer advertiser-supported productions broken up by annoying commercial messages consisting of as much as a third of their run time. They were shows you paid for, costing less than a latte, and viewed without interruption. You could download them anytime and view them wherever you were, using your iPod.

They were podcasts.

The 5G iPod represented a turnaround for Jobs, who for years had been insisting that people would have little interest in viewing video on the tiny screens of handheld devices. ("It's the music, stupid," he once said during a conference call with reporters. "Music is a wonderful thing because, A, it's music, and, B, it can be listened to as background activity. You can't drive your car when you're watching a movie.") A number of companies had released versions of a Microsoft-designed handheld video player. But it wasn't selling. The Microsoft devices required some geek skills to get the video content you wanted, and in some cases it was nearly impossible because the Hollywood studios refused to permit translations of their productions to this weird format. This jam-up was typical of what was happening as television content met the Internet. Whenever anyone talked about the future of television, they would begin with a golden promise, embodied in the mantra "Any program, anytime, on any device." But this was terrifying to Hollywood's lawyers (who feared copyright infringement) and accountants (who were alarmed at the threat to the tried-and-true business models).

Into this stalemate swept Steve Jobs. Of course, by linking this revolution to the iPod, he wound up in the middle of a potentially embarrassing change of direction. After all, before that day he'd been ruthless in mocking products that resembled the one he'd just introduced. Naturally, when I talked to him after the launch, the first thing I did was to remind him that he'd always said that people had no interest in watching video on tiny screens.

"I have said that," he admitted. Then he embarked on a spin session that occupied a middle ground on the issue. He didn't go so far as to say his previous pronouncements had been *wrong*. But he did soften his blanket condemnations of the tiny-screen experience. Video on iPods, he said, was similar to the previous introduction of photos on iPods. "These are *extra* things," he said. "They're great, they're the peas on the side, [but] they're not the entrée. The entrée is music. That's the most important thing." On the other hand, he suggested that adding video to the iPod was a breakthrough. iPod users "may not even use it for video right away. But they'll discover it. Because millions of people are going to buy it as the best music player in the world, we will rapidly become the most popular portable video player in history. So if anything is going to happen on video, it's going to happen on the iPod. And we're going to push it along to see if we can move it along by two thousand music videos and Pixar short films and, I think, a plate-tectonic-shift relationship with Disney for these five shows. And so we'll find out what happens. But we don't know."

Please note, if you will, the seismographic locution. Any other CEO would have used a phrase like "groundbreaking" or "pioneering" to describe an innovative collaboration such as Apple was forging with Disney. With Jobs, it's "plate-tectonic-shift," as one adjective. Talk about the earth moving.

I asked him if he'd actually sat down and watched an entire television show or movie on an iPod. He said that he had tried it a few weeks ago to see what it was like. So what *was* it like? "Fine," he said. "I watched an episode of *Lost*. It's fine. It's not bad." (Again, please note: this from a guy whose vocabulary usually abounds with words like "fantastic" or "insanely great" or "tectonic shift relationship.") I pressed on: Had he held it in his hand for the whole show?

"Yes. I generally held it like this"—here he took the iPod, crossed his legs, and balanced it on the crook of his knee—"rested against my leg."

I tried it myself a few days later, while waiting for the people at a tire warehouse to put new rubber on my aging automobile. I'd downloaded an episode of *Lost* the night before. Like Jobs, I considered the experience . . . not bad. The picture was very sharp, and with the earphones blocking out the low-level din of the tire salesman being paged and the distant wheezing of electric socket wrenches, the experience was moderately immersive. Not that I'd want to watch the *Lord of the Rings* trilogy on an iPod.

Of course, Apple did not invent the idea of à la carte television. Cable companies had been urging broadcasters to supply programming so their customers could order on demand. Fledgling Internet start-ups were coming up with ideas for "IPTV," where television channels would be as plentiful as Web sites. But as it had done with digital music, legal downloads, and audio podcasts, the iPod pushed a conceptual probability into a hard market reality. In the first two weeks, Apple sold a million downloads of music videos, television shows, and Pixar shorts. By early December, when the iTunes store added some NBC shows, including *Law & Order,* highlights from Jay Leno and Conan O'Brien, and old episodes of *Alfred Hitchcock Presents,* the total had gone up to 3 million. But by then, iTunes wasn't the only place where tube-heads could go to for television shows. CBS began streaming episodes from its Web site. And Google jumped in with its own service, including episodes of *CSI* and NBA basketball games.

But at the head of the class was iTunes. The three-legged iPod system, consisting of an adorable device, quietly powerful software, and a bone-simple online store, had been built for music. But with podcasts and podcastlike television shows, the iPod was suddenly at the center of the two biggest and most disruptive trends in digital media: a grassroots uprising of a wisdom-drenched crowd of the self-appointed and an à la carte disintegration of the traditional packaging of broadcast and cable programming. Would the iPod destroy the networks by allowing us to cherry-pick and shuffle *all* our media, the same way it lets us shuffle our music?

Whether or not this happens, one thing is as clear as a high-bit-rate musical tone: Podcasting should not be viewed as a doomed technology like CB radio. Whether or not it survives decades into this century, it has already made its mark. Think of podcasting as shorthand for the way the world changes when digital distribution mixes with the ubiquitous and surprisingly flexible device that Apple introduced solely as a music player. Think of the disruption that comes when the established giants of broadcast no longer have the artifices of broadcast licenses and cable distribution fees to fend off competitors. Think of the empowerment that comes when a copy of GarageBand—Apple's music-making program, revamped to make people podcasters—an internal mike, and a mouse click make you a radio station.

Then take a look at what Apple might do with iPods in the future, and imagine what might come from this. The company has taken patents on wireless technology for handheld devices. Think what happens when the process of downloading podcasts untethers from the computer—and your wireless iPod retrieves your audio dispatches instantly, no matter where you are, with the reach of a network and the intimacy of an instant message. Podcasting could quite literally become, as Apple exec Greg Joswiak had told me, the radio of the twenty-first century. Only this time, *everybody* could be broadcasting, belly to belly with NPR, Harry Potter audiobooks, and highlights from last night's baseball game. More stuff to shuffle. More novelty. More surprise. Once again, to quote Steve Jobs, the iPod has moved tectonic plates.

Oh, and when *The New Oxford American Dictionary* chose its "word of the year" for 2005, guess which word it picked.

Podcast.

Coda

❯How will we remember the iPod? As something that embodied who we were—and who we were going to be—in the early part of a century bound to take us places we couldn't hope to imagine? It was our fetish and our future. Its irresistible contours made us hungry to possess it. But it possessed us. Taking full advantage of the flexibility and fungibility of digital technology, the iPod changed our behavior, made business winners and losers, and made everything it touched just a little bit cooler.

But none of it would have happened if not for the music. Steve Jobs knew that. "We all grew up in the golden age of music, the golden age of rock and roll," he once told me. "[Music is] going to be around as long as humans are around. So it's not like we're making a gizmo and taking it out in the world and trying to convince everybody they need it. We don't have to convince people that they love music. People know that already. So all we're doing is reinventing the experience of enjoying music, because you have your whole library with you."

Apple's 6.4-ounce baby wasn't the first stab at this, and it won't be the last. But for this age, at this moment, the iPod was . . . the perfect thing.

Afterword:
iPod, iSaw, iConquered, iPhone

❯The iPod is a story that won't stand still. Not that I thought it would. Even as I reported in this book how many iPods were sold by the end of 2005 (42 million), I realized that by publication date in October 2006 there would be many more (around 70 million, as it turned out). And that was at the beginning of a holiday selling season, which promised to be the biggest three-month crush of iPod buying in history.

Indeed, it was. And as of this update, in April 2007, Apple has taken out full-page ads congratulating itself on selling over 100 million iPods.

I also knew that Apple wasn't going to wait around to introduce new iPods, or iPod-related products or services. Sure enough, at a Jobs-athon in October 2006, Apple introduced a slightly upgraded flagship iPod (brighter screen, more storage, lower price), a spiffier iPod nano (pick your color), and a revamped iPod shuffle barely bigger than a commemorative postage stamp (you can clip it to the sleeve of your T-shirt). You can now buy movies on the iTunes store. Jobs also announced a totally new product, Apple TV (at the time he called it iTV, but apparently the British ITV network had other ideas). Released in early March, Apple TV is a small box that works like an iPod for the living room, allowing you to enjoy on your widescreen television your iTunes songs and videos, as well as the photos on your computer.

Earlier in the book I quoted Apple's Jon Rubinstein commenting that every Christmas, company executives marveled that no competitor had emerged to poach iPod sales. In 2006, though Rubenstein had retired, his former colleagues continued marveling. This was true in spite of the appearance of what had been billed as the most serious threat to Apple's dominance in music to date: Microsoft's much-hyped Zune. After a couple of abortive tries at getting its traditional hardware partners to develop MP3 players using Microsoft software, Bill Gates turned over the challenge of producing an iPod killer to the whiz kids who had developed the company's successful Xbox game console. They adopted a system much like the iPod's: a hard-disk device tightly integrated with jukebox software that in turn was bound with an online music service. The interface was well designed and the screen a bit bigger than the iPod's, though the boxy device looked like a clunkier version of the original iPod. It came in black, white, and brown. *Brown?* Oh, my.

But the Zune did have one thing that the iPod did not—wireless connectivity. Microsoft's people explained that eventually the Zune could use this connectivity innovatively, but the original Zune utilized the Wi-Fi for only one thing—sending (or "squirting") a song to a nearby Zune.

When I asked Jobs about Zune not long before its release, he literally laughed it off. He had seen an Internet video depicting the process by which one transmits a song from one Zune to another "It takes forever," he said. "By the time you've gone through all that, the girl's got up and left! You're much better off to take one of your earbuds out and put it in her ear."

The problem with squirting, though, wasn't the speed with which songs moved. It was the digital rights management (DRM) restrictions slapped on the songs you wanted to share. After three plays or three days—whichever came first—the song you received from a fellow Zune-ster would expire, and be as worthless as a ticket to yesterday's concert. What's more, these limitations would be imposed on every song or sound file you sent from one Zune to another, whether or not the copyright owners actually demanded that level of protection. The recording of your daughter singing a lullaby she made up that you hoped to send to your mother for repeated listening would be burdened with the same restrictions as the latest hit from an *American Idol* star. Since Zune sales were very slow, spontaneous exchanges between Zune owners were rare. (Try to find two in the same place.) Only once did the screen of my own Zune prompt me to receive a song some stranger was willing to send to me. It turned out to be a tune actually recorded by an amateur musician who found my Zune in the wild only because on my blog I had advertised my availability at a book appearance. The sender later explained to me that if he had his way, I could have not only kept the song forever, but sent it to my friends. But of course due to the Zune restrictions I could keep it only three days and could not share it with anyone. DRM had pretty much ruined Microsoft's innovation.

The more significant developments in DRM involved Apple and iPod. As I mentioned earlier, Apple's DRM software, Fairplay, prevented songs sold on iTunes from being played on devices that competed with the iPod; likewise, Apple did not take steps to allow songs sold on other online music emporiums to play on iPods. Jobs continually shrugged off complaints, including mine, about this lack of interoperability. As late as October 2006, when I interviewed him for the fifth anniversary of the iPod, he insisted that no problem existed: "Nobody's ever demanded [interoperability]," he said. "People know up front that when they buy music from the iTunes stores it plays on iPods, and so we're not trying to hide anything there." But officials in several European countries saw the process as one by which Apple, with its dominant market share, "locked in" customers, and began legislative or regulatory processes to alter this scheme. Also, the growth in online song sales wasn't as rapid as some had anticipated—could it be that customers were balking at the DRM that hobbled the songs?

In February 2007, Jobs took the unusual step of going directly to the public on the issue. He published an essay on the Apple site entitled "Thoughts on Music." After explaining why he could not make iTunes interoperable without compromising Fairplay, he suggested that the record labels allow him to provide the ultimate solution: "abolish DRMs entirely." After all, he argued, the labels sell billions of DRM-free songs already—on CDs, which are easily ripped into unprotected digital files. "What benefits do they get from selling the remaining small percentage of their music encumbered with a DRM system?" he asked, and then answered his own question: "There appear to be none." He sounded like a cypherpunk digital-rights activist as he rhapsodized: "Imagine a world where every online store sells DRM-free music encoded in open licensable formats. In such a world, any player can play music purchased from any store, and any store can sell music which is playable on all players. This is clearly the best alternative for consumers, and Apple would embrace it in a heartbeat."

He would soon make good on his promise. Early in April 2007, Jobs flew to London to share a podium with Eric Nicoli, the head of one of the big four labels, EMI. (Some people assumed that the press event would be the long-awaited announcement that the Beatles were finally going to sell their songs online.) Nicoli and Jobs announced that EMI would hereafter sell its songs on iTunes (and other stores) without DRM. There was some bad news, however. The new format, which also boasted better sound quality, would cost thirty cents more per track than protected songs.

(The Beatles announcement would have to wait. A few months earlier, I'd asked Jobs whether it was a dream of his to be able to make that announcement at one of his keynotes and then bring out Paul McCartney to perform. "No," he said, deadpan. "My dream would be to bring out John Lennon.")

Dropping DRM on legal downloads was a giant step in the history of digital music. But the biggest iPod news of all involved something that was not an iPod, but a possible successor as Apple's signature product. On January 9, 2007, Steve Jobs took the stage once again for a two-hour keynote address at the Macworld Expo and pulled one more thing out of his pocket. A phone.

Actually, he explained, the "iPhone" was three devices. It was a new iPod, it was an Internet navigator, and it was, yes, the long-awaited Apple phone handset that had been the subject of fanboy rumors for years. (I'd mentioned the speculation in a *Newsweek* account of the 2003 Macworld Expo.) It was also a typically gorgeous Jonathan Ive–designed objet d'art, a dense black palm-size slab ringed in silver. At less than half an inch thick, it made a cigarette case look obese.

Apple, Jobs explained with his customary disregard for humility, had reinvented the phone. It also reinvented the iPod. Gone was the wheel—which had been an iPod stalwart in the form of scroll wheel, click wheel, and (in the case of the shuffle) faux wheel—consisting of buttons laid out on the points of a circle. Instead there was a spacious three-and-a-half-inch screen (not an oxymoron when you're talking about something that goes in your pocket) that consumed almost all of the device's front surface. There was but a single button on the device, one step away from Jobs's and Ive's interface nirvana, where controls disappear. (Okay, there's a ring-tone volume control hidden on the side, but it's almost imperceptible.) You work the iPhone by direct contact with the screen, which takes advantage of custom technology cooked up by Apple engineers to create a "multi-touch" experience. You pinch, tap, and swipe your way around. Instead of twirling your finger along a circular track to find a song, you brush your finger down a menu and the songs spin by, almost as if they were on a giant roll. The harder you flick, the faster they go.

It seems obvious that the iPod features on the iPhone will eventually become standard on all full-size iPods, but the iPhone's main advances reflect what Apple has done best for years—transforming tasks that we perform on small computing devices in a somewhat unsatisfactory way, and simplifying and adding delight to the process so that it becomes a different experience entirely. The idea is to reinvent not only the phone, but everything one can possibly do on a palm-size, wirelessly connected object—surfing the Net, e-mail, chatting, and imposing organization on a complicated life while still listening to an entire song collection. Just as the iPod brought life to a dead-upon-delivery digital-music-player industry, the iPhone wants to bring excellence to a product sector where even the best devices frustrate their users.

The iPhone has another thing in common with the original iPod: an eye-popping price. Jobs set the initial cost at $499 with a meager four gigabytes of storage, and $599 with eight gigs. (That's one tenth the storage of a $349 iPod. If you've got one movie and three TV shows on the lower-price model, you've barely got room for enough songs to last you for a decent run in the park.) And that price comes on top of a two-year mandatory contract with AT&T, the sole mobile phone network that works with the iPhone.

Jobs was ebullient after the announcement. In recent weeks he had been coping with two big problems: keeping news of the iPhone secret, and dealing with investigations inside and outside of Apple concerning the dating and reporting of stock options. (Apple had pinned the problem on a couple of departed executives, and Jobs himself seemed confident that the options matter would be put to rest without affecting his ability to continue as CEO.) Now he seemed at ease as he pushed the iPhone at me and watched carefully as I put it through a few paces. When I asked him why Apple had made a phone, he answered playfully.

"We looked at the market, did buying research, and figured out if we could make a lot of money," he said. When he saw my startled look, he laughed. "No, that's not us. We started working on the phone because we wanted one [for ourselves]."

The complete story is more nuanced. While people had been waiting for an Apple phone for years, the company had been on the project only a little over two years. The genesis of the phone was not a driving need to call home using something with the Apple logo, but a project designed to build a tablet computer, an idea that Microsoft had been pursuing for years without success. Jobs and his team felt that they could improve touch-screen technology to make that category a winner. Instead, as Apple's engineers experimented with the multi-touch screen, they realized that this would work well on an iPod-size mobile phone. The same thing, says Jobs that "everyone was asking us" to do.

Jobs had previously resisted the phone for one very good reason: the mobile phone world is ruled by carrier networks that do not think the way Silicon Valley companies do. Instead of creating open platforms that welcome innovators to write their own software, the carriers closely police what goes on the handsets connected to their network. The most coveted phone applications are ones that create the most revenue for the carrier, not value for the customer. Jobs disdained this model. At one point, during a *Wall Street Journal* conference, he referred to the carriers as "orifices." (Thankfully, he did not specify which orifice he was thinking of.)

Nonetheless, when Apple decided that it could reinvent the phone, Jobs concluded that it would have to choose an orifice and be done with it. Though he flirted with Verizon, he settled for Cingular, which was itself controlled by giant AT&T. (In fact, soon after the iPhone launch event, Cingular announced that it planned to give up its name and adopt that of its parent, AT&T. Not exactly a cuddly moniker.) What appealed to Jobs was that Cingular gave Apple a lot of rope—more control that any carrier had allowed any manufacturer. In fact, according to the *Wall Street Journal*, Jobs would not even demonstrate the phone for the CEO of Cingular Wireless until a month before the public product launch.

"*We* decided what the phone is," Jobs said. "*We* decided what software would be on the phone. And so we could make the product we wanted. That was a big deal. There was a lot of contention about whether we could build OS X [the Macintosh operating system] on it. But that's what we did because we really wanted to build that class of apps."

The iPhone, however, is not an open system. Like other phones, there will be strict limitations on what software can be installed on it, even though it uses the Macintosh operating system. "This thing is more like an iPod than it is a computer in that sense," says Jobs, who observes that with a phone one must be careful that rogue applications don't mess up the fragile nature of the communications system.

Though I've only played with the iPhone in highly controlled circumstances as of this writing, it's clear that Apple has used imagination and fresh technology to improve the cell-phone experience. Consider the use of sensors on the phone. An accelerometer determines whether you're holding the device horizontially or vertically, and adjusts the screen display to accommodate. An ambient-light sensor measures the illumination in the area and tweaks the brightness of the screen accordingly. A proximity sensor detects when the handset is at your ear and instructs the phone to ignore any touches on the screen (as they are more likely to be made by your cheek than your finger).

Apple has also included software to simplify formerly cumbersome tasks and thus overcome the resistance of hardcore skeptics to smart phones. In one demo, a user scrolls through a contact list (which works like the song listing on the iPod function), makes a call with two touches on the screen, puts the caller on hold while he takes another call, then merges the calls into a conference with another touch. Apple also claims to break ground with "visual voicemail," which lets you listen to the messages you want to hear instead of slogging through voicemails in chronological order. And e-mail looks as good on the iPhone as it does on a full-size computer (though it's not clear whether multi-touch typing on a virtual keyboard will be an effective way of replying).

Some of the innovations are less obvious. Apple spent millions of dollars and unleashed a squadron of PhDs to compress the necessary antenna length into a gizmo thinner than a pencil. Every day, and into the night, they went into battle, fighting for every tenth of a millimeter. "No one's seen an antenna like this in the world!" insists one Apple engineer.

"This is five years ahead of what everybody's got," Jobs gushes. "If we didn't do one more thing, we'd be set for five years!"

Will the iPhone be as significant as the iPod? Certainly more people use mobile phones than listen to digital music players: in 2006, the world snatched up a billion new handsets. Nonetheless, even if the iPhone succeeds (Jobs wants one percent of the market by 2008), it will be tough for Apple to match the iPod as a life-changing, and world-changing, phenomenon. For many of us, the iPod rekindled a dormant passion for music. It made us want to hear more songs, it encouraged us to go out and find new bands to love, it offered new ways to organize music and take it with us. Will the iPhone encourage us to make . . . *more phone calls*? I don't want more phone calls, I want fewer; and when I'm on the road or staring at hummingbirds in my garden, I don't want any. In fact, if you take into consideration the universal loathing that comes from being around people who talk on cell phones, it can be argued that if the iPhone encourages more conversation, it will have done us a universal disservice. At least iPod users keep to themselves.

In short, I do look forward to getting my own iPhone, but choosing which of my voice mails to hear first isn't quite on the thrill level of having a shuffle session enlivened by Arcade Fire's "Wake Up," followed by a great version of Tom Waits's "San Diego Serenade" that I didn't even know I had. And since the iPhone's memory is so skimpy, I'm still going to carry my iPod around with me.

This is not to say that the iPhone doesn't have the potential to be a breakout product—especially if Apple eases up on the innovative software outsiders can put on it. The potential is huge. Nonetheless, the iPod's mojo was unique. As I documented in these pages—with maybe too much enthusiasm for those not in tune with the magic—the iPod was one of those perfect-storm events where everything came together. Those things don't often happen.

When they do, the consequences keep on happening. On the

same day that Jobs unveiled his iPhone, he made another announcement that was almost lost in the excitement. Believe it or not, Apple Computer was no more. Jobs had shortened the company name, which had come to him in a brainstorm over thirty years back, to Apple, Inc. The company now was identified with the tiny music player Jobs had pulled out of his pocket in 2006 (and its consumer-electronics successors) as much as with its famous Macintosh.

From Apple Computer to just plain Apple. Chalk up another change to the iPod.

Notes

Unless otherwise cited, *The Perfect Thing* is based on my own reporting, primarily personal interviews with people within and outside Apple. Of course my views benefited from the journalism and commentary of the countless people who have addressed themselves to the iPod in print and on the Internet.

Perfect

2   *quaffing beer:* Associated Press report (June 8, 2006) of a survey by the Student Monitor research firm. Seventy-three percent of 1,200 students surveyed said that the iPod was the number one in thing—beating a long winning streak by the previous champion, beer.

4   *"younger listeners think the way the iPod thinks":* Alex Ross, "Listen to This," *The New Yorker,* February 16, 2004.

5   *"iPod of the brain":* David Malakoff, "iPod of the Brain," NPR Morning Edition, March 14, 2001.

5   *"Nothing fits better":* William Powers, "The Happy Dance," *National Journal,* January 13, 2006.

5   *premiums:* David Bernstein, "The Free Toaster? Today, It's an iPod,"

The New York Times, Aug. 18, 2005; Bob Tedeschi, "An iPod for Your Thoughts: A Website Offers Incentives to Reviewers," *The New York Times,* August 15, 2005.

6 *"a little iPod in swaddling clothes":* Joe Morgenstern, "A Thriller to Bank On," *The Wall Street Journal,* March 24, 2006.

6 *"iPod Theology":* "Houston Pastor Preached iPod Theology," Associated Press, January 24, 2006.

13 *an article published on CNET:* Joe Wilcox, "Apple to Unveil Digital Device," *CNET News,* October 17, 2001.

18 *"I'm a bike guy":* Elisabeth Bumiller, "White House Letter: Not the Decider, but Stirring Anxiety," *The New York Times,* February 6, 2006.

Identity

21 *iPod Wars:* Trace Crutchfield, "iPod Wars," *The Brooklyn Rail,* April 2005.

23 *rock snobbery:* Michael Crowley, "Washington Diarist," *New Republic,* September 9, 2005.

24 *"Obscure ain't what it used to be":* Kelefa Sanneh, "Sounds That Missed the Charts but Merit a Hearing," *The New York Times,* December 22, 2005.

25 1966 recording session: Xeni Jardin, "Sun Ra and Blues Project Do Batman and Robin," *Boing Boing,* February 5, 2006.

27 *"a special place in celebrities' hearts":* Karen Wood was interviewed by *Newsweek*'s Jordana Lewis.

29 *Bush's iPod:* Elisabeth Bumiller, "White House Letter: Some Favorite Tunes for the Freewheelin' George Bush," *The New York Times,* April 11, 2005; Katrina vanden Heuvel, "Bush's iPod: Take Two," *The Nation*

blog, April 19, 2005; Amy Argetsinger and Roxanne Roberts, "POTUS iPod: Totally Random," *The Washington Post,* December 16, 2005; Tuskegee transcript from White House Press Office, www.whitehouse .gov/news/releases/2006/04/20060419-5.html.

30   *Tony Blair:* Michael White, "God Will Judge Me, PM tells Parkinson," *The Guardian,* March 4, 2006.

31   *Dick Cheney:* Richard Benedetto, "Cheney's Feet Solidly Planted in Number Two Spot," *USA Today,* January 20, 2005; Nedra Pickler, "Notebook: Cheney Comfortable in the Air," Associated Press, December 21, 2005.

31   *Queen Elizabeth:* "Britain's Queen Plugging into Her iPod," Agence France Presse, June 16, 2005 (via Yahoo News).

32   *the pope:* Carol Glatz, "Vatican Radio Employees Present Pope with Specially Loaded iPod Nano," Catholic News Service, March 3, 2006.

33   *Joe Paterno:* Mark Blaudschun, "Elder Statesman," *The Boston Globe,* May 28, 2004.

33   *Laveranues Coles:* Karen Crouse, "New Trust Lets Coles Share Secret," *The New York Times,* September 18, 2005.

34   *Vince Carter:* Ina Fried, "NBA Gives iPod a Technical Foul," *CNet News,* November 17, 2004.

35   *midnight visits from female students:* Mitch Ratcliffe, "iPods Get People Laid and Improve Their Memories, Too!" RatcliffeBlog, December 9, 2005.

35   *Georgia Institute of Technology:* Amy Voida, Rebecca E. Grinter, Nicholas Duchneaut, W. Keith Edwards, and Mark W. Newman, "Listening In: Practices Surrounding iTunes Music Sharing," in *CHI 2005* (Portland, Oreg.: ACM, 2005). My researcher Jodi Mardesich interviewed Voida.

Notes

37 *Jennifer Hartstein:* "iPod Guilty Pleasures," Don Fernandez, *Atlanta Journal-Constitution,* September 10, 2004.

38 *"Kenworld":* John Schwartz, "To Know Me, Know My iPod," *The New York Times,* November 28, 2004.

Origin

43 *Personal Jukebox:* In addition to my interviews with Wobber and Redell, information about the PJB was drawn from the Wikipedia entry (http://en.wikipedia.org/wiki/PJB) and Andrew Birrell's PowerPoint presentation of the Personal Jukebox team (www.birrell.org/Andrew/talks/pjb-overview.ppt).

51 *I felt like a dope:* From Brent Schlender, "How Big Can Apple Get?" *Fortune,* February 21, 2005.

52 *Audion and SoundJam:* A good account of Audion's history by its cofounder Cabel Sasser is posted at http://panic.com/extras/audionstory. An addendum by Bill Kincaid (www.panic.com/extras/audionstory/popup-sjstory.html) describes the origin of SoundJam.

54 *Anthony Michael Fadell:* Tony Fadell's now-dark Web site provided background, as did Pamela Kruger and Katherine Miezknowski, "Stop the Fight," *Fast Company,* September 1998; Stephen Roskoff, "U-M Students: They're Bullish on Business," *Michigan Alumnus,* November–December 1989; and John Markoff, "Oh, Yeah, He Also Sells Computers," *The New York Times,* April 25, 2004.

64 *PortalPlayer, Pixo:* Besides personal interviews, my account of the iPod's outside suppliers drew on Erik Sherman, "Inside the Apple iPod Design Triumph," *Electronics Design Chain,* Summer 2002; Mathew Yi, "Little Known Startup Was Behind iPod's Easy-to-use Interface," *San Francisco Chronicle,* August 16, 2004; and John H. Day, "Inside iPod," *Electronic Design,* January 20, 2005.

68   *Ben Knauss:* Leander Kahney, "Inside Look at the Birth of iPod," *Wired News,* July 21, 2004.

Cool

75   *Carl Rohde:* Information on Rohde is on his Web site www.signsof thetime.nl; and in D. Parvaz, "They're on a Quest for What's Cool—Here, There and Everywhere," *Seattle Post-Intelligencer,* November 20, 2003.

80   *2004 press conference:* Phone conference on first anniversary of iTunes Music store, April 28, 2004.

80   *"somebody who's not cool trying to be cool":* Rob Walker, "The Guts of a New Machine," *The New York Times Magazine,* November 30, 2003.

81   *Lee Clow:* Stuart Elliott, "Behind 'Think Different,' " *The New York Times,* August 3, 1988.

84   *Company 3:* "Company 3's Alex Brodie Rocks with Apple's iPod," Company 3 press release, January 4, 2004.

84   *"orgiastic boogaloo-ing":* Randall Stross, "After 20 Years, Finally Capitalizing on Cool," *The New York Times,* January 16, 2005.

85   *The O.C.:* My *Newsweek* colleague Jordana Lewis talked to Josh Schwartz.

86   *Ron Gillyard:* Gillyard spoke to my *Newsweek* colleague Jennifer Ordonez.

87   *Ford:* Seth Stevenson, "Apple Jacking," *Slate,* January 30, 2006.

87   *"'cool factor'":* The Diffusion Group, "Understanding iPod's Dominance: A Consumer Perspective," Research study, November 1, 2005.

89   *Virginia Postrel:* Virginia Postrel, *The Substance of Style* (New York: HarperCollins, 2003). Postrel also discusses the iPod and coolness in her blog, www.dynamist.com.

Notes

90　*"the aesthetic is in the artifact"*: Leander Kahney, "Bull Session with Professor iPod," *Wired News*, February 24, 2004.

90　*"I kissed it good night"*: Julio Ojeda-Zapata, "Invasion of the iPod People," *St. Paul Pioneer Press*, May 15, 2005.

91　*"Pigwidgeon"*: Regina Lynn, "For the Love of iPod," *Wired News*, July 29, 2005.

92　*polled by the BBC*: Sheryl Garratt, "The iMan," *London Times*, December 3, 2005.

93　*Design Museum*: The Ive "Designer of the Year, 2003" interview is posted on the London Design Museum Web site, www.design museum.org/design/index.php?id=63.

93　*"Fruit—an apple"*: My first in-depth interview with Jobs was in November 1983, while he was in the final stages of Macintosh development. My article "The Whiz Kids vs. Darth Vader" appeared in the April 15, 1984 issue of *Rolling Stone*.

99　*"bathroom"*: Luke Williams, "The iPod and the Bathtub: Managing Perceptions Through Design Language," *Design Mind* articles, www.frog design.com.

Personal

107　*little white wires*: Andrew Sullivan, "Society Is Dead, We Have Retreated into the iWorld," *The Times Online* [London], February 20, 2005.

108　*"a whole new hazard in campaigning"*: Chris Smith, "Four Donkeys on a Trail," *New York*, July 4, 2005.

108　*Wayne Coyne*: The Flaming Lips singer was interviewed by *Newsweek*'s Vanessa Juarez.

Notes

110 *"mobile privatization"*: Raymond Williams, *Television: Technology and Cultural Form* (London: Fontana, 1974).

111 *Andreas Pavel:* In addition to my interview with Pavel, I drew on Larry Rohter, "An Unlikely Trendsetter Made Earphones a Way of Life," *The New York Times,* December 17, 2005; and the copious descriptions and drawings in Pavel's U.S. Patent 5,201,003 (April 6, 1993).

112 *Walkman:* Books consulted on the history of the Walkman include Sony's official history, *Genryu* (Tokyo: Sony Corporation, 1996); Akio Morita with Edwin M. Reingold and Mitsuko Shimomura, *Made in Japan* (New York: E. P. Dutton, 1986); John Nathan, *Sony: The Private Life* (Boston: Houghton Mifflin, 1999); Paul du Gay, Stuart Hall, Linda Jones, High Mackay, and Keith Negus, *Doing Cultural Studies: The Story of the Sony Walkman* (London: Sage Publications, 1997); and Lincoln Caplan, "The Walkman," *The New Yorker,* September 21, 1981.

115 *"The shirt-pocket-portable"*: Michael Brian Schiffer, *The Portable Radio in American Life* (Tucson: University of Arizona Press, 1991).

120 *"I remember my first Walkman"*: Joi Ito, "My First Sony Walkman," Joi Ito Web, November 20, 2004.

121 *"intensely insular"*: Vincent Jackson, "Menace II Society," included in du Gay et al., *Doing Cultural Studies.*

121 *cooperating in a sociological study:* Michael Bull, *Sounding Out the City* (Oxford: Berg, 2000).

121 *"the ultimate musical means in mediating the media"*: Iain Chambers, "A Miniature History of the Walkman," in du Gay et al., *Doing Cultural Studies.*

122 *William Gibson:* May 1994 interview with Giuseppe Salza, archived at www.eff.org/Misc/Publications/William_Gibson/salza.interview. Gib-

Notes

son has also attributed his 1981 introduction to the Walkman as the inspiration for his concept of "cyberspace."

122   *Herbert Marcuse:* Herbert Marcuse, *One Dimensional Man* (Boston: Beacon Press, 1964).

122   *"deaf to the loudspeakers of history":* R. Chow, "Listening Otherwise, Music Miniaturized: A Different Type of Question About Revolution," in du Gay et al., *Doing Cultural Studies.*

123   *Michael Bull:* In addition to an interview I did with Bull in 2004, I drew on *Sounding Out the City,* ibid.; Leander Kahney, "Bull Session with Professor iPod," *Wired News,* February 25, 2004. Bull's writings on the iPod include "The Intimate Sounds of Urban Experience: An Auditory Epistemology of Everyday Mobility" and "No Dead Air! The iPod and the Culture of Mobile Listening," in *Leisure Studies,* vol. 24, no. 4, October 2005.

123   *"As long as they have the Walkman on":* Bloom is quoted in du Gay et al., *Doing Cultural Studies.*

124   *Cardinal William Keeler:* Kevin Eckstrom, "Cardinal Warns Parents About Giving Wireless Devices as Christmas Gifts," Religion News Service, November 15, 2005.

124   *Norman Lebrecht:* Cited in Christine Rosen, "The Age of Egocasting," *The New Atlantis,* no. 7, Fall 2004–Winter 2005.

124   *"The autism of the Walkman listener":* Chow, "Listening Otherwise."

124   *"the look and sound of the Walkman dead":* Paul Farhi, "Akio Morita, a Man of Great Import," *The Washington Post,* October 5, 1999, p. C1.

128   *"the technology of the disconnected individual":* Rosen, "Egocasting."

129   *"trapped in a self-imposed bubble":* Gabriel Sherman, "Behind the Music: Deaf to the World, an iPod Addict Unplugs," *New York Observer,* August 30, 2004.

Notes

129 *impact of iPods on hearing loss:* Jane Spencer, "Behind the Music: iPods and Hearing Loss," *The Wall Street Journal,* Jan. 10, 2006; Pete Townshend, "No New Resolutions," Pete's Diaries (www.petetownshend.co.uk), December 29, 2005.

130 *Placard Headphone Festivals:* "The London Headphone Festival," Bagatellen blog, May 24, 2004.

132 *"It's gotten to be my baby":* Carmichael was interviewed by *Newsweek's* Vanessa Juarez.

132 *jumped onto the tracks:* Thomas Beller, "iPod on the Tracks," *The New York Times,* February 12, 2006.

133 *iPod crimes:* Tales of iPod muggings include Sewell Chan, "Ears Plugged? Keep Eyes Open, Subway's iPod Users Are Told," *The New York Times,* April 28, 2005; Erika Martinez, "iPod Muggers Will Face the Music," *New York Post,* September 9, 2005; "Dianne Wiest's Daughter Pleads to Larceny," *USA Today,* May 15, 2005; CNN Transcripts, "Showbiz Tonight," December 27, 2005. Bryce Wisell was interviewed by Jodi Mardesich.

133 *Christopher Rose:* Kareem Fahim, "Apple Executive Calls Family of Teenager Killed for iPod," *The New York Times,* July 6, 2005.

Download

136 *MP3:* The history and early applications of MP3 were informed by my own reporting as well as many sources including Mark Coleman, *Playback: From the Victrola to MP3, 100 Years of Music, Machines and Money* (Cambridge, Mass.: Da Capo Press, 2003); Mark Katz, *Capturing Sound: How Technology Has Changed Music* (Berkeley: University of California Press, 1974); and Charles C. Mann, "The Heavenly Jukebox," *The Atlantic,* September 2000.

139 *MP3.com, Napster, WinAmp:* In addition to my own reporting, I consulted Coleman John Alderman, *Sonic Boom: Napster, MP3, and the*

New Pioneers of Music (Cambridge, Mass.: Perseus, 2001). My researcher Jodi Mardesich also supplied me with earlier interviews of MP3.com's Michael Robertson.

142   *Long Tail:* The best explanation of this by far comes in Chris Anderson's *The Long Tail: Why the Future of Business Is Selling Less or More* (New York: Hyperion, 2006).

146   *"the false lesson of Napster":* Walt Mossberg, "Personal Technology," *The Wall Street Journal*, February 7, 2002.

148   *a major military campaign:* Besides my interviews with people inside Apple and at the record labels, I drew on Peter Burrows, "Show Time!" *Business Week*, February 2, 2004; Devin Leonard, "Songs in the Key of Steve," *Fortune*, May 12, 2003; and Jeff Goodell, "Steve Jobs: The Rolling Stone Interview," *Rolling Stone*, December 25, 2003.

159   *"reprogram the order of cuts":* David Denby, "My Problem with Perfection," *The New Yorker*, August 26, 1996.

159   *Heather McNeil:* Interviewed by *Newsweek*'s Ron Depasquale.

160   *"The promise of Coachella":* Kelefa Sanneh, "Embracing the Random," *The New York Times*, May 3, 2005, p. D1.

162   *"they are getting greedy":* "Quote of the day," CNET News, September 20, 2005.

163   *Grokster:* Supreme Court of the United States, *Metro-Goldwyn-Mayer Studios, Inc., et al. v. Grokster, Ltd. et al.* Argued March 29, 2005, decided June 27, 2005.

Shuffle

169   *the Steely Dan problem:* I first addressed this in "Does Your iPod Play Favorites?" *Newsweek*, January 31, 2005.

Notes

278

174   *Kapgar*: Kevin Apgar, "Kapgar: My Life in HTML/XML," http://kapgar.typepad.com.

178   *"About a year ago I was diagnosed with cancer"*: The complete text of Jobs's graduation speech is stored on the Stanford Web site at http://news-service.stanford.edu/news/2005/june15/jobs-061505.html.

183   *"the human mind does badly with randomness"*: Steven D. Levitt, "What Do the Kansas City Royals and My iPod Have in Common?" Freakonomics Blog, August 20, 2005.

185   *OmniNerd*: Brian Hansen, "How Much Does My iPod Like My Five-Star Tunes?" *OmniNerd* blog, August 25, 2005.

190   *"The almost anything-goes eclecticism"*: Ben Sisario, "Jack and Bob and Hank and Ben: Meeting Radio's Hottest Nonentities," *The New York Times*, July 17, 2005.

191   *The PD nixed that idea*: Jeff Leeds, "Fade-Out: New Rock Is Passé," *The New York Times*, April 28. 2005.

193   *"the segue is in imminent danger"*: Dave Mandl, "In Praise of the Segue," *The Brooklyn Rail*, February 2005.

195   *"Automatic Record Reviews"*: Brian Whitman and Daniel Ellis, "Automatic Record Reviews," unpublished paper.

Apple

197   *"I'd shut [Apple] down"*: Jai Singh, "Dell: Apple Should Close Shop," *CNET News*, October 6, 1997.

201   *Mac team*: I addressed the dynamics of Jobs and the Mac team in *Insanely Great: The Story of Macintosh, the Computer that Changed Everything* (New York: Viking, 1994).

214   *"Style is nice"*: Colleen Ryan was interviewed by my *Newsweek* colleague Brad Stone.

216   *Sony:* In addition to several personal interviews with Howard Stringer and other Sony executives, my discussion of Sony was informed by Phred Dvorak, "At Sony, Rivalries Were Encouraged; Then Came iPod," *The Wall Street Journal,* June 29, 2005; and Frank Rose, "The Civil War Inside Sony," *Wired,* February 2003.

218   *Neistat:* My researcher Jodi Mardesich interviewed the Neistat brothers. You can view the movie on the Neistat Web site http://www. ipodsdirtysecret.com.

221   *The iPod Economy:* Damon Darlin, "Add-ons Have Become a Billion-Dollar Bonanza," *The New York Times,* February 3, 2006.

226   *"Michael Dell wasn't perfect at predicting the future"*: John Markoff, "Michael Dell Should Eat His Words, Apple Chief Suggests," *The New York Times,* January 16, 2006.

Podcast

230   *iPod-based tour commentaries:* Hannah Karp, "Hearing the Sights," *The Wall Street Journal,* April 21, 2006.

231   *ShasPod:* My researcher Jodi Mardesich interviewed Shmidman. I also consulted Alex Mindlin, "2000 Talmud Tapes, or One Loaded iPod," *The New York Times,* March 17, 2005.

238   *Think Secret:* Tom McNichol, "Think Belligerent," *Wired,* May 2005.

240   *"Podcasting will shift"*: Doc Searls, "DIY Radio with Podcasting," *Doc Searls' IT Garage,* September 28, 2004.

244   *six thousand podcasts:* Vauhini-Vara, "Now Playing on iTunes: Adult-Oriented Podcasts," *The Wall Street Journal,* July 22, 2005.

245　*"A student starts a script"*: Mikael Blaisdell, "Academic MP3s: Is It iTime Yet?" *Campus Technology*, March 1, 2006. Another helpful source on academic podcasts was Brock Read, "Seriously, iPods Are Educational," *The Chronicle of Higher Education*, March 18, 2005.

245　*Georgia College and State University*: Greg Bluestein, "Rural college pushed iPod use for lectures," AP, March 11, 2006; and college site, http://ipod.gcsu.edu/index.html.

246　*National Semiconductor*: Press release, "National Semiconductor Equips All Employees with 30-Gigabyte Video Apple iPods to Cap Off Most Successful Year in Company's History," June 12, 2006.

246　*www.toodou.com*: Thomas L. Friedman, "Chinese Finding Their Voice," *The New York Times*, October 21, 2005.

247　*Even the Vatican*: "The Gospel According to iPod," Agence France Presse, October 27, 2005.

247　*podcast from outer space*: "Steve Robinson: First Podcaster from Outer Space" is available at www.nasa.gov/returntoflight/crew/robinson_podcast.html.

Notes

Acknowledgments

First, I'd like to thank all my iPods, especially my latest one. It holds 3,999 songs at this moment (along with a bunch of podcasts and some episodes of *Lost, 24,* and a Ricky Gervais video or two), and it has kept me delighted as I flew back and forth across the country to visit Apple for various events.

Apple CEO Steve Jobs provided encouragement from the moment I told him about this book, and Apple Computer's cooperation has benefited this book tremendously. Katie Cotton and Steve Dowling provided contacts, guidance, and answers during my research, and the people who helped create and develop the iPod, iTunes, and the iTunes store were more than generous with interview time. The same goes for my sources in the tech industry, the music world, colleagues in the media, and enchanted users (as well as a few disgruntled ones). *Everybody* likes to talk about the iPod, with the exception of my sources at other companies, including Microsoft, Creative Technologies, Hewlett-Packard, Real Networks, and Sony. But they were kind enough to speak to me anyway, and I thank them.

It was at *Newsweek* where I realized that I was on a collision course with this book. The moment came when I was working on a July 2004 cover story about the iPod which was suggested not by me but by Devin Gordon, a writer in the arts section. That story benefited from reporting by the usual great team of *Newsweek* journalists, including Brad Stone, Jennifer Ordonez, Catharine Kipp, Jamie Reno, Ron Depasquale, Jordana Lewis, Claire Sulmers, Dana Thomas, and Vanessa Juarez. I'd also like to thank my editors: George Hackett, Kathy Deveny, Jon Meacham, and Mark Whitaker.

Once I engaged in a round of interviews and investigation for the book, I was aided in my work by Jodi Mardesich, a truly overqualified researcher. Victoria Wright did her usual terrific job of transcribing tapes (and this time, MP3 files). Kevin McCarthy and J. Gabriel Boylan painstakingly fact-checked the manuscript. Brooke Hammerling and Julie Panebianco helped with music industry connections. Thanks also to J. J. Jacobi, Carl Malamud, Bruce Schneier, and John Markoff.

My agent, Flip Brophy, not only supplied the usual good advice but the perfect place to work during crunch time. (Thanks also to everyone at Sterling Lord Literistic.) I'm happy that David Rosenthal of Simon & Schuster finally bought one of my books, and happier still to be edited by Bob Bender, who even kept his cool when I told him my idea about shuffling the book. Johanna Li kept things moving. And kudos to the S&S production staff for enthusiastically rising to an unusual challenge.

Andrew and Teresa were more than patient with me while I documented and pondered the lure of a very special gizmo. Of course they had their own iPods to keep them busy. I love you both.

Index

Index

Index

Index

Index

Index

Index